Brand JAMAICA

Brand JAMAICA

REIMAGINING A NATIONAL
IMAGE AND IDENTITY

*Edited and with an introduction
by* HUME JOHNSON *and*
KAMILLE GENTLES-PEART

UNIVERSITY OF NEBRASKA PRESS   LINCOLN

Chapter 1 is adapted by permission from
Springer Nature: *Place Branding and Public
Diplomacy*, "JAMAICA: A Famous, Strong
but Damaged Brand," by Hume N. Johnson,
special issue on "Managing the Reputation of
Places in Crisis," 10, no. 3: 199–217. © 2014.

Library of Congress
Cataloging-in-Publication Data
Names: Johnson, Hume N., editor. |
Gentles-Peart, Kamille, editor.
Title: Brand Jamaica: reimagining a
national image and identity / edited by
Hume Johnson, Kamille Gentles-Peart.
Description: Lincoln: University of
Nebraska Press, [2019] | Includes
bibliographical references and index.
Identifiers: LCCN 2019015631
ISBN 9781496200563 (hardback: alk. paper)
ISBN 9781496217486 (epub)
ISBN 9781496217493 (mobi)
ISBN 9781496217509 (pdf)
Subjects: LCSH: Jamaica—Civilization—
21st century. | Group identity—Jamaica. |
National characteristics, Jamaican. | Jamaica—
Public opinion, Foreign. | BISAC: HISTORY
/ Caribbean & West Indies / General.
Classification: LCC F1887 .B73 2019 |
DDC 972.92/06—dc23 LC record available
at https://lccn.loc.gov/2019015631

Set in Chaparral by Mikala R. Kolander.
Designed by N. Putens.

Dedicated to the people of Jamaica,
on whose backs the remarkable story
of Jamaican achievement stands.

CONTENTS

ACKNOWLEDGMENTS

It has taken a Herculean effort by the editors to pull together this collection to reimagine Jamaica and craft an alternative prism through which this famed Caribbean nation can be seen and engaged. We are grateful to each of our contributors for their perspectives and to everyone who provided insights that shaped our arguments, commented on the various drafts of the chapters, or simply engaged us in conversations around issues having to do with the brand image and reputation of places.

The origin of this volume was the first ever interdisciplinary symposium on Jamaica's global image and identity entitled "Re-Imagine Jamaica: Unlimited Possibilities," organized by the nation branding think tank The Re:Imagine Jamaica Project at the University of the West Indies (UWI) in July 2015. The symposium brought together scholars as well as leading professionals and practitioners in business, tourism, creative industries, sports, science and technology, media communication, marketing, politics, and academia to discuss key issues, trends, challenges, and practices that are shaping Jamaica's public international image as well as to share experiences, perspectives, insights, and the latest developments in the national drive to lift, promote, and protect "Brand Jamaica." Overall, the conversations at the conference were rich and deeply engaging, and they sparked the idea of creating an innovative volume that would look at Brand Jamaica through a fresh lens.

We wish to thank the moderators of the symposium's nine panels and three speaker sessions—Cordel Green, Carole Beckford, Dimario McDowell, Rodney Campbell, Sharon Haye-Webster, Patrick Barrett (aka Tony Rebel), Raymond Pryce, Donald Oliver, Kathy Francis-McClure, and Saudicka Diaram—all of whom not only added to the richness of the symposium but also succeeded in keeping it on schedule. We also wish to thank keynote speaker Samantha North, who flew all the way from Istanbul, Turkey, to join us in Jamaica. Her enthusiastic participation and insightful remarks were well received.

We wish to express our gratitude to the Spanish Court Hotel, and particularly hotelier Christopher Issa, whose idea it was to stage a symposium around Brand Jamaica, after Hume Johnson's lengthy conversation with him about Jamaica's global reputation, and for his generous support in the planning phase of the event. We thank the Jamaica National Building Society (JNBS) and Peart Consulting Group for the financial support that made the project possible. The project also benefited from the support of Roger Williams University's Foundation for Teaching and Research (Rhode Island), the University of the West Indies Centre for Leadership and Governance, and the Institute of Caribbean Studies (ICS).

We are particularly indebted to June Pinto of the University of the West Indies and policy analyst Rohan Wright, with whom we worked from the outset on the design and running of the symposium that led to this book. That the symposium ran so smoothly was largely the result of June Pinto's energy and efficiency and Rohan Wright's dedication and excellent organizational and interpersonal skills. We are also grateful to Newton James and Lorna Lewis of Power 106 FM for their help with the brand management aspects of the symposium and to Andre Gordon and Sabrina Caserta for their administrative assistance.

We are especially indebted to the editors at the University of Nebraska Press, particularly Alicia Christensen for her unflagging interest, engagement, and support; and the reviewers for their constructive comments on each draft and whose perspectives truly helped us to refine the argument of the book.

Finally, Hume Johnson wishes to acknowledge the encouragement and support she received at the outset from former prime minister of Jamaica, the Most Honorable P. J. Patterson. Kamille Gentles-Peart wants to thank specifically Prince Peart, whose support of her endeavors has been unwavering.

INTRODUCTION

Hume Johnson and Kamille Gentles-Peart

Jamaica is awaiting its due. Despite being one of the world's most highly recognized nation brands and a central player in world culture, Jamaica has yet to prosper from the great value embedded in its brand name and culture. It remains a moribund economic environment and a country battling decay and underdevelopment. In short, Jamaica's impoverishment is out of sync with its global fame. The nation has also not yet accounted for or resolved the major deficits of governance it confronts, nor has it adequately promoted the rich, complex identities and culture of the nation. Instead, Jamaican authorities promote a top-down, elite approach to constructing and projecting the national image, one that is grounded in *destination tourism* and relegates the vast majority of Jamaican citizens to the periphery of the society, denying them agency in the making of their nation's image.

As the nation recognizes more than a half-century as an independent nation, the time is apt for Jamaican authorities to interrogate, deconstruct, and reimagine how they constitute the nation's public image and the way they project the nation in the world. *Brand JAMAICA: Reimagining A National Image and Identity* offers such a rethinking. It provides the first scholarly exploration of the current manifestations, implications, and future directions of Jamaica's nation branding project: "Brand Jamaica." The volume offers a critique of the existing models within which Jamaica's global image is framed. As a point of clarification, Jamaica currently does not have a formal and centralized Brand Jamaica organization or entity responsible for shaping the country's image in the international arena—in the way that countries such as Australia (Brand Australia), South Africa (Brand South Africa), Spain (Marca Espana), New Zealand (100% Pure), and Colombia (ProColombia) do. Instead, a few government agencies currently maintain and undertake a diffuse set of activities, efforts, and initiatives that are designed to promote the nation's public image. These dispersed efforts are what we refer to as the "Brand Jamaica Project." Historically, the Brand Jamaica Project locates itself predominantly within a destination tourism paradigm. Through a series of critical interrogations, the volume problematizes the current tourism model of "sun, sand, and sea," particularly within the context of postcoloniality, and examines the ways in which it excludes and obscures other crucial aspects of Jamaica's public international image and ignores the unintentional images, vistas, and stereotypes it creates. The volume thus critically assesses nation branding from the perspective of Jamaica's formal international tourism promotion.

To be clear, our objective is not to provide a complete appraisal of every aspect of Jamaica's public image and reputation. Nor does the volume offer prescriptions or "how-to" formulas for nation branding in Jamaica. Rather, our primary aim is to highlight some of the problematic aspects of Jamaica's nation branding project (which is exclusively tourism-centric) and advocate for a paradigmatic shift in the model of nation branding that Jamaica undertakes—one that is more comprehensive and complete and offers a critical articulation of the nation that locates the Jamaican people at the center and acknowledges, if not addresses, the realities of Jamaica. Although the primary focus is Jamaica, the arguments that we expound have utility for rethinking more broadly the study and practice of nation branding in postcolonial societies of the Global South. By integrating institutional, cultural, ethnographic, and linguistic analyses, we offer an ethno-political framework to examining nation branding practices at large.

As a point of departure, we provide an overview of nation branding and highlight and locate the Jamaican branding project within the context of the contemporary global thrust toward nation branding. Later we take a critical look at some of the problems with the concept itself and its application and relevance to postcolonial societies such as Jamaica.

Defining *Nation Branding*

It is largely accepted that nations have always had a brand image and identity—a sense of themselves that they project in the world or that is projected onto them. In other words, whether their images are formally managed or not, dominant perceptions already circulate about nations. Moreover, in our technological, globalized age, powered by the internet and dominated by social networking, in which transnational interaction and trade is inescapable, no nation-state wants to, or can, be anonymous. So, nation branding has emerged as a powerful strategic tool adopted by many countries with emerging market economies to manage and build positive reputations in order to gain competitive and economic advantage. In spite of the ubiquity and almost inevitability of the practice today, and after almost two decades of scholarly investigation, nation branding remains a contested phenomenon.

It is important to distinguish a nation's image and its branding initiatives. A nation's image is the sum total of all mental associations about a nation in the mind of international (and local) stakeholders and may have components related to the economic, political, and cultural environment and history of the nation (Fan 2008; Scott et al. 2011). *Nation branding* refers to "the application of branding and marketing communications techniques to promote and manage a nation's image; thus, a nation's brand is what a nation's people want the world to understand about their nation and seeks to incorporate its most central, enduring, and distinctive features (Scott et al. 2011, 229). In general terms, "nation branding can be defined as the result of the interpenetration of commercial and public sector interests to communicate national priorities among domestic and international populations . . . [with the primary aim of helping] . . . the nation-state successfully compete for international capital in areas of tourism, foreign direct investment, import-export trade, higher education, and skilled labor" (Aronczyk 2013, 16). Aronczyk sees nation branding as having diplomatic, recursive, and communicative dimensions. She asserts that the practice not only wins state leaders a seat at the table in multilateral decisions or membership in transnational organizations but also conveys an image of legitimacy and authority. The challenge is being able to control and manage impressions or use these opportunities to repair reputations damaged by political and economic legacies.

In terms of its recursive function, Aronczyk (2013) maintains that the practice of nation branding can allow national leaders to attain international distinction abroad and in this way generate positive foreign public opinion that will reverberate at home, fostering domestic consensus or approbation of their actions as well as pride and patriotism within the nation's borders (16). As a communication strategy, nation branding promises to generate international awareness of a nation through marketing and promotional techniques. To carry influence or leverage, Aronczyk argues that national representatives are obliged to find ways to make their jurisdiction visible in a noisy, competitive global media environment. In this sense nation branding conveys to the world that the nation is not only visible but well regarded in international circles (17).

Simon Anholt, who is often credited with coining the concept "nation brand" (ca. 1996), insists that all nations have brands, that is, their reputations. He contends that when a place conjures the same meanings and images for most people, it is an indication that it has a strong reputation. The opposite is also true: if a place means very little to most people who are aware of it or has widely different meanings depending on whom you ask, it has a weak reputation. Moreover, if it is known by a lot of people, it is a famous place (Anholt 2007, 8). This national reputation, he argues, cannot be constructed but has to be earned. It is the new currency for nations because "the brand powerfully affects the way people inside and outside the place think about it, the way they behave towards it, and the way they respond to everything with regard to that place, for instance, its products, sporting and cultural events, relationships with other regions, cities, and countries, tourism and heritage attractions, investment and business potential, etc. The brand image of a country has a direct and measurable impact on just about every aspect of its engagement with other countries, and plays a role in its economic, social and political progress" (Anholt 2006, 9).

For Anholt, one of the fundamental duties of a government in nation branding is therefore to understand and manage the *reputation* of its country and trade this good name to achieve success in the global marketplace. This means monitoring its international image in the countries and sectors where it matters most to the nation; collaborating with business, civil society, and governments on a national strategy and narrative that articulates the story of the nation—where it is going and how it will get there—in order to reflect the genius and will of the people; and maintaining a stream of innovative products, services, and policies in every sector, which keeps the country at the forefront of the world's attention and admiration, affirming its right to achieve the reputation its government and people desire (Anholt 2010, 6–7).

Anholt asserts that most countries communicate with the rest of the world and deliberately create their brand image through six common channels: tourism promotion; exports; the policy decisions of the government; how it solicits foreign direct investment; cultural exchange; and the activities and the people, from high-profile leaders and stars to immigrants. In other words, because nations have essentially become brands, Anholt sees nation brand (which he now calls "competitive identity") as a new and vital approach to statecraft, economic development, and international relations.

Nation branding can also be seen as a means of communicating "soft power" as opposed to "hard power." American political theorist Joseph Nye first introduced the concept of soft power in the late 1980s to refer to the ability of a country to persuade others and shape their long-term attitudes and preferences through the power of example—their values and culture. So, rather than using hard power such as raw military might as a means to success in world affairs, Nye (2004) argues, the United States deploys its soft power assets—such as its well-known companies, famous Hollywood films and movie stars, foundations, universities, churches, and other institutions of civil society—to foster favorable international public opinion. Similarly, van Ham (2001) speaks of the emerging phenomenon of the "brand state." The brand state represents the ideas that the outside world holds about a particular country. This obliges countries and cities to deploy their history, geography, and ethnic and emotional motifs to construct a distinctive image. This image, according to van Ham, is a form of identity politics. He posits that in old-world politics, influence was based on ideology and raw power, but in the postmodern world, influence is based on image. Strong nation brands, he argues, are important in attracting foreign direct investment, recruiting the best and the brightest, and wielding political influence. In other words, smart states are building their brands around reputation and attitudes in the same way smart companies do.

For Clancy, "nation branding sheds light on how a state presents the nation, not just to an external audience but to an internal audience as well" (2011, 290). In other words, nation branding is seen as a conscious effort by nations to shape internal and external conceptions of a place; the branding narrative distinguishes what is unique and important about the nation. In essence, countries market themselves not only to sell products but to shape more generally how they are perceived. While the primary audience may be external, branding directly and indirectly shapes national identity (the domestic sphere) to the extent that citizens at home also consume marketing messages and respond to external expectations of who they are (Clancy 2011, 290). Nation branding and its impacts are therefore "glocal"—both global and local. This brings us to one of the main motivating forces for nations involved in nation branding: the desire for global competitiveness.

Branding and Global Competitiveness

Scholars agree that in today's crowded, busy, and fiercely competitive global marketplace, all nation-states are obliged to develop, manage, and leverage their images in order to stand out and succeed. This means nations must adopt conscious branding strategies (Kotler and Gertner 2002) or face difficulty in attracting economic and political attention and constructing and ameliorating their own images. A country, in other words, engages in nation branding primarily to improve its global standing, to boost trade and investment, to attract higher education students and skilled workers, and to embrace (or distance itself from) its heritage and culture (Dinnie 2014; Anholt 2007) as well as promote its core values in such a way that it appears more attractive than its peers in the global community (Aronczyk 2013).

For these reasons, it is no surprise that over the last few decades many countries, including highly developed countries of the Global North with buoyant industrialized economies—among them Australia, Britain, China, France, Germany, Ireland, Japan, Spain, and the United States—have been committing tremendous resources to the development of their nation's brand. These practices include cosmetic efforts, such as the creation of logos and slogans; strategic approaches, such as huge advertising campaigns and media blitzes as well as events and content marketing aimed at reimagining these countries in the minds of global publics; and more institutional approaches, such as the establishment of governmental and quasi-governmental bodies to oversee long-term nation branding efforts. The United Kingdom's Public Diplomacy Board, South Korea's Presidential Council on Nation Branding, and South Africa's International Marketing Council are current examples. Here nation branding is a component of national policy tied to the planning, governance, and economic development of the country (Kaneva 2011).

These practices have become necessary tools for gaining competitive advantage in global politics and the global economy (Olins 2000; Anholt 2010), and without question these countries are now reaping the benefits of having established strong nation brands, thanks to clear, concise, well-articulated, and well-understood brand footprints embedded in business and cultural products, supported by fairly stable political, social, and economic environments as well as strategic international relations and public diplomacy. In the mid-1990s, for example, former British prime minister Tony Blair became convinced of the need for Britain to rebrand and reposition itself in the world. According to Leonard (1997), "a gulf [had] opened up between the reality of Britain as a highly creative and diverse society and the perception around the world that Britain remains a backward looking island immersed in its heritage" (8). The result was a hastily effected "Cool Britannia" campaign. Although heavily critiqued, it was designed to remake Britain to reflect not just traditional values, heritage, and class but to showcase the cultural renaissance that Britain was undergoing and the best of what the country had become in the modern age.

Ireland and Spain have also completely refashioned their identities over the past few decades. Ireland rapidly transformed its image from a rural, insular traditional Catholic country plagued by political violence to an innovative "Celtic Tiger," with Dublin recast as one of Europe's most exciting cities (Leonard 1997). Former Irish prime minister Brian Cowen, in a speech in 2010, underlined the significance of branding the country: "Ireland is a brand. People know us. Our country, her landscape and her culture are known the world over. We must connect with that brand now and use it to give us the competitive advantage in a globalized world that is increasingly the same. We must ourselves portray the positives that others see in us" (qtd. in Pelan 2012, 4). Similarly, starting in the mid-1980s, but particularly following its hosting of the Barcelona Olympics in 1992, Spain was in vogue, marked by the internationalization of Spanish companies and the increasing promotion and popularity of Spanish products in global markets. The result was a period of economic development that turned Spain into a powerful example of the power of nation branding—positive international image, credibility, and prestige (Mars 2012). The same is true for Australia, France, Germany, Italy, Japan, New Zealand, and Switzerland: Germany is today associated with quality manufacturing, Italy with fashion and style, Switzerland with trustworthiness, France with quality living and a chic lifestyle, and New Zealand and Australia with environmentalism and conservation. After the disastrous Japan earthquake and tsunami of 2011, Japan—known for technology—has reinvented itself and is expanding its nation brand in the world through a carefully crafted national strategy premised on cultural transformation, including fashion, film, and music.

Even the United States, as powerful and looming as its presence already is in the world—built on a mix of militarism, Hollywood, and the ethos of freedom and openness—realized that its international image, especially post 9/11 and its controversial occupation of Iraq, is sullied and international opinion of it is less favorable than it once was. Americans, no doubt, wanted their brand and reputation back. In 2008, Barack Obama, America's first black president, was elected to the United States presidency on a platform of change. A large part of Obama's campaign rested on his determination to reengineer and restore America's global image. Americans bought into his idea. In many ways Obama had a positive impact on America's global image. According to a Pew Research report by Richard Wike, Jacob Poushter, and Hani Zainulbhai (2016), favorable views of the United States endured throughout the Obama administration. U.S.-led military action against ISIS in Iraq and Syria, for example, won broad approval. By the close of Obama's presidency, the overall image of America among key publics in North America, Europe, and the Asia-Pacific region was, according to the report, generally favorable. Yet, with the 2016 election of Donald Trump—bent on American isolationism, restrictions on Muslim immigration, and his seeming support for what many see as a white supremacist agenda and a dangerous form of nationalism—America is again confronting sweeping unfavorability (Sanger 2017).

Branding and reputation management is, however, not just the prerogative of developed countries. A plethora of developing countries, including The Bahamas, Costa Rica, Ecuador, Kenya, Namibia, Nigeria, South Africa, and Uganda, are also embarking on carefully crafted programs of nation branding and country promotion. Referencing South Africa, which historically had a controversial public image (with its decades of racial segregation through its policy of apartheid and the arrest and conviction of black freedom fighters, most notably Nelson Mandela), Viosca, Bergiel, and Balsmeier (2005) posits that developing countries can reap benefits from embarking on professional country branding strategies, including the ability to win more investment business, because a country's image communicates to a global public the right things about taxation, labor skills, safety, the environment, and political stability. The authors argue that there is the chance to apply "made in" labels, for example, which positively aid the sale of a product in an overseas market. Nigeria is another developing nation that has begun to recognize the links between its international reputation and its business success and potential to attract investment. Despite being one of the largest oil producers in the world, Nigeria maintains a reputation as one of the world's most corrupt nations. Nigerian authorities admit that this reputation, coupled with other sociopolitical issues, affects Nigeria's global image and undermines its ability to attract investment, tourists, and respect. Over the last fifteen years Nigeria's public and private sectors have invested millions of dollars to rebrand the country, reorient its cultural and ethical reputation, and ameliorate its global image (Nworah 2008). Yet, at the same time, as developing countries hop aboard the "brand wagon," so to speak, they need to take account of the problematic nature of the concept of nation branding itself and its implications for countries with a colonial past.

Nation Branding: A Critical Perspective

In spite of the growing body of literature and increased energy with which nations now pursue the process, nation branding itself is at a watershed moment. On one hand, projects of nation branding have grown exponentially within the last two decades, reflected in the numerous publications, studies, and consultancy projects in this area as well as intensive and widespread attention in the media. On the other hand, nation branding faces a crisis of legitimacy ranging from cynical skepticism to outright objections emerging among the public. Indeed, a growing area of critical scholarship problematizes nation branding. First, there is much discussion and ambivalence about the relationship between national identity and nation branding. National identity is largely seen as a "nebulous and complex" entity (Fan 2006, 9), one that is imagined or socially constructed. In this regard some scholars postulate that since nations are being "imagined," the challenge "is to identify and track who or what precisely is imagining the nation as well as how different conceptions of national identity conflict and evolve over time" (Clancy 2011, 281). This fluid and contested nature of national identity poses a challenge for even the most well-thought-out branding strategies as it is impossible and improbable to encapsulate the complexities and fluidity of a nation and its identity into a neat, concise brand image or slogan (O'Shaughnessy and O'Shaughnessy 2000).

Second, nation branding projects are criticized for projecting a singular and incomplete narrative of national identity, one that is constructed and maintained by the dominant groups of the country. In their analysis of nation branding in postcommunist nations, for example, Kaneva and Popescu assert that nation branding was used by elites in these countries to provide a "highly visible and deceptively simple way to address the urgent need for rejecting communist identity markers and construct renewed national subjectivities" (2011, 193). In other words, these scholars insist that nation branding narratives tend to reflect the particular choices and agendas of the most powerful people who wish to shape national identity.

Furthermore, some scholars also highlight the ways in which nation branding in contemporary global political relations works to secure and maintain the existing global hierarchy and is perceived as a mechanism to prop up the power structures created by old-world colonialism. As Ishita Sinha Roy argues, "Nation branding is a strategic act to secure ideological terrain in the global/national cultural imaginary, and symbolically reinforce the notion of a 'natural' hierarchy of nations within the world order" (2007, 572). Specifically, Roy posits that nation branding functions to position industrialized nations as modern owners and consumers and developing nations as the "other." The most economically and politically powerful countries have the ability and resources to define, construct, and maintain their own image as well as those of others, thus establishing themselves as "'masters' of globalization." These mega-brand nations, such as the United States, are perceived as brand leaders, and postcolonial countries and others of the Global South are presented as "spaces of 'lack' or underdevelopment" (Roy 2007, 570). In this way nation branding is an enterprise of neocolonialism. In sum, the nation brands of developing countries have historically been shaped and influenced by more dominant countries for their own advantage. Nation branding in postcolonial societies—even when undertaken by local organizations and agencies—reinforces the exoticization of nations and the empowerment of the "first world." Given the global hegemonic and geopolitical implications of nation branding, participation in branding itself can be problematic for postcolonial societies as it can reinforce existing ideas about nations and preserve power hierarchies.

Jamaica is caught in this ideological and practical bind. The country has to negotiate complexities related to shaping its reputation and global image within the context of an uneven global environment. Unfortunately, the Jamaican authorities' response to this dilemma has been to oversimplify the nation by creating a singular tourism narrative as the main expression of Jamaican identity.

Welcome to JamRock: The Branding of Jamaica

Jamaica is a tiny island situated in the Caribbean Sea—a mere speck on the world map inhabited by only 2.8 million people. Yet Jamaica's remarkable presence on the world stage is well established, as the nation has drawn, over time, much attention in the international public sphere. The island has developed a strong reputation for its vigorous creative industries and customs, particularly its popular music and dance styles and its extraordinary athletes as well as its symbolic culture embedded in its flag, colors, artifacts, and language. Like other Caribbean islands, Jamaica also has a rich heritage and history shaped by its indigenous populations and its long encounter with slavery, colonialism, resistance, and the independence and de-colonization movements. As a consequence, the nation today preserves and upholds a passion for the values of freedom, justice, and equality and for a voice in the management of their affairs (Sherlock and Bennett 1998). Existing alongside these positive credentials, Jamaica is also associated with less favorable attributes, such as violence, homophobia, corruption, and poverty. Thus, while Jamaica has a strong and famous nation brand, its reputation is not always positive. As Anholt (2007) posits, a strong and famous brand does not always mean a positive reputation.

With regard to the branding of Jamaica, it may be illuminative to distinguish between what may be termed "intentional" and "unintentional" branding. To some degree Jamaica benefits from unintentional branding; the symbolic global narratives associated with Jamaica—extraordinary athletes, strong music culture, rich heritage, and recognizable national colors, for example—are not the result of deliberate branding strategies per se but, rather, are reflections of Jamaicans' activities and contributions in the world arena. Essentially, Jamaica has just been exercising its *Jamaicaness*— through the presence and activities of its citizens in its diasporas; the performance of its natives in sports, fashion, and beauty; the innovation of its artists in all spheres of the arts (music, dance, drama, and fine arts); the breakthroughs made by its scientists; and the noted scholarship by some of its intellectuals. Therefore, outside of formal, or intentional, branding campaigns, Jamaica maintains an undeniably strong presence and reputation overseas, ranging from notable accomplishments and associations with vibrancy and what Bob Marley refers to as a "natural mystic" quality to connections to crime, underdevelopment, a poor human rights record, and infrastructure weaknesses due to weak governance and other deficits.

We also acknowledge, however, the crucial role and impact elite stakeholders play in the intentional development of Jamaica's nation brand. Jamaica at present does not have a formal or coherent nation branding strategy. Nevertheless, the government of Jamaica, through its entities the Jamaica Tourist Board (JTB) and Jamaica's Trade and Promotions Agency (JAMPRO), pursue aspects of branding and are the agencies responsible for communicating the nation to global publics. Historically, the branding efforts of these organizations have emphasized tourism marketing. Anholt's Nation Brand Index holds that tourism is often the most visibly promoted aspect of a nation brand, and tourism assets have a disproportionate effect on people's perception of the country as a whole. Many foreigners come to know distant countries as tourists or would-be tourists. In addition, tourism is a valuable economic sector, with international tourists spending more than $1.4 trillion (World Bank 2015). It is therefore not surprising that government officials, such as those of Jamaica, frequently center their brand strategies on how their nations are perceived abroad as tourist destinations. As tourism has become increasingly lucrative, the modern state itself has become more and more involved in "staging the nation" through overseas marketing and through funding for the creation and maintenance of important tourist sites (Clancy 2011).

As far back as 1890, the British colonial authorities made a concerted effort to market the island as a health and pleasure retreat. Before then, tourism was a relatively small part of Jamaica's domestic economy. In fact, the Caribbean in general was known as a place of tropical plantations and the "white man's graveyard." (Taylor 1993, 9). At one point "diseases were so rampant in the Antilles and the mortality rate so high that travel to (or residence in) the region was thought by whites to be quite unwholesome" (4). Therefore, in order to capitalize on the global tourism industry that emerged during the Industrial Revolution at the turn of the twentieth century, Jamaica and other islands had to overcome major practical and social complications. The island had to be transformed into an island paradise.

To foster the tourism trade, Jamaica staged an international exhibition in 1891. The main products exhibited were grand hotels with luxurious accommodations and spacious grounds, all designed to create and communicate the idea of being in an exotic locale and the island as a place of relaxation and retreat. The hope was that Jamaicans and external stakeholders would see how lucrative it would be for the island if Jamaica could be sold as a winter paradise to northerners (Taylor 1993). The British colonizers wanted to lay the foundation for a steady and increasing flow of tourists to the island, creating the catalyst for tourism and investment. This signaled the beginning of the Jamaican authorities' commitment to the tourism brand. In the early 1960s, when the country gained independence from Britain, the new Jamaican government continued this projection of the tourism brand. Extraordinarily, much of the postindependence imagining and projection of Jamaican identity has been left to the tourism authorities and other elite groups both within and outside of the country. Like many other islands of the Caribbean region, Jamaica incorporated tourism as a central pillar in the country's economic development plan. In this way the authorities conceptualized and shaped the island as a tourist destination and constructed a tourism product essentially for consumption by foreigners and with the primary aim of attracting foreign investment, growing the economy, and providing employment for the Jamaican people. According to the World Bank, Jamaica's tourism expenditure in 2015 was US$411 million. With tourism earnings of some US$2.6 billion from more than three million visitors in 2016, tourism contributes enormously to Jamaica's national income and developing infrastructure (Tingling 2016).

Jamaica's past and current destination tourism model anchors itself on the island's aesthetic features, on paradise, so to speak—rustic landscapes, year-round warm temperatures, and white sand beaches and the magnificent all-inclusive resorts where the foreign tourists are housed—while Bob Marley, reggae, and Rastafari provide the literal and metaphorical backdrop and the "natural mystic" that would entice foreigners to come to the island and "feel all right." The image of Jamaica and its people that has emerged is singular and sanitized and based upon a set of ideological narratives constructed on neocolonial ideas that feature Jamaica as an exotic island paradise of beautiful beaches and friendly but docile and undereducated people. In other words, in place of a nuanced, holistic image that acknowledges and embraces the Jamaican people and their history and culture, the Jamaican authorities have historically (and problematically) defined the nation as a tourist destination and, as such, have focused its nation branding efforts primarily, if not exclusively, on tourism marketing, ignoring the broad, multidimensional reputation and image that Jamaica maintains in the world.

The Jamaica Tourism Master Plan of 2002 suggests that the government is interested in taking the country's image to the next level by including attention to heritage, culture, and community. The government of Jamaica acknowledged the need to move the tourism industry to a sustainable development model, based, among other things, on Jamaica's heritage (natural, cultural, historic, and built). The idea is to enhance the visitor experience by increasing the type and quality of attractions and including community-based development in which local communities are involved in defining, developing, and managing the tourism experience, that is, a bottom-up versus top-down elite model tourism development and an inclusive industry that benefits not just a few but the Jamaican people and the country. For Jamaican tourism officials its success is to be measured "not only by the amount of GDP, foreign exchange or jobs it provides but more importantly by the extent to which the industry serves as a vehicle for providing economic and social opportunities for the Jamaican people" (Ministry of Tourism 2002, 12).

Similarly, the Jamaica Promotions Agency (JAMPRO) appears keen to engage in activities that promote overlooked aspects of the Jamaican identity. Its president, Diane Edwards, asserted in early November 2017, in an interview with the popular place branding website the Place Brand Observer: "'Destination Jamaica' has stamped Jamaica into the consciousness of the world traveler, has successfully drawn visitors to the island since the 1960s and continues to exude an exotic appeal. However, this positioning does not fully and consistently reflect the many faces of Jamaica, the industriousness of its people and the breadth and depth of the diverse economy of the island. We need to expand the nation's brand recognition to a broader positioning which situates Jamaica as the business hub of the Caribbean, a place you want to visit and to do business with. We need to define the Jamaica that's beyond the beach."

JAMPRO has embarked on several initiatives to this end. For example, the agency established a Jamaican village at select Olympic Games, sponsored food festivals, and hosted film festivals to showcase indigenous products. In 2017, as part of JAMPRO's strategy to increase exports to regional markets, the agency led eighteen companies on export promotion missions to regional neighbors—Barbados, Trinidad and Tobago, and The Bahamas. The Caribbean Market Mission, part of the agency's export development program Export Max, gives companies the opportunity to promote Brand Jamaica in the region and increase the export of Jamaican products to regional markets. The companies were to undertake scheduled business meetings with buyers to promote their products, execute trade visits to key retail outlets, and have important discussions with private and public sector partners to garner market intelligence. The goal is to increase overall exports for the participating companies by 50 percent (JAMPRO 2017). Similar to the efforts by the Jamaica Tourist Board, JAMPRO, according to Edwards, "measures success in terms of the level of investment we attract, the number of jobs we can create, our export success and success of our social media and online campaigns" (Place Brand Observer 2017).

These initiatives by JAMPRO and the JTB indicate a desire to move beyond Jamaica's tourism image. However, the plans remain incomplete in several ways. First, nowhere do the agencies articulate that success will be measured by the creation of a positive national identity and reputation. In other words, the initiatives fail to address the definitional and reputational issues that Jamaica faces. The varied and contrary reputation of Jamaica is largely ignored in the "new" branding project of the nation. In short, notions of national image and identity are not seen to be tied to the country's larger social and economic objectives. Noted Jamaican political commentator Robert Buddan explained the definitional dilemma of Jamaica in a 2016 column for the *Jamaica Gleaner* newspaper:

A number of current issues seem to suggest that Jamaica needs a clear definition of what kind of country it is, what it stands for, and where it is going. But Jamaicans need to take the lead in defining themselves or else others will define us for their own purposes, out of their own stereotypes, and based on their own prejudices. Lately, for instance, some organisations have described Jamaica as homophobic. Transparency International describes Jamaica as corrupt. International credit agencies have at times said Jamaica is a bad place in which to invest. There is a general perception that Jamaica is a violent place. This struggle over definition is not just one between Jamaicans and foreigners, but between Jamaicans themselves, both at home and abroad. (2004)

As a result of these continual intentional and unintentional associations, Jamaica needs to communicate a coherent definition and image of the country. Even Diane Edwards of JAMPRO admits that in spite of her agency's non-tourism work, Jamaica's reputation as a destination brand is difficult to change; it is difficult to get the world to think about Jamaica outside of the narratives of beach and underdevelopment (in an interview with Place Brand Observer 2017). This means that an important part of Brand Jamaica has to be definitional, working to reframe the identity of Jamaica.

Second, the initiatives are dispersed and do not present a cohesive plan that consolidate all sectors that are marketing Jamaican products and services abroad. The challenge for Jamaica is to forge a nation brand that develops and promotes the country's credentials in the traditional sectors such as sports and music for which the country is known as well as the nontraditional sectors such as literature, science and technology, gastronomy, education, and entrepreneurship that have had little resonance in the existing and established image of Jamaica.

Finally, in spite of the plans to expand Jamaica's global reputation, these efforts are subordinated to the tourism-centric narrative. In other words, the "sand, sea, and sun" narrative of Jamaica—which dominates the imagination of foreigners and Jamaicans alike—has been institutionalized as the primary global promotional strategy. Clancy (2011) posits that tourism nation branding, such as that engaged in by Jamaica, can create an essentialized image of the nation that influences conceptions of the place both at home and abroad. Although the sources of national identity formation among citizens are multifaceted, nuanced, and a product of complex factors, it is now widely accepted that tourism nation branding constructs, promotes, and maintains a limited image of the nation. Specifically, tourism brands tend to project images of idealism that obscure evidence of poverty, violence, and internal tumult. Nation branding of this kind thus commodifies "people, culture, and space for the affluent tourist market" and creates "exclusionary stereotyping of the indigenous population" (Kerrigan, Shivanandan, and Hede 2012, 325). These tourism narratives are consumed not only by foreign tourists but by citizens residing in the country, encouraging them to take on or live up to the ideals promoted in the images. In other words, to the extent that the state formulates and accepts branding or marketing tourism content, it is officially sanctioning particular national narratives not only for consumption abroad but also for its own citizens (Clancy 2011).

These problematic offshoots of tourism marketing are evident in Jamaica's nation branding campaigns. State actors, such as the JTB, have produced a narrative of Jamaica that has excluded its history, culture(s), multidimensional identity, and complex global reputation. Jamaica's tourism authorities, in their promotion and articulation of Brand Jamaica abroad, have not made significant attempts to incorporate into their projects other aspects of Jamaica's global reputation (such as successes in sports, music, and fashion), nor have they addressed the less favorable reputational issues (such as crime and homophobia) that also circulate about Jamaica. Furthermore, they do not seem to recognize or take seriously the ideological implications of projecting Jamaica through the prism of tourism.

In addition, the ongoing and proposed initiatives by the JTB and JAM-PRO continue to reflect the kind of cultural self-commodification and "ethnopreneurialism" that Comaroff and Comaroff have documented in their 2009 book, *Ethnicity, Inc.* This ethnopreneurialism is often promoted and financed by, and largely benefits, global venture capital and "requires 'natives' to "perform" themselves in such a way as to make their indigeneity legible to the consumer of otherness" (142). This formation fosters an open-ended, unresolved dialectic that creates "ethno-commodities"—cultural properties, heritage, and bodies packaged and marketed for consumption by others and themselves. In this sense capital and economic possibilities become the driving force behind nation branding and the crafting of national identity. According to the Comaroffs, ethnopreneurialism can be economically beneficial and is able to foster conditions of "insurgent possibility,"—"new forms of self-realization, sentiment, entitlement, enrichment" (2009, 139), even as it intensifies intergroup inequalities and the exoticization of peoples and cultures. The latter is particularly salient in the case of Jamaica: The ethnopreneurialism of Jamaican state actors in marketing Jamaica as a tourist *destination*, while relatively profitable, has reinforced an essentialized, stereotypical caricature of Jamaica that does not address or acknowledge all the issues that the country faces and that has significant consequences for the nation's economic and social progress as well as the well-being, agency, and self-realization of its citizens at home and abroad.

For these reasons the editors and contributors of *Brand JAMAICA: Reimagining a National Image and Identity* argue that Jamaica's tourism-centric marketing model is problematic; it is out of sync with the realities of Jamaica and the global presence and reputation (negative and positive) of the country and is inimical to Jamaica's economic, cultural, and social goals. In other words, we posit that Jamaica's current promotional global strategy illustrates the country's reluctance "to see the potential economic value of its own cultural symbols" (Mussche 2008, 4). Furthermore, the strategy fails to acknowledge the potential consequences for national identity when Jamaican cultural symbolisms and discourses are excluded and silenced in the formal conception of the nation.

Drawing on a variety of approaches from the realms of cultural studies, postcolonial studies, political science, and literary analysis, the contributors to this volume address issues that complicate the current nature of Brand Jamaica.

Chapter 1, "Between Fame and Infamy: The Dialectical Tension in Jamaica's Nation Brand," by Hume Johnson, provides a detailed overview of Jamaica's global reputation, exploring its strengths and challenges. Johnson argues that positive global coverage of Jamaica's outstanding brand achievements in sports, music, and as a premier tourism destination is undermined, even negated, by what she calls "rival brands"—economic instability (debt, poverty, unemployment), violent crime, corruption, and perceptions of declining human rights. She contends that the consequence of this duality in Jamaica's image is a contradictory, perplexing, and problematic public image of Jamaica, with severe consequences for inward investment, tourism promotion, and economic and social progress. The chapter points to the imperative for Jamaican authorities to evaluate the nation's public image, manage the impact of prolonged crises on its brand, and attempt to reimagine Jamaica, in order to remain relevant in changing times.

In chapter 2, "The Branding of a Nation: A Rhetorical Analysis of the Jamaica Tourist Board's Commercial Campaigns," Nickesia Gordon presents a more focused analysis of the tourism brand constructed by the Jamaican authorities. She foregrounds the implicit meanings and stereotypes embedded in the "destination" brand that are largely overlooked by these state actors. Specifically, she offers a sociocultural analysis of the images and other representations of Jamaica in television commercials produced by the Jamaica Tourist Board as part of its marketing campaigns between 1955 and 2012. Using Barthes's (1977) idea of the rhetoric of the image as a theoretical framework along with critical and cultural studies, Gordon examines eight video commercials, one from each of the JTB's eight campaigns launched between 1955 and 2012, to explore what meanings about Jamaica's national identity are being produced by the various images and rhetorical messages embedded in the projection of Jamaica as a "premier Caribbean tourism destination."

Building on Gordon's analysis of tourism marketing, Kamille Gentles-Peart explores the implications of such images in the lives of Jamaican women in chapter 3, "Women of Paradise: Tourism Discourses and the Lived Realities of Jamaican Women Abroad." Injecting a humanistic component into the discussion of Jamaican nation branding, Gentles-Peart explores the impact of Jamaica's contemporary tourism brand on the lived experiences of Jamaican women living abroad. She argues that while the intent of the tourism brand may be to attract tourists to the island, the image of the island that is constructed by this discourse complicates the experiences of Jamaican women abroad who have to live with the implications of being the natives of "paradise." This chapter specifically interrogates the ways in which the discourses of race, gender, class, and nation disseminated in the tourism marketing of Jamaica influence and shape the diasporic experiences of first- and second-generation Jamaican women in the United States.

Chapter 4, "Brand Jamaica and the Economic Cost of Homophobia: Initiating a Conversation," by Anna Kasafi Perkins, also highlights the ways in which Jamaica's tourism nation branding projects are detrimental to the Jamaica economy. Here Kasafi Perkins illustrates how the focus on paradise as Jamaica's national identity is contradicted by the unintentional reputation of homophobia in the country. In this chapter Perkins addresses the implications of not centering issues of governance in conceptions of Brand Jamaica, specifically focusing on the failure of Jamaican authorities to address the perceived and real marginalization of LGBTQ+ people in Jamaica and the impact this silence may have on economic earnings from Brand Jamaica. Perkins argues that one often overlooked area of loss of earnings comes from the country's reputation as one of the most homophobic nations on earth. Drawing on ongoing empirical research into the economic impact of homophobia in Jamaica, this chapter aims to expand the conversation to examine the economic implications of homophobia (real and perceived) for branding Jamaica. In so doing, Perkins considers the micro and macro impacts of homophobia—its effects on individuals and on the nation's development.

In chapter 5, "An (Un)easy Sell: Rebrandings of Jamaica in Marlon James's *A Brief History of Seven Killings* and Its French and Spanish Translations," Laëtitia Saint-Loubert exposes the potentialities that exist for the creative industries of Jamaica to challenge the existing brand of Jamaica and present a more "plausible" image of Jamaican culture. Saint-Loubert uses a case study of acclaimed Jamaican author Marlon James's novel *A Brief History of Seven Killings* to assess the ways in which literature from and about Jamaica can project a more complex image of Jamaica in the world, disrupting the Edenic tourism narrative that currently exists. Her contribution shows that James's re-politicization of Jamaica as well as his various attempts at complicating the notion of cultural authenticity play a determining role in the reconfiguration of the country's image for external consumers. In turn both the French and Spanish translations regenerate in their own terms Brand Jamaica so as to offer a more complex representation of the country, away from the sun, sand, and sea model with which it is often associated.

In chapter 6, "Brand Kingston: Reimagining Jamaica's Capital City," Hume Johnson continues the conversation regarding future directions for Brand Jamaica. Johnson examines the brand image of Jamaica's capital city, Kingston, to better comprehend its potential to contribute to the Jamaica's contemporary nation brand. Johnson argues that global recognition of Kingston as one of the world's "creative cities" is an opportunity for Jamaican authorities to reimagine the city and fundamentally alter its image from dangerous to benign and to design a new future based on urban regeneration, good governance, and creative economy. The chapter specifically proposes what a (reimagined) Kingston city brand might look like, drawing on aspects of the city's identity; cultural, geographic, and other attributes; what takes place in the city; as well as current and future marketing strategies that might be implemented.

In chapter 7, "Hold On to What You Got: Intellectual Property and Jamaican Symbols and Culture," Steffen Mussche-Johansen and Hume Johnson discuss the impact that Jamaica's tourism marketing approach to nation branding can have on the meaning of its national symbols and its ability to protect the "brand." The authors illuminate the ways in which Jamaican symbols and cultural expressions have been misappropriated by external factors and their meanings diluted, devalued, and detached from their original signifiers. The authors argue that this narrative misplacement of Jamaica is detrimental to Jamaica's national identity and economy. The chapter ends by discussing the judicial viability of a more structured and proactive approach to reclaiming and protecting Jamaica's symbols and how Jamaica could greatly improve its strategic position vis-à-vis a more structured governance of its cultural products and intangible resources.

Together the chapters included here provide a rich, nuanced, and multidisciplinary exploration of the validity, impact, challenges, and implications of the intentional and unintentional brand of Jamaica. The collection presents a sustained reflection upon Jamaica's nation brand, in terms of economic impacts, potential for copyrighting, impediments to the positive branding of Jamaica, impacts upon its residents and Jamaicans living abroad of the notion of Jamaica as a "magical paradise", and future suggestions. Because of its singular focus, the collection's essays are able to look deeply into questions of general relevance concerning the commodification of Jamaica, its culture and people.

In addition, overall the volume provides scholars from multiple fields (e.g., political science, tourism and hospitality studies, Caribbean studies, cultural studies, and postcolonial studies) with sociocultural and political frameworks as well as analytical tools for understanding and interrogating practices of nation branding, particularly for postcolonial nations of the Global South.

Brand JAMAICA

1

Between Fame and Infamy

The Dialectical Tension in Jamaica's Nation Brand

Hume Johnson

Jamaica—a former colony of Great Britain and the third most populous Anglophone country in the Americas—is among the world's most recognized and highly identifiable nation brands. Despite its miniscule size—both in terms of landmass (4, 244 sq. miles, 10, 911 sq. km) and population (2.8 million)—Jamaica has achieved fame and prestige from boasting a strong global image and symbolic portfolio as the home of one of the world's most iconic artistes, Robert Nesta Marley (Bob Marley); some of the fastest sprinters in the world, including the legendary Usain Bolt, who is considered the planet's fastest human; a hugely popular indigenous culture featuring reggae, Rastafari, great food, and ganja (otherwise called marijuana or weed, which is said to be the best in the world); Jamaica is also internationally famous for having a year-round sunny climate, beautiful beaches, and landscapes described by many as a mythical, enchanting island, a "paradise." On the other hand, Jamaica is known for virulent crime, corruption, poverty, underdevelopment, and homophobia. In 2013 the United Nations Office of Drugs and Crime (UNODC) *Global Study on Homicide* ranked Jamaica among the top six "most murderous" countries in the world, Transparency International, in its 2018 Corruption Perceptions Index (CPI), continues to rank Jamaica among the world's most corrupt, scoring the country 44 out of 100 where zero is highly corrupt and 100 is very clean (Francis 2019), and in 2006 *Time* magazine called Jamaica "the most homophobic place on earth" (Padgett 2006; Jackson 2015), locking this nation brand between fame and infamy.

The latter is worrying, as a problematic national image is seen to be a major obstacle for a country's social, economic, and cultural progress. In this era of globalism/globality—defined by globalization, competition, technological advancements, and social networking—nations are competing for buyers of their products; for students, talent, aid, and investment; as well as for attention and respect in the international community. Extant scholarship (e.g., Avraham and Ketter 2013; Avraham 2009; Anholt 2006, 2010; Viosca, Bergiel, and Balsmeier 2005) draws attention to nations' enduring prolonged crises and negative images caused by long-lasting problems such as economic hardship, high crime rates, continuous war, and political instability. The prevailing argument is that nations that have poor reputations (or that are not well-known) are more likely to suffer marginalization and will not easily witness economic success. In short, a bad reputation is bad for business. This means that the stakes are high for countries such as Jamaica that confront troubling and controversial public image and perceptions. Jamaican political authorities, including foreign affairs, tourism, industry and commerce ministries, along with its promotion and trade agency (JAMPRO) and other players, confront an extremely difficult challenge regarding the nation's conflicting and ambiguous public international image. These interests believe that Jamaica's international reputation and success in sports, music, and as a top tourism destination is enough to make the country attractive and respected on the global stage as well as potentially economically successful. Jamaican authorities must, however, consistently address the negative and controversial aspects of the Jamaican brand if it is to construct a successful and sustainable brand and reap economic harvests.

In this chapter I explore the existing challenges confronting "Brand Jamaica." I argue that positive global coverage of Jamaica's outstanding brand achievements in sports, music, and as a premier tourism destination is being potentially negated, if not undone, by the destabilizing impacts of its rival brands—crime, economic instability (debt, poverty, unemployment), corruption, and perceptions of declining human rights.

The consequence is a contradictory, perplexing, and problematic public image of Jamaica, with severe consequences for investment and tourism promotion as well as economic and social progress. Jamaica represents a nation that finds itself in a troubling situation of prolonged negative images and stereotypes even alongside positive perceptions. It is this contradiction that I see as the "dialectical tension" in Jamaica's national image, a friction between fame and infamy. The chapter thus points at the imperative for Jamaican authorities to evaluate the nation's formal public image, manage the impact of prolonged crises on its brand, and attempt to reimagine Jamaica beginning with a focus on its people and the nation's creative and cultural credentials in order to ensure economic success and remain relevant in changing times. As a point of departure, I will provide an overview of Jamaica's famous nation brand, popularly called "Brand Jamaica," and then introduce dialectical tension as a conceptual framework that may help us to make sense of the contradictions in Jamaica's nation brand. Finally, I look more closely at challenges Brand Jamaica currently confronts and how they may be reconciled as well as the role the Jamaican authorities might play in the construction of the brand that is Jamaica.

Jamaica's "Claim to Fame"—An Overview

Despite its inescapable status as a former colony of Great Britain, shaped by centuries of slavery, violence, and plunder, Jamaica has made an indelible mark on the global arena through a massively successful troika of brands—reggae music, sports, and destination tourism. Since the 1960s and 1970s Jamaica's rising popularity and esteem in the world has been premised on the ballooning success of the nation's vibrant music culture, featuring forms such as ska and rocksteady but particularly its indigenous reggae, which was then the world's newest music genre. Jamaica is known as a musical force, having the highest per capita musical composition of any country in the world (Mussche 2008, 31). The list of reggae's megastars is extensive, but Bob Marley is undeniably the genre's greatest celebrity icon and ambassador. Through Marley's timeless music and powerful messages of peace and love, Jamaica found itself a significant player in the global movement for equality, peace, and justice. As a lyrical art form and cultural expression, reggae has had a penetrating local and global impact as a vehicle for sociopolitical commentary, critiquing oppressive political systems and engaging listeners about issues of identity, love and relationships, perseverance, and hope.

Consistently addressing issues such as poverty, justice, and education as well as a resistance to Babylon (the social and political structures of the state), Marley transcended culture and language and cultivated a strong social consciousness especially among the younger generation (Mussche 2008). Songs such as "One Love" and "War" resonated with oppressed peoples on every continent and inspired a desire to fight for and protect their fundamental human rights. The expression *One Love* itself became a widely understood expression of love and respect for all peoples regardless of race, creed, or color. This was Jamaica's gift to the world and the beginning of the nation's symbolic presence on the world stage in the modern period.[1] In 2000, global media recognized Jamaica's significant contribution to world culture. The British Broadcasting Corporation, BBC, for example, named Bob Marley's "One Love" as the song of the millennium. This is while the popular U.S. newsmagazine, *Time*, in a piece entitled "The Best of the Century," listed Marley's 1977 album *Exodus* as the best album of the twentieth century, asserting that "the album is a political and cultural nexus drawing inspiration from the Third World, then giving voice to it the world over" (*Jamaica Gleaner* 2007).

Emerging alongside the rise of Bob Marley as global superstar were Jamaica's indigenous cultural practices, such as the lifestyle and ideology of Rastafari, which—thanks to Marley—had begun to take on a fad-like following across the world. Developed in Jamaica in the 1930s, Rastafarianism espouses racial pride and identity as well as repatriation of blacks to Africa, the home of their ancestors. Rastas base their philosophy on the teachings of Jamaican black activist and national hero Marcus Garvey, who advanced a Pan-African philosophy of black pride, empowerment, and black racial identity—which became known as Garveyism. Marcus Garvey became one of the most influential leaders emerging from Jamaica during the 1920s and 1930s; he defined Pan-Africanism not just for the

Harlem Renaissance but for the whole world. His philosophy had a huge influence on the global civil rights movements, particularly on the views of Martin Luther King, Malcolm X, and Nelson Mandela, and provided an important inspiration to the Rastafari movement and other activist movements around the world (Mussche 2008).

The followers of Rastafari, which now number in the thousands worldwide, sport the distinctive dreadlocks hairstyle (as a resistance to Babylon), observe various rites and customs such as the smoking of weed (marijuana, or ganja) as a religious sacrament, and revere the late emperor of Ethiopia, Haile Selassie, who they see as the Black Messiah; they also sport the signature colors of red, green, and gold, which represent the Ethiopian national colors. Rastafari is intrinsically tied to the expansion of reggae internationally, as many of Jamaica's reggae artistes adopted a Rastafarian aesthetic and philosophy and are seen to be largely responsible for popularizing and contributing to the expansion of Rasta culture globally. Rastafari, in other words, played a critical role in situating Jamaican culture in the international arena. It is this symbolic culture that essentially concretized Jamaica's sense of place in the world.

It is the Jamaican people, however, who ought to be given credit for Jamaica's global fame and strong brand name.[2] A significant example of this is the modern athletic revolution being led by legendary Jamaican sprinters such as Usain Bolt (considered the fastest man in the world) and compatriots Asafa Powell, Veronica Campbell-Brown, Shelly-Ann Fraser-Pryce, Elaine Thompson, and, before them, Merlene Ottey and Herb McKenley and his compatriots Arthur Wint and Donald Quarrie. Breaking record after record, Jamaican athletes have set new bars of achievement in world athletics. Known as the "sprint factory," Jamaica has given the world new sprinting techniques and coaching tactics and in the process helped to transform track and field from a fading sport to the most popular event at the Olympic Games.[3] Other outstanding citizens in fashion, the arts, film, and food technology as well as tech-savvy entrepreneurs and intellectuals are promoting Jamaica abroad through their notable achievements. Cultural studies scholar Donna Hope, for example, writes extensively on the critical contribution of "dancehall culture" (dance, fashion, and lifestyle) in the internationalization of Jamaican culture (Hope 2006). In addition, Jamaica's local language, patois, which has, for a long time been fighting for recognition, found space in Volkswagen's 2013 Super Bowl commercial and in a plethora of Hollywood films, including the 1990 flick *Marked for Death*, starring Steven Seagal; the popular *Cool Runnings* in 1993; *Meet Joe Black* (1998), starring Brad Pitt; and in the 2017 Marvel series *Luke Cage*. Jamaican export products are also strong signifiers of its "claim to fame." Blue Mountain Coffee (one of the most expensive and sought after coffees in the world), Appleton Jamaica Rum, patties (meat pies), Red Stripe Beer, jerk, and the grapefruit drink Ting are fully established around the world, contributing to the nation's presence and strong symbolic culture. If this was not enough, white sand beaches, lavish all-inclusive resorts, and a tropical climate have catapulted Jamaica into one of the world's premier destination tourism brands, attracting on average some 3.5 million tourists annually—including stopover and cruise ship passengers (Caribbean360 2016; Jamaica Tourist Board 2015).[4]

Yet the discourse about Jamaica is not always positive. Accompanying Jamaica's largely positive public international image is the development of what may be called a "rival brand" image. Since the early 1960s (when the island gained independence from Great Britain) and 1970s, Jamaica's emergence as a progressive nation—legislating new political and social rights to its poor, improving education, and actively participating in the global civil rights and social justice movements—has also been attended by international media coverage of the country's internal political civil war, featuring intense warfare between opposing gangs loyal to the country's two main political parties (the People's National Party [PNP] and the Jamaica Labor Party [JLP]), mushrooming crime, inflation, unemployment, and impoverishment. Today this negative image persists. Regular reports in the global media of Jamaica featuring gang warfare, upsurges in violent crime, corruption, and economic instability lead to troubling perceptions of the country as unsafe—a dangerous paradise, so to speak. Overall, the result has been a contradictory and problematic public image of Jamaica, with severe consequences for investment, tourism promotion, and the nation's economic and social progress.

The Brand Jamaica Dialectic

Despite the centrality of tourism in Jamaica's nation branding project and this sector being the bedrock of the economy, it is essential that Jamaican authorities bear in mind that Brand Jamaica is a nation brand of striking contradictions. A contradiction exists "whenever two forces or tendencies are interdependent yet mutually negate each other" (Miller 2002). Whereas all nation brands contain both positive and negative aspects, Brand Jamaica exhibits a perplexing combination of competing forces that are struggling for dominance. Dialectical theory appears to be a good model by which to explain these tensions and contradictions. Dialectic, in the Hegelian sense, is an interpretive method that explains the dynamic interplay between two opposing forces or entities (Rawlins 2008; Baxter and Montgomery 1996). It suggests that some proposition (a thesis) is necessarily opposed by an equally contradictory proposition (antithesis). The contradiction is often reconciled on a higher level of truth by a third proposition (synthesis). Dialectical theory has its philosophical roots in the idea that the world is in constant flux, with creative and destructive forces constantly operating upon each other. Baxter (1996), for example, in applying dialectics to communication and relationships, argues that dialectical tension is the "tugs and pulls" that are present in relationships as a result of the coexistence of both repelling (centrifugal) and attracting (centripetal) forces. Drawing on this theory, figure 1 illustrates the dialectical tensions inherent in the Jamaican brand.

This figure goes to the heart of the dilemma confronting Brand Jamaica. First, the figure points to the extraordinary presence, influence, and promise (both formally projected or informally created) of many aspects of the Jamaican national brand (e.g., tourism; sports, particularly athletics and bobsled; a vibrant culture featuring the popular reggae and dancehall music genres; a unique language and accent; an indigenous Rastafari movement; vibrant lifestyle; world-famous export products such as Blue Mountain Coffee; and a multiplicity of iconic citizens, among them Bob Marley and Usain Bolt). Second, it points to dangerous deficits and the prolonged crisis facing the Jamaican brand embodied in ostensible weaknesses in the institutions, structures, and processes of governance—deep

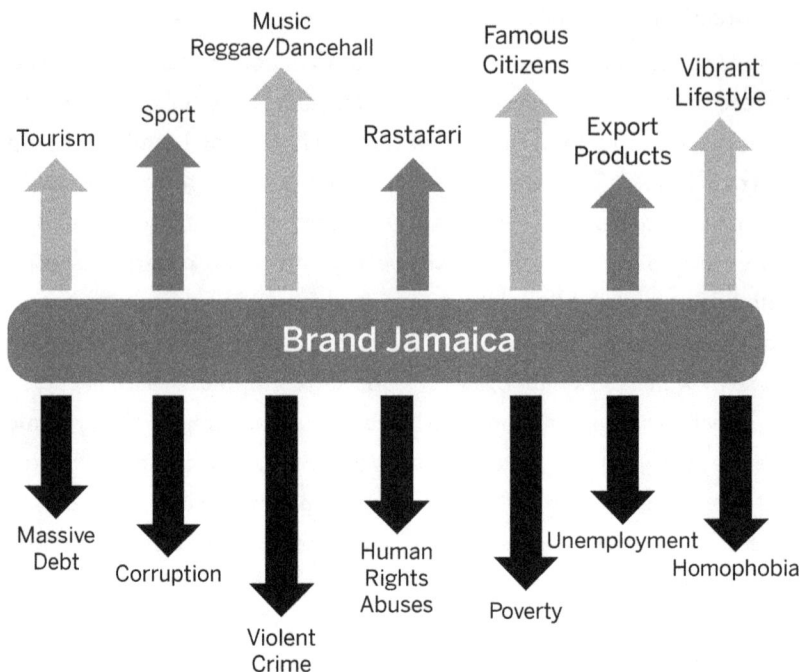

Fig. 1. Brand Jamaica Dialectic

debt, corruption, violent crime, breaches of human rights, poverty, rising employment, and perceptions of homophobia.

This glaring dichotomy exhibits the dialectical tension within this nation brand, reproducing Brand Jamaica's relative strength versus its profound vulnerability. The positive brand narratives evident in the top half of figure 1 have historically served to elevate and position Brand Jamaica as one of the world's most popular nation brands. However, it is worth noting that the negative discourses displayed in the bottom half of figure 1 have simultaneously served to undermine Jamaica in international public opinion and disrupt its capacity to take full advantage of its moral, social, economic, and cultural capital. This dialectical contestation between opposing brand attributes in Jamaica suggests that some variables may be performing brand-building functions while others are equally and simultaneously performing brand-reducing functions. In other words, both negative and positive brand narratives are vying to become the dominant discourse in Jamaica.[5]

As the case of Jamaica indicates, nation brands can exemplify constructive and progressive features as well as destructive and undesirable features. This tension causes them to mutually negate each other, leaving the brand at risk of stagnation. This is the position in which Brand Jamaica finds itself. Despite having a globally recognizable brand, Jamaica is yet to truly prosper from the great equity embedded in its brand name and culture. Scholars agree that nations that manage their country images and external reputations are more likely to create more conducive and attractive conditions for foreign direct investment, tourism, trade, and political relations (Viosca, Bergiel, and Balsmeier 2005). Positive brand narratives must no doubt win in order for Brand Jamaica to improve its brand equity and ultimately ensure its economic and social progress. If negative brand features such as crime, poverty, and corruption are allowed to dominate, it will not only have a considerable negative impact on the nation's socioeconomic goals but also will detract from, and even undermine, its existing brand achievements. This chapter aims to establish the basis for a presumption in favor of proactively managing these unfavorable aspects of Jamaica's nation brand, that is, positioning and promoting its many positive aspects while strategically addressing and reframing its negative features (socioeconomic problems).

The Lived Reality of Brand Jamaica

It is difficult, if not impossible, to separate a country brand from the lived experience and material conditions of the people of that place. Beyond its idyllic portrayal as paradise lies the reality of Jamaica—a lived reality Jamaican citizens know firsthand. Consequently, one cannot begin to talk about Brand Jamaica or embark on "branding" Jamaica without starting at home, acknowledging the country's brutal history of violence, slavery, and colonization and addressing, inter alia, the ongoing challenges of economic instability (debt, unemployment, poverty), corruption, and crime that the country confronts. Government policy and leadership with respect to economic growth, infrastructure development, employment, national security, and education are fundamental aspects of what defines and determines a country's brand. The everyday lived experience of the

Jamaican people and the effects of these challenges on the country's public image are thus fundamental to ongoing and future efforts to brand Jamaica.

Economic Instability

The Jamaican economy, for the last several decades, has been characterized by a brutal combination of low growth, high debt, and rising levels of poverty as well as external shocks that have crippled the economy. In 2012, for example, Jamaica's debt reached 145 percent of GDP, and the country's average annual per capita growth has been a mere 1 percent over the past thirty years, making Jamaica one of the slowest-growing developing economies in the world. Indeed, Jamaica is cited as having "the slowest growth rates in the Americas since 2000, even behind disaster-ridden Haiti," and "runs fiscal deficits for 44 of the 50 years of its Independence" (*Economist* 2012; Johnston 2013; World Bank 2017a). Debt servicing accounted for the largest portion of the national budget, hampering spending on critical social sectors such as health, education, and infrastructural development. Low economic growth also meant rising unemployment. As of July 2016, Jamaica's unemployment rate stood at 12.9 percent, and it was considerably higher for youth, at 28.6 percent (Statistical Institute of Jamaica 2016; *Jamaica Observer* 2013a). This is while per capita income stands at only US$5,500 (compared to neighboring Barbados and Singapore, which stand at US$13,400 and US$46,241 respectively) (Williams 2013; *Jamaica Observer* 2013a). Of its 2.8 million population, over 540,000 live below the poverty line and struggle to pay for basic amenities such as food, clothes, shelter, and access to education and public transportation. Although Jamaica experienced rapid economic growth and remarkable levels of prosperity in the 1950s and 1960s through foreign direct investments and foreign exchange earnings from manufacturing and tourism as well as the bauxite and alumina industries (*Jamaica Observer* 2013b; Manley 1974), by the early 1970s it was all over.

Coupled with political unrest as the country's two main political parties—the Jamaica Labour Party (JLP) and the People's National Party (PNP)—struggled for power in a bloody political civil war that polarized the country, unnerved the international community, and frightened investors, there was the world oil shock of 1973. Jamaica's economic decline coincided with a massive global recession that upended the world economy. Developing countries such as Jamaica were forced to undertake a fundamental restructuring of their economies. The structural adjustment (SA) conditionalities, while aimed at reducing fiscal deficits and achieving greater competitiveness, dealt a severe blow to an already enfeebled Jamaican economy, leaving social and economic sectors in a state of crisis (Johnson 2011). The Jamaican government found it virtually impossible to boost its economy, repay debts, improve standards of living, create employment, and give its poor any kind of meaningful life. Yet this was the beginning of a long period of economic downturn that some analysts refer to as "the multilateral debt trap." For example, Johnston argues that since 2010, in an effort to address an unsustainable debt burden, Jamaican state leaders "undertook severe austerity measures, freezing wages and cutting spending. Even after the debt exchange, Jamaica was left with the highest debt interest burden in the world; interest payments alone amounted to 11 percent of GDP" (Johnston 2013, 1).

Jamaican state leaders have been blamed for failing to address socioeconomic problems. Some analysts and commentators admit that Jamaica's economic troubles are largely homemade, caused by poor economic management, unnecessary bureaucracy, inequitable distribution of wealth, periods of political instability, and widespread corruption (*Economist* 2012). The economic misery confronting the Jamaican population—including a general depreciation in the exchange rate over the last two decades, massive jumps in inflation reflected in rising costs of utilities and food, and new taxes imposed on basic commodities—has been laid squarely at the feet of successive governments (Johnson 2011). The historic inability of political leaders to generate the kind of policies that are conducive to growth makes Jamaica vulnerable and largely unattractive to foreign investors. In a 2016 Global Resilience Index report published by the property insurance group FM Global, Jamaica was ranked among the riskiest countries to do business with in the world and the second most risky country in the Caribbean to do business with (Bennett 2017). At the time of writing, the World Bank ranked Jamaica 75 of 190 economies in its 2019 *Doing Business* report. This represents a 5-point decline from 70 in 2017 and 67 in 2016 (World Bank 2018).

Jamaica's economic situation is thus bad for its brand. Generalized poverty and the high costs of doing business in the country, including high energy charges, inadequate provision of public infrastructure services (both physical and nonphysical), and increases in security costs, diminish investor confidence. Economic instability also lowers the stocks of available social and human capital, thereby weakening the foundation for long-term economic growth and prosperity. It is noteworthy that the government of Jamaica has moved to stabilize the economy and reduce debt through a comprehensive program of reforms that has already begun to improve the investment climate and restore confidence in the Jamaican economy. According to noted financial forecasters, Jamaica's GDP grew by 1.7 percent in 2016, and this rate was estimated to carry into 2018 (Regan 2019; World Bank Group 2017b; *Economist* 2012). In addition, Bloomberg declared the Jamaica Stock Exchange the world's best-performing stock market for 2018 (Regan 2019). Despite these positive strides, the country continues to confront mushrooming levels of crime and violence, a situation with crippling consequences, particularly its ability to attract investment and project a strong and positive international image. Indeed, popular tourism marketing techniques—namely, "Jamaica No Problem" and "Jamaica, Feel All Right"—used to promote Jamaica are at odds with the reality of the country's dire economic situation and the untenable security situation.

A "Dangerous Paradise"—The Impact of Crime on Brand Jamaica

Crime remains Jamaica's biggest problem and has the most damaging impact on the country's international image. As far back as 2000, leading criminologists described Jamaica as wedged in the midst of an intractable and profound "crisis of public safety" (Harriott 2000). For a population of 2.8 million people, Jamaica's homicide rates are staggering. In 1970 Jamaica's murder rate was 8.1 per 100,000. By 2002 it had escalated to a record 40 per 100,000 and 44 murders per 100,000 in 2001 after a record 1,138 murders that year. Jamaica's murder rate climbed to close to 1,500 by the end of 2004. By 2005 this figure had risen to 1,674 murders, putting the murder rate at 64 per 100,000, which was then the highest murder rate in the world (Gray 2007, 3). Although murders ebbed in 2012, falling to 1,097 following the extradition to the United States of top criminal boss Christopher "Dudus" Coke, by the end of 2013 homicides again jumped to 1,200. By 2015 the figure was 45 murders per 100,000 people, with 1,129 murders (*Jamaica Observer* 2016). In 2017 alone there were 1,616 murders in Jamaica, one of the highest figures on record (Graham 2018).

With this deteriorating security situation, and limited success at tackling violent crime, Jamaica is now ranked among the most violent countries in the world and the most murder prone. For example, in the United Nations Office of Drugs and Crime's (UNODC) *Global Study on Homicide 2013*, Jamaica came in at number 6 in a list of countries with the world's highest murder rates. It is notable that Central America and the Caribbean have surged ahead of the rest of the world in terms of intentional homicides for countries not at war. Honduras continues to hold the top spot for the most homicides in the world, with a rate of 90.4 per 100,000 residents. Venezuela, Belize, El Salvador, Guatemala, Swaziland, St. Kitts and Nevis, South Africa, Colombia, and Trinidad and Tobago round out the top twelve countries with the highest murder rates in the world. South Africa and Swaziland—ranked seventh and ninth, respectively—are the only countries among them outside the Latin America and Caribbean region (UNODC 2013a).

Organized crime and gang-related activity as well as the inability of the state to make a real dent in the crime rate contribute to Jamaica's desperate security situation. The police are only able to make arrests in 45 percent of homicides annually, and they only convict perpetrators in 7 percent of the homicide cases. This leads both the public and police to doubt the effectiveness of the criminal justice system, leading to vigilantism, which exacerbates the cycle of violence (OSAC 2016). Many civilians do not have confidence in the ability of the authorities to protect them; they fear that the police are corrupt and could be colluding with criminals, leading citizens to avoid giving evidence or witness testimony, a situation that I have elsewhere called "informerphobia" (Johnson and Soeters 2015).[6] This extraordinary rate of violent crime has not only undermined the rule of law in Jamaica, but it has also underscored Jamaica's reputation as lawless and unsafe while elevating the level of citizen vulnerability and the fear (of crime) by visitors. When asked in 2013 what they thought about the current quality of Jamaica's nation brand, one well-known citizen characterized it as follows: "Violence, music, laissez faire-ism in terms of pseudo-liberal kind of lifestyle; if you want to find somewhere to go where you can get away with breaking the law, that kind of thing, Jamaica would factor in on the radar; very violent gangs that you fear; criminals who you should fear, scammers, a place to honeymoon, good ganja, yes and depending on how granular you get, a stable democracy in the Caribbean region, religious tolerance, etc." (pers. comm.).

The perception that Jamaica is a kind of "dangerous paradise" has become embedded—historically tied to the presence of garrisons, captive communities ruled by criminal overlords called "dons" with extraordinary political connections and influence; the emergence of a drug economy at home; and its integration into the international narco-trafficking industry and, with it, a notable shift in the position of Jamaican gangs in transnational crime. With the arrest or killings of notable dons and a crackdown on gangs by the Jamaican authorities in recent years, the criminal network has refined their operations, largely dispersing, splintering to avoid detection, as well as diversifying their operations, turning to the famed "lottery scams" to access new rents (Yagoub 2017). With the escalation of nonviolent crimes such as scams and fraud in recent years, this negative reputation of Jamaica has increased. The U.S. Federal Trade Commission, for example, reported that in 2011 alone the Jamaican lottery scam generated some thirty thousand complaints from American citizens, who were scammed between US$30 million and US$1 billion per year. The lottery scam has also generated significant negative international media attention for Jamaica, forcing American police departments to issue warnings to their elderly residents to be wary of calls from Jamaica's 876 area code (Fox News 2012). Although the Jamaican authorities have cracked down on scammers through arrests and new legislation, without question the proliferation of scams and fraud has negative consequences for Jamaica's international reputation and brand image. Scams compromise the money transfer mechanism by which crucial remittances vital to the economy flow into the country from the Jamaican diaspora, thwart potential investments, and leave the impression to an international onlooker of an insecure, dangerous country. (Anna Perkins, in chapter 4, also discusses the impact of scams on Jamaica's international reputation.)

Former prime minister P. J. Patterson, in an apocalyptic remark way back in 1993, confirmed the centrality of Jamaica's crime problem when he remarked: "It affects us all. It threatens our personal security; it severely affects the investment climate. It impacts negatively on our tourism industry. All our efforts at economic stabilisation and development will come to nothing if the monster of crime is not controlled." It is no longer possible for Jamaica to think of crime as a minor social problem. It remains the number one concern for most citizens. It is noteworthy that over the last fifty years Jamaica has undergone a fundamental revolution in the values, attitudes, and behavioral norms that guide the society. These powerful changes have led to more crime and violence, greater civil disorder, and other manifestations of social deviance (Johnson 2011 and 2005; Gray 2004; Boyne 2003; Munroe 1999).

Arguably, the most serious manifestation of Jamaica's declining social order and the gravest threat to the state in decades erupted in May 2010, when dissidents gathered in the Jamaica Labor Party (JLP) stronghold of Tivoli Gardens, the constituency of then prime minister Bruce Golding, barricaded themselves in to protect the "area leader," or don,[7] and alleged criminal Christopher "Dudus" Coke. Coke who was to be extradited to the United States to face drug and gun-running charges. In attempting to halt the escalating political and security crisis, the Jamaican government instituted a state of emergency for the parishes of Kingston and St. Andrew for a month and called in the military. This decision resulted in sixty-nine civilian fatalities. These developments serve to reinforce popular perceptions of the Jamaican social landscape as aggressive, dangerous, unfriendly, and impolite. Indeed, there is general consensus, according to the Jamaica Vision 2030 National Development Plan, that "there are aspects of Jamaica's culture that are not conducive to innovation and increased productivity. These include inadequate attention to punctuality, declining appreciation and respect for civic rights and responsibilities, and disturbingly low levels of interpersonal and institutional trust. These are aspects of our social capital that must be corrected to create an authentic and transformational culture and support our process of national development" (qtd. in Aronczyck 2013, 152).

This view of the public sphere in Jamaica illustrates the breakdown of the social system and paints a bleak picture of the nation among its own citizens at home, those in the diaspora, investors, tourists, and other overseas populations. The overall situation challenges and contradicts the familiar "no problem" and "come and be all right" representations of Jamaica long projected internationally by the country's tourism authorities. Ignoring crime and social disorder and pretending it is a separate construct unrelated to Jamaica's overall image are unwise, only serving to weaken the brand and limit its potential.

Corruption Perceptions and Brand Jamaica

Another major challenge to Jamaica's international branding project is the perception of corruption. Despite recording respectable levels of human development, Jamaica is ranked among the worst in the world with regard to governance indicators such as corruption. For example, of the twenty-five countries measured in a 2010 Latin American Public Opinion Project (LAPOP), the people of Jamaica (and Trinidad and Tobago) perceived their country as the most corrupt. External perceptions are the same. Transparency International Corruption Perceptions Index, which measures corruption among public officials and politicians around the world—where 10 is the most clean and 1 is the most corrupt—ranks Jamaica below 5, among the most corrupt in the world (Transparency International 2013). This negative appraisal is bad for Jamaica's public image. International organizations such as Transparency International assert that corruption destabilizes a society as it thwarts public investment and undermines the democratic process. In a recent report the Jamaican anti-corruption agency National Integrity Alliance (NIA) suggests that corruption also increases poverty and causes a brain drain because contributors to the economy may choose to leave due to frustration. Corruption, the NIA contends, causes citizens to lose faith in their political leaders, leading to a system that is neither transparent nor trustworthy.

Recent surveys carried out by the Centre for Leadership and Governance at the University of the West Indies and Vanderbilt University affirm a general decline in quality governance in Jamaica. The findings of a 2010 poll revealed that the levels of trust Jamaicans have in social and political institutions and in public officials is generally low. On a 100-point scale, the police and political parties were the least trusted, receiving mean scores of 33 and 34, respectively. This is while the army and the mass media enjoyed the highest levels of trust, scoring 66 and 61 points, respectively. The Electoral Office and Supreme Court received marginal scores of 50 points (Powell, Lewis, and Seligson 2010). It is clear that the Jamaican population has lost confidence in its government. Many share the view that the absence of quality governance at home has negative consequences for Brand Jamaica in a global context. One Jamaican executive interviewed in my ongoing study on Jamaica's nation brand summed it up this way in August 2013: "I would say it must be very hard for you to convince anybody to do business in a country which ranks as low as Jamaica does in the world competitiveness report, the doing business report and where you have such heinous crimes occurring; where corruption is so high; with a justice system that is operating, functioning but not at a level which causes a lot of confidence on the part of the Jamaican population. I don't know how you go and tell people to come and do business in Jamaica when they have other options." Although Jamaica has improved its world ranking, leading the Caribbean with regard to the ease of doing business (World Bank Group 2017a), the interviewee's point is well taken. Furthermore, the insistent promotion of the "no problem," "come and feel all right" image in the tourism marketing of Jamaica does not help to create or restore trust in the government. In fact, it exacerbates the distrust and the perception of corruption in Jamaican society as citizens and potential visitors and investors alike read it as disingenuous, as seeking to cover or hide real issues in the country. It is therefore in the country's best interest for the branding strategists to rethink the largely tourism-centric model as they address the real issues with corruption in the nation.

Human Rights and Jamaica's Brand

Jamaica's human rights record has long been a stain on its public international image and, as such, a troubling issue for Jamaican authorities responsible for the country's brand. The weak observance of civil and human rights in areas of law enforcement, children rights, violence against women and girls, as well as gay rights has received much negative attention from international organizations and global media. Amnesty International's 2016 report on Jamaica asserts that unlawful killings and extrajudicial executions continued; violence against women and discrimination against lesbian, gay, bisexual, transgender, and intersex (LGBTI) people persisted; while children continued to be detained in violation of international standards. With regard to law enforcement, the historical record on Jamaica reveals a systematic practice of violence by members of the country's security forces. Police crime statistics reveal that an average of 100 to 140 people are shot and killed annually by the Jamaican police, one of the highest rates of lethal killings in the world. In 2001 Amnesty International, in a damning report on Jamaica's human rights situation, argued that "the manner in which deadly force is frequently employed, and the absence of prompt, thorough, and effective investigations are consistent with, in many instances, a pattern of extra-judicial killings."

Amnesty International admits that high levels of gang-related murders and killings by the police persist in inner-city communities but assert that a bad record exists with regard to holding the responsible officers to account and providing justice or reparations to the families of victims. Indeed, the human rights authority suggests that of the 2,220 fatal shootings by the police recorded between 2000 and 2010, only two police officers have been reportedly convicted (Amnesty 2012). It is noteworthy that the government of Jamaica in 2014 established a Commission of Enquiry into alleged human rights violations during the 2010 state of emergency that left sixty-nine people dead. The report by the commission published in 2016 identified a number of cases of possible extrajudicial execution and made significant recommendations for police reform. According to Amnesty (2016), the Jamaican police continued to refuse to accept any responsibility for human rights violations or extrajudicial executions during the state of emergency, and there is no indication by the government on how it would implement the recommendations of the commissioners.

In terms of violence against women and children, as well as observing the rights of children, Jamaica is not faring well. In 2016, 24 women were murdered by their partners (*Jamaica Gleaner* 2016), while over 470 women and girls had reported being raped (Amnesty 2016). Although the figures are trending downward, sexual violence against women is still very high and remains a real concern. In 2011 the police recorded 748 cases of rape, a 6 percent increase when compared to 704 reported in 2010 (Barnett 2012; *Jamaica Gleaner* 2016). Sexual assault is the most common cause of injury for women. Amnesty International argues that violence against women in Jamaica persists because the state has failed to tackle discrimination against women, allowing social and cultural attitudes that encourage discrimination and violence. This, the organization, argues violates the government's most basic treaty obligations under the UN Convention for the Elimination of Violence against Women (CEDAW), among others. It also suggests that the Jamaican government has not adequately addressed shortcomings in national legislation related to marital rape, incest, or sexual harassment, thereby encouraging impunity and leaving women without the protection of the law.

Meanwhile, international organizations such as Human Rights Watch and Amnesty International continue to draw global attention to the controversial issue of child offenders being housed alongside adults in prisons in Jamaica. The reports suggest that

> children as young as ages twelve and thirteen are locked up for long period of up to six months in filthy and overcrowded police lockups . . . The children are often held in the same cells as adults accused of serious crimes, vulnerable to victimization by their cellmates, and ill-treatment by abusive police; and virtually always they are held in poor conditions, deprived of proper sanitary facilities, adequate ventilation, adequate food, exercise, education, and basic medical care. Some of these children have not been detained on suspicion of criminal activity but have been locked up only because they are deemed "in need of care and protection." (Human Rights Watch 1999)

This situation does not augur well for Jamaica's public image. The treatment of women and children speaks loudly about the quality of a nation's brand. Yet it may be homophobic violence that puts Jamaica's human rights under the most international scrutiny. Jamaica is perceived to be among the world's most homophobic countries. In its 2013 report noted human rights organization Amnesty International reports that attacks, harassment, and threats were increasing against members of the Jamaican lesbian, gay, bisexual, and transgender community. The Jamaican law expressly prohibits homosexual expression. Section 76 of the Offences against the Person Act (1864) prohibits the "abominable crime of buggery," for which the punishment is imprisonment at hard labor for up to ten years. Although Amnesty and other international and local human rights bodies criticize Jamaica for retaining what it sees as an outdated "buggery law" on the grounds that the law is unconstitutional and serves to promote homophobia within the culture, no attempt has been made to amend or repeal it. Indeed, 76 percent of Jamaicans oppose amending the law. Even larger majorities believe that homosexuality is immoral (Jackson 2015).

In reality successive governments have in effect given legitimacy to gay discrimination. For example, former Jamaican prime minister Bruce Golding, in a 2008 interview with the BBC's *HardTalk* program, declared that "there is no room for gays in my Cabinet." Former prime minister Portia Simpson Miller—while declaring her support for gays in her 2011 reelection campaign, stating that no one would be discriminated against due to their sexual orientation—made no attempts to remove the discriminatory laws or raise the debate about gay rights in the Jamaican parliament. Indeed, in 2016 Jamaica's attorney general, Marlene Malahoo-Forte, used social media to criticize the U.S. embassy in Kingston for flying a pride flag after the killings of LGBTI people in a nightclub in Orlando, Florida. For scholars such as Williams, "the notion of a gay or homosexual person is not one that has any standing worthy of protection in Jamaica. The law, of course, is merely a reflection of wider social attitudes where the reality of a gay person or a gay community is not readily acknowledged" (2000, 110).

That gayness is not given political legitimacy or allowed to enter the Jamaican "national arena" is also explicitly manifested in Jamaica's music culture, which, paradoxically, has been one of the most strident pillars of the country's global brand. Although Jamaica's music is celebrated around the world, and reggae and dancehall artistes have helped to articulate the concerns and grievances of the poor—often mounting a lyrical counter war against oppressive power structures and being at the forefront of the global movement against inequality and injustice—some of its contemporary music transmits intensely violent, homophobic messages and lends support to antagonistic values and uncivil norms (Johnson 2011; Boyne 2003). Popular dancehall songs bear a call to arms against "batty bwoy" (male homosexuals) and lesbians calling for their murder. A textual analysis of popular dancehall songs reveals that dancehall artistes publicly issue threats to members of the gay community with impunity (Charles 2013).

Jamaica's anti-gay political stance, assumed by the country's political leadership, the church, and members of the artistic community, is detrimental to Jamaica's international image. It sends a negative signal about Jamaica to potential investors, other countries that look to Jamaica as a regional leader, tourists, and other members of the international community. It also marginalizes and endangers its own citizens, who cannot find institutional refuge or recourse for discriminatory actions taken against them. The unwillingness to engage in activism or to challenge prevailing attitudes toward homosexuality in the culture has the effects of isolating Jamaican artistes and prevents them from securing economic and other advantages in the global arena. For example, because aspects of Jamaican music have been tagged "murder music" in some quarters, Jamaican artistes are subject to an international campaign, which urges sponsors to pull funding from offending artistes, pressures venues not to book them, and stage boycotts and protests when they perform (Nelson 2010). In addition, Jamaican artistes have, in recent years, been banned from performing at international venues across the United States, Europe, Canada, and the Caribbean. The United States has also revoked the visas of several artistes, preventing them from traveling to that country (Petridris 2004; McKenzie 2010).

These are worrying developments. Anna Perkins, in chapter 4 of this volume, explores the impact of homophobia on Jamaica's economic development. She argues that the prevailing negative image of Jamaica as one of the "most homophobic nations on earth" carries consequences for the economic advancement of the country, first, at the micro-level, that is, on the lives of individuals who are victims of stigma and discrimination and as a result live less productive lives and their productive contribution to the nation is lost or significantly lessened; and second, Jamaica, having been branded as a homophobic nation, has suffered from losses in earnings, thereby further limiting growth in an already moribund economic space. Generally speaking, people outside the country, including Jamaicans in the diaspora, investors, students, and tourists, have expectations of political stability, the rule of law, tolerance, and respect for justice. Global media coverage of bad governance, poverty (which itself breeds social ills), crime, corruption, and failings of justice and homophobia have persisted rather than lessened and have served to weaken Jamaica's public image, its brand. It is clear that on some platforms, such as sports, music, and destination tourism, Jamaica's brand remains famous and strong, but in many ways it is being severely undermined. Yet it is the kind of brand that is so formidable that nobody gives up on it. So what now? Can Brand Jamaica reconcile its negative features and design a new future?

Moving Forward: Branding Jamaica into the Future

What are some of the efforts that Jamaican authorities can and should undertake to reimagine, reframe, and reconstruct its national image? First, Jamaica, for its small population size and economy, is an undeniably powerful national brand and needs to take full advantage of its current presence on the world stage. As Jamaica finds itself in a problematic and perplexing situation of prolonged negative images and labels (even alongside positive perceptions), it is important that the Jamaican government seeks to cater to more than just the current sun, sand, sea, and all-inclusive resorts, tourism-centric model as the singular expression of Jamaican identity in the world and illustrate and express the true complexity of Jamaica's brand. To successfully accomplish these changes, the Jamaican authorities must undertake several key initiatives.

Improve Governance

The Jamaican brand cannot be distinguished from the lived reality and material conditions of the Jamaican people as well as the experience of those who come to the island. The Jamaican government must initiate and expand policy with respect to building world-class infrastructure and facilities (e.g., roads, ports, and transportation), improving education, growing the economy, cutting unemployment, lessening corruption, reducing crime levels, and attendant to this, improving human rights and reforming the justice system. The political leadership must also seek to fast-track efforts at "de-tribalizing" the country's politics (i.e., making it less partisan and polarized) and at "de-garrisonization" (dismantling communities controlled by criminals and rebuilding them through social intervention). The Jamaican authorities must also make efforts to invest in the people of Jamaica in order to improve their quality of life with regard to housing, health, environment, youth, and sports as well as taking care of women and children. Undertaking these crucial developments at home are inextricably tied to how people see and talk about Jamaica and are thus imperative to improving Jamaica's reputation and reimagining the Jamaican brand in a global arena.

Recognize the Importance of Public Relations

If a nation fails to control and manage its international reputation, it facilitates the widening gap between reputation and reality, and hence, the image remains prey to ignorance and stereotypes (Mussche 2008). The fierce competition among places to gain positive media coverage and to attract tourists has made advertising the publicity tool of choice for place marketers. The World Tourism Organization reports that governments spend some $350 million annually on destination marketing (Morgan and Pritchard 2001, qtd. in Avraham and Ketter 2008). Although extremely costly, advertising has the benefit of giving campaign managers direct control over the message and its timing. Yet advertising has the disadvantage of consumers' tendency to distrust ads and question their credibility. It is thus important for Jamaican authorities to supplement its repertoire of Jamaica promotions strategies with effective public relations. Public relations is an intentional strategy that aims to build and sustain good relationships between an organization and its various publics, on whom its success or failure depends. It does so by obtaining favorable publicity, building up a good public image, and handling unfavorable publicity, rumors, stories, or events when these relationships go awry (Cutlip and Centre 2009). Deploying neutral mediated tools such as press connections, event publicity, and lobbying to portray a place positively, public relations are vital components in place promotion.

At present Jamaica public relations efforts largely takes place through representatives from the Jamaica Promotions Agency and tourism authorities (e.g., Jamaica Tourist Board, primarily the ministers of tourism) as well as external PR firms such as RuderFinn, New York. Generally, public relations people focus their efforts on both the positive and negative aspects of a place's image. For example, Burston-Marsteller (London), which handles public relations for the Jamaica Tourist Board, works mainly to promote the positive side of the nation's tourism product. Negative news such as the outbreak of a mosquito-borne virus, Chickungunya, and in the recent past the violence and unrest associated with the extradition to the United States of wanted drug kingpin Dudus Coke in 2010 and the controversy surrounding VW's Super Bowl commercial in 2013 are handled as needed by local representatives of the Jamaican government. It is important that Jamaican decision makers effect more organized public relations and work to prevent or mitigate the fallout of bad publicity via global news coverage about crime and the myriad social problems that may cause Jamaica to be perceived as dangerous. Public relations, over and above advertising, thus become crucial, particularly during times of sudden crisis. Recent negative publicity stemming from upsurges of crime and violence, natural disasters, economic instability, corruption, and declining human rights require strategic public relations responses, not merely advertising.

Promote Jamaican Credentials (Creative Arts, History, Business, Sports)

The articulation of Jamaican identity should begin at home. Promoting the country's credentials in the creative arts, sports, and business as well as its unique history and the genius of its people, as part of a coherent national brand build strategy, is required. For example, within the context of Jamaica's efforts to fight its way out of a severe economic downturn, the arts and culture have a fundamental role to play in getting the nation on track. The arts in general (dance, drama, and fine arts) and music in particular are a substantial part of what Jamaica is about. The country's diverse and vibrant culture represent its "calling card" abroad and the most dominant expression of Jamaican identity at home. Jamaican culture—expressed in popular songs, dance, and dramatic theater—has been important especially during difficult times. Reggae itself has largely been a reaction to society and a sort of soporific for the political dissatisfaction of the population with poor governance and a substandard way of life. Yet this musical form has managed to become part of the global mainstream, with many of its artistes known worldwide and its revolutionary message part of the political expression of oppressed people's worldwide, particularly those engaged in various liberation struggles throughout the 1960s and 1970s onward. Overall, the majority Afro-Jamaican population laid the foundation for the nation's "rich national culture by retaining their sense of spiritual values, by creating a vivid creole language, preserving their natural love for drama, music, song, drumming, for laughter, sympathy and wit" (Sherlock and Bennett 1998, xi). All of this gives Jamaica rights to an enormous intellectual property that must be leveraged to add value to the economy. This is all the more important now, when these cultural products are being redistributed by nonindigenous actors abroad without any credit or benefits being given to Jamaicans at home.

Jamaican authorities must not only position sport, particularly athletics, as a part of the expression of Jamaican identity, but it must hasten to build a viable sports economy, including sport tourism, now valued at US$632 billion, 14 percent of the overall tourism product (Franklyn 2009; Beckford 2007). Jamaica's astonishing accomplishments in sport is well known. At the London Olympics in 2012, the country recognized sixty-four years of participation in the Summer Olympic Games, stretching from its debut at the London Games in 1948. The nation's dazzling performances at these games is well known. At the Beijing Games of 2008, Jamaica captured its largest medal haul of twelve, winning both the popular men's and women's 100-meter sprint, thanks to the likes of Usain Bolt and Shelly-Ann Fraser-Pryce. Indeed, it was the first time—since the men from the United States did it in 1912—that athletes from a single country won all the medals in the 100-meter races (Franklyn 2009).

Although track and field is where Jamaica has had the most dominant presence, producing world records for well over five decades, Jamaica has also produced internationally acclaimed athletes in multiple sporting fields, including boxing, swimming, cycling, netball, football, volleyball, weightlifting, wrestling, and bobsled, and has won multiple medals across these areas. For example, beyond Usain Bolt's acclaim as the planet's fastest sprinter, the extraordinary success of swimmer Alia Atkinson, who in 2014 became the first black woman in the world to win a world swim title in the 100-meter breaststroke, is noteworthy (*Telegraph* 2014). Of remarkable note is also Jamaica's historic qualification and participation in the bobsled competition at the Winter Olympics in 1988 (Montreal, Canada) and 2014 (Sochi, Russia) as well as the historic participation of the "Reggae Boyz" at the Football World Cup in France 1998 and the historic qualification of the "Reggae Girlz" for the Women's Football World Cup in France in 2019. These combined achievements have the potential to catapult the nation into a global sports brand, with huge potential to contribute to the Jamaican economy (Beckford 2007).

Exploit the "Made in Jamaica" Label

Jamaican authorities should seek to accelerate the process of getting Jamaican manufacturers to capitalize on the "Made in Jamaica" label to gain "country equity" and economic traction for its popular export commodities such as Blue Mountain Coffee, Wray and Nephew Jamaica Rum, Red Stripe beer, and jerk sauce. Country equity is essentially an emotional value that stems from consumers' association of a brand with a country. In global marketing, perceptions and attitudes toward particular countries often extend to products and brands known to originate in those countries. These perceptions can be positive or negative and are impacted by past promotion, product reputation, and product evaluation and experience (Viosca, Bergiel, and Balsmeier 2005). For example, on the positive side, in the same way that Italy is associated with style, Japan with technology, and Brazil with football, Jamaica is currently linked with entertainment, notably reggae, tourism, and athletics, but can also take advantage of its association with certain products that carry the Made in Jamaica label. Jamaican manufacturers and business interests, for example, must become more alert to the "country of origin effect" (or geographic indicators—a name or sign used on a product to designate where it is from) on the market's perception of a country's products and services and seek to improve the brand equity of its export commodities. The government of Jamaica passed a Protection of Geographical Indications Act in 2004 to identify goods originating in Jamaica. Given the increasing flood of other coffee brands on the global market, for example, Blue Mountain Coffee must find a way to stand out and still be the coffee of choice for consumers of this beverage. Other products that manufacturers want to become competitive in the global market, such as Jamaica's jerk sauce, Jamaican rum, Red Stripe beer, Jamaican ginger, and scotch bonnet peppers, require immediate attention. Jamaican marketers should also seek to develop and strengthen the impressions global consumers have of the country's products. Brands with greater equity are less vulnerable to competitive markets and crises. They also benefit from greater trade cooperation and support. It is also important that Jamaica improve the brand of its products in the global marketplace through evaluating choice of labels, packaging, and positioning in new markets beyond the diasporic community. (See chapter 7 for Steffen Mussche-Johansen and Hume Johnson's more detailed discussion of intellectual property and Jamaica's cultural symbols and products.)

Return Jamaican People to the Center of the National Imagination

The Jamaican people must be positioned at the center of Jamaica's articulation of its national and international identity. The remarkable story of Jamaican achievement must be told through the prism of its people, and the Jamaican people ought to be made more visible in the global understanding of Jamaica. Jamaica boasts an exceptionally gifted people, many of whom have made a remarkable and substantial impact in their various fields and have helped to shape the nation's image in the international arena. Groups such as the Maroons, Rastafarians, and early freedom fighters as well as modern nationalists have all contributed to the country's unique history. All of these developments characterize the identity of Jamaica and Jamaicans. This aspect must find a place in any current and future Brand Jamaica project.

Despite its popularity in the world community for its astounding successes in sport, music, and destination tourism, Jamaica remains a strong and famous but troubled and misunderstood brand. Although exoticized in global media and endorsed by Jamaican tourism authorities as an island paradise of beautiful beaches, lavish resorts, and a laidback lifestyle, Jamaica is nevertheless experiencing an enduring crisis—economic instability, unemployment, high levels of crime and violence, corruption, and some human rights issues. These conflicting impressions, and "either/or" narratives, ultimately serve to weaken the Jamaican brand in international public opinion. They oversimplify the nation and do not tell the complete story of this remarkable country. Good advertising has been essential in creating the model tourism destination brand enjoyed by Jamaica today, but "that's not the same thing as a positive, famous, well-rounded, nation brand that stimulates attention, respect, good relations and good business" (Anholt 2006). The Jamaican authorities, through its Jamaica Tourism Board, Jamaica Promotions, and other agencies, are obliged to call upon the multiple, complex narratives that define Jamaica in their promotion of the country, not just articulate a singular sun, sand, and sea narrative of Jamaica.

Fundamentally, Jamaican authorities must ensure that the articulation of Brand Jamaica begins at home, that Jamaicans take the lead in defining themselves. Every Jamaican organization, company, and citizen must have the same mission in mind; their energies and behavior ought to be channeled in the same direction, one that is positive and productive for the country's reputation. All Jamaicans should be able to articulate the same powerful, credible, and interesting story about what their country is about;

what their tourism, sports, and cultural products are about; what the nation stands for and does not stand for. This consensus is crucial to Jamaica's brand success. It is also critical that Jamaica's authorities accelerate steps to address the enduring challenges of governance, including economic underdevelopment, unemployment, crime, corruption, and a decline in human rights, if they hope to gain control over Jamaica's public image. They also need to build on the power of the nation's creative industries and establish new intellectual property, aligning this innovation with a comprehensive (not merely cosmetic) national strategy for enhancing the nation's reputation and achieving its economic and social goals.

NOTES

1. No formal research has yet to trace Jamaica's internationalization as a nation brand. But anecdotal claims could be made about Jamaica's early entry on the world stage on the back of Jamaican national hero and civil rights activist Marcus Garvey and his United Negro Improvement Association (UNIA), a Pan-Africanist organization that was very active in the 1920s; the successes of Jamaica's sprint legends George Headley, Arthur Wint, Herb McKenley, and Donald Quarrie in the 1948 and 1952 Olympic Games; Jamaica's hosting of the 1966 Commonwealth Games in Kingston; as well as the nation's mythical role in the James Bond franchise—as many as twelve novels were written by author Ian Fleming at his vacation home in Jamaica, GoldenEye.
2. While I argue for the centrality of the Jamaican people in the formal branding and imagining of the nation, I acknowledge the role of the media, as well as other agencies and structures that condition how they become known to the world, because these have a significant impact on the resulting nation brand. For example, Usain Bolt is an iconic aspect of Brand Jamaica because of his superlatively strong personal brand and self-identity, yet his image and the way the world interprets him are filtered through his sponsor, Puma, which manages his image and how global media elects to frame the athlete.
3. Jamaica's historic participation in the bobsleigh competition at the Winter Olympic Games in Calgary, Canada, in 1988, although hailing from a country where snow does not exist, also positioned the nation as an example of courage, confidence, and triumph over adversity for many people around the world. The inspired participation and performance of the bobsled team

at the Winter Olympics became the subject of the popular Disney Film *Cool Runnings*. Many other nations with tropical climates, among them Nigeria, have since participated in the Winter Games, drawing inspiration from Jamaica. At the Sochi Winter Olympics in 2014, the Jamaica bobsled team was the center of international media attention for the enduring glory it brings to the games (Olympic.org 2014).

4. The Dominican Republic, Cuba, and St. Lucia are strong competitors in the tourism market for Jamaica, with St. Lucia recording the highest percentage of visitor growth in 2017.

5. It is important to note that the political reality is a bit more nuanced than this diagram suggests. For example, although Rastafari is seen as a positive element of Brand Jamaica, the Rasta community and culture has historically struggled against negative perceptions. Tourism, seen as a positive here, also has negative implications. The diagram also indicates homophobia as a negative development, but it does not capture the ongoing and incremental positive changes in attitudes toward the LGBTQ community in Jamaica.

6. *Informerphobia* refers to the fear people have about reporting information on (threatening) violence, crime, and terror to the state agencies formally tasked to respond to these threats. This includes giving witness testimony in court, filing police reports, and in extreme cases general participation in the justice system.

7. A don draws explicitly on the idea of the Italian Mafia don or mob boss. In Jamaica he is a self-styled politically connected local leader who wields power, status, and prestige from multiple sources—legal and illegal—and who assumes leadership over specific geographical areas called "garrisons"; hence, they are also called "area leaders." I discuss extensively their negative impact on civil society and governance in Jamaica elsewhere (Johnson 2011).

2

Branding the Nation

A Rhetorical Analysis of the Jamaica Tourist Board's Commercial Campaigns

Nickesia Gordon

This chapter offers a sociocultural analysis of the images and representations of Jamaica in television commercials produced by the Jamaica Tourist Board (JTB) as part of its marketing campaigns between 1955 and 2012. Using Barthes's (1977) idea of the rhetoric of the image as a theoretical framework along with critical and cultural studies, the author examines eight video commercials, one from each of the JTB's eight campaigns launched between 1955 and 2012, to explore what meanings about Jamaica's national identity as well as its brand as a "premier Caribbean tourism destination" are being produced by the various images and rhetorical messages embedded in the selected advertisements (JTB 2016a). Specifically, the author focuses on the images of the Jamaican landscape present in the commercials, the actors performing, as well as the narration that accompanies each video. Given the intentionality of the marketing process, in which advertising plays a significant role, it is important to critically examine the associated meanings or significations produced by such processes as they are actively cultivating particular perceptions about Jamaica as a place and space.

The premise of this line of investigation also stems from the notion that the images chosen by advertisers purposefully signify meanings, which are communicated by certain signs that tell us how those images should be understood. Barthes (1977) agrees that "in advertising, the signification of the image is undoubtedly intentional" (32), and since the accompanying images are designed to convey certain attributes of the product being advertised, they are thus "formed with a view to the optimum reading" (33). It is therefore appropriate to ask, What "readings" of Jamaica do the JTB commercials invite? And what are the political and cultural implications of the discourses that may be produced by such readings? Dali (2014) admits that advertising acts as "a tool for the expression and reinforcement of ideological consensus" (91), not just among local power brokers but those from the global stage as well. Often the frameworks at play in construing particular cultural identities, such as those from the Global South, are ideologically charged and coded a priori to persuade the observer to adopt a worldview that is normative and desirable to the power structure. To this end, the working "hypothesis" of the current discussion is that the dominant reading that the examined JTB commercials invariably invoke is that of the native and exotic other. The author thus argues that such portrayals are closely linked to the political and economic processes of globalization and culture. This implicates the JTB's branding efforts through its various marketing campaigns as being complicit in producing a form of neocolonialism that "depoliticizes and obscures the struggles and negotiations through which national identities are produced" (Kaneva 2011, 131).

The conclusion is that the articulation of a Jamaican aesthetic in the JTB commercials is part of a struggle for cultural identity within the context of a global economic and political system that positions such expressions as part of the syndrome of private ownership to be bought, sold, and traded for profit to the highest bidder (Nettleford 1979). Cultural marketing endeavors like the JTB's consequently create a vortex for the manipulation of world cultures from the less industrialized side of the hemisphere and come "dangerously close to the exoticization of Caribbean places and peoples that . . . take place through the [neocolonial] dynamics of tourism, culture industries and sexual labour" (Pertierra and Horst 2009, 109).

The JTB: A Brief Overview

The Jamaica Tourist Board (JTB) was founded in 1955 to promote Jamaica as a tourist destination exclusively oversees. This was not the first organized attempt to promote tourism as an industry in Jamaica. In 1910 the Jamaica Tourist Association (JTA) was created by nongovernment actors with the primary intention to "enhance the claims of the colony as a health and pleasure resort." Twelve years later, in 1922, the colonial government embarked on its own project to promote tourism on the island, which led to the establishment of the Tourist Trade Development Board (TTD). Both the JTA and TTD were amalgamated in 1926. This body was the forerunner to the current JTB. Initially, during the 1930s, funds for advertising tourism in Jamaica overseas were derived from a special tax levied on passengers traveling to the island by air or boat (JTB 2016a). However, once the JTB was created, on April 1, 1955, through the Tourist Board Act, this funding structure changed as the operations of the board became entirely funded by the government.

As stated on its website, the JTB has as its mission "the promotion of Jamaica as a preferred destination; identifying new and emerging customer groups, cultivating new relationships with travel partners and the dissemination of timely and useful marketing information to its offices and travel partners across the world" (JTB 2016a). Most of this promotion is done through aggressive advertising campaigns, such as the ones examined for this study, and other marketing strategies, such as maintaining offices in key locations across Europe, the Americas, and parts of Asia. These efforts are also part of the JTB's branding strategy, that is, to promote a specific image or identity of Jamaica that will lure tourists to its shores. What exactly is this brand that the JTB has been selling over the past fifty years? Scholars have noted with some concern the overarching vision of Jamaica and the Caribbean in general as a perennial "paradise" just waiting to pleasure (nonlocal) tourists that is typically found in tourism promotion material (Gordon 2012; Wilkes 2016). Such representations invoke the specter of colonialism, by presenting not only Caribbean locales as passive and backward but its people as servants who naturally inhabit positions of vassalage. These observations were made about the Caribbean tourism industry in general, not the JTB specifically. This current study focuses on the JTB, a state-sponsored organization, to examine the nature of the representations of Jamaica in its branding efforts. To do this, the author employs rhetorical analysis to investigate the visual images and verbal texts that accompany the selected JTB television commercials.

Rhetorical Analysis and Visual Images

Rhetorical analysis is a form of textual analysis that is increasingly being used by scholars to examine mass mediated culture. Although traditionally reserved for evaluating speech and the written word, rhetorical analysis is now recognized as an important tool for critiquing popular culture in visual forms. As Berger observes: "We watch around 4 hours of television each day and spend time looking through magazines; watching videos on YouTube; and checking Facebook, Pinterest, and other social media sites in a typical day. In all of these activities, we are exposed to visual images. So it makes sense to extend our use of rhetorical methods of analyzing written texts to visual images" (2016, 102).

In general textual analysis, or the close reading of a text, offers a critical approach to looking at the messages that may be embedded in a piece of work. Formerly the province of literary criticism, as previously stated, textual analysis has now crossed over to communications studies as a key methodological tool in film and television analysis (Gibbs and Pye 2005). In television and film textual analysis offers the opportunity for the critical appraisal of the thematic, formal, and stylistic qualities of a piece of work (2005). However, it also presents a framework for the exploration of representation and ideology in visual media as well as the sociocultural contexts within which such visual texts may operate. The latter is the main concern of this chapter, given that critical textual analysis approaches "often view culture as a narrative or story-telling process in which particular 'texts' or 'cultural artifacts' consciously or unconsciously link themselves to larger stories at play in the society" (Reed n.d.). In this respect the key thing here is representation, that is, how texts produce a version of reality that may be altered. They thus represent or symbolize the likeness of an object or subject and are portrayals that seek to leave an impression of what is real in the minds of viewers. As such, visual mass media texts create subject positions or identities for those they represent as well as for those who use them (Reed n.d.). Where subject positions or identities are established based on ideology, certain cultural information is conveyed that promotes stereotypical ideas about such subjects.

For the purposes of this study, Barthes's (1977) idea of the rhetoric of the image is especially relevant since it focuses on the image in advertising. According to Barthes: "In advertising the signification of the image is undoubtedly intentional; the signifieds of the advertising message are formed a priori by certain attributes of the product and these signifieds have to be transmitted as clearly as possible. If the image contains signs, we can be sure that in advertising these signs are full, formed with a view to the optimum reading: the advertising image is frank, or at least emphatic" (1977, 33).

Advertisements therefore offer a storehouse of meanings that can potentially make an impression on an audience. Commercials usually have thirty seconds in which to communicate their messages and so use highly charged and intensive images to accomplish their goals (Panzaru 2012). It is not surprising therefore that commercials are rife with ideological persuasion. According to Barthes, such acts of persuasion are conveyed predominantly through the visual images advertisers employ to sell their messages. An important utility offered by Barthes's approach to visual rhetoric rests with its allowance of simultaneous criticism of both image and text in visual media by acknowledging that the latter usually rely on linguistic and visual means of sending messages. The image is in constant communication with the accompanying text, and as such, words and images occupy their own defined spaces contiguously, thereby demanding discrete analysis (Barthes 1961).

Barthes defines the image as "an object endowed with structural autonomy" (1961, 195). Consequently, any analysis of images necessitates dividing them into units that are then constituted as signs. In rhetorical analysis signs may be denotative or connotative. According to Barthes, the image itself is denotative, while the messages they convey are connotative, that is to say, signs are read by recipients against a collected traditional stock of signs and codes, which cue us about how to read the literal image. In other words, ads "rely on a vocabulary of images stored in our brains over the years . . . [and] are based on our way of looking at reality" (Dali 2014, 92). The process of reading is thus interpretative; as "meaning is not transmitted to us, we actually create it according to a complex interplay of codes or conventions" (Panzaru 2012, 409). It is also ideological since in advertising signification is intentional. As a result, ads are replete with various cultural and political messages, all beckoning readings that promote the interests of the dominant classes. The present study is concerned with uncovering what dominant ideologies inform the message structure of the selected JTB ads and what cultural myths are being created or circulated by these commercials. To do so, the author developed a coding scheme that relies on key rhetorical devices as espoused by Barthes (1961; 1977), specifically the idea of denotation and connotation and signifier and signified. These were then used to identify specific signs and symbols used in the commercials to convey certain kinds of messages.[1]

Methods

As part of the study's analytical framework, the term *signs* refers to the "the countless meaningful items, images and so on [found in the selected JTB ads]" (Brummett 2012, 4) and that, as previously stated, have specific cultural import that may be ideological in nature. Signs are both visual and verbal in nature and are internally related through the idea of the signifier and the signified. In the current study visual images are operationalized as possessing the following attributes: being composed of visual signs such as signifiers and signified as well as symbols; representing something real or imagined; containing objects and people in various places and sometimes also words; generating meaning in those who see them; having denotational and connotational significance; and often generating emotional responses (Berger 2016).

Verbal texts refer to the language and narration that accompanies the visual text. Finally, both visual images and verbal text, at the level of the signified, are comprised of two messages, that is, "a denoted message, which is the analogon itself, and connoted message, which is the manner in which the society to a certain extent communicates what it thinks of it" (Barthes 1961, 197). Therefore, the visual images and verbal texts contained in the commercials being studied were coded both at the denotative and the connotative levels of meanings, *denotation* here referring to the "objectivity" of the signs and *connotation* referring to the "implicit" aspects of the sign (198). In other words, the "denotation is the dictionary meaning of the sign/word and it denotes something in the real world. The connotation is the interpretive association that comes with the sign and is something which is culturally and context dependent" (Panzaru 2012, 410). Every sign supposes a code constituted by what Barthes calls a "universal symbolic order," or a stock of stereotypes such as schemes, colors, gestures, and expressions that cue the audience to the preferred or dominant reading of the conveyed message. Along those lines the author also considered as part of the analytical structure used to assess the selected commercials issues such as mise-en-scène, or formal codes of construction such as setting, props, codes of nonverbal communication, and codes of dress; and technical codes, including shot size and camera angles (Selby and Cowdery 1995).

A total of eight JTB television commercials were analyzed, using the coding structure outlined here. The commercials were selected based on the JTB's campaign history since its inception, which yielded eight campaigns over the past fifty years: "Come to Jamaica" (1955–63), "Come Back to Jamaica" (1963–75), "Discover Jamaica" (1975–84), "Make It Jamaica Again" (1984–94), "One Love" (1994–2003), "Once You Go You Know" (2003–7), "Once You Go" (2008–11), and "Home of All Right" (2012–). Due to the space limitations of this study, only one commercial from each campaign was selected for analysis. These were the ones available on the JTB website as an example of the reigning ad campaign. All videos for these commercials were retrieved from the JTB website at the time of the study.

Branding Jamaica: Thematic Outcomes

Two dominant ideas about Jamaica's brand as a tourist destination emerged from the analysis of the eight commercials—namely, Jamaica as authentic and Jamaica as magical. These ideas are conveyed both through the verbal text or linguistic messages as well as the visual images that reference signs about the experiences one will get as a tourist if one spends time in Jamaica.

Brand Authentic

From a linguistic point of view the commercials invariably yield a message that references Jamaica as authentic. Within much of the tourism literature, the idea of authenticity is usually associated with cultural tourism (Ramkissoon 2015). It is usually presented as an important part of the value-added chain that tourist destinations can capitalize on in order to draw visitors to their products (Lee et al. 2016; Wang, Huang, and Kim 2015; Chambers and McIntosh 2008). That the analysis of the JTB commercials reveal the emergence of *brand authentic* as a theme illustrates that the JTB is perhaps trying to capitalize on this conceptual selling point. After all, studies in tourism tend to link tourists' perceived authenticity of a place to visitor satisfaction and potential repurchase of the tourism product (Ramkissoon 2015). From a purely commercial point of view, one can surmise that the JTB's branding of Jamaica as authentic in its commercials is good business strategy. However, such an uncritical understanding of the JTB's marketing approach belies several problematic issues associated with representing Jamaica as authentic. As Sharpley argues, "The search for authenticity in tourism is based around myth and fantasy about a cultural ideal" (1994, 127). In other words, authenticity is frequently staged. It is also a production, not unlike the JTB commercials, that in the case of Jamaica reimagines the anthropology of colonization as innocuous and even natural.

In the commercials the linguistic codes for authenticity come from the narration as well as captions present in the ads that use language such as "Come back to Jamaica, come back to yourself" or "Once you go, you know," words that beckon some belief in the genuineness of what the place and people have to offer. Visually, images of the Jamaican landscape as untouched and virginal reinforce this message. For example, there are repeated depictions of pristine white sand beaches that are empty of people except for the lone tourists or of uninhabited forests with only birds flying across its canopies. The JTB's "One Love" campaign (1994–2003) is especially redolent with these images. One such commercial begins with an aerial shot of a misty mountaintop surrounded by wispy clouds in what appears to be the early dawn. The scene then fades to a superimposition of an older, bearded gentleman standing on a colonial style veranda, dressed in expedition type clothing, looking out over the mountains contemplatively. He does not stay but quickly fades in and out of the picture. The rest of the ad continues to feature aerial shots of the landscape with flocks of birds flying over it. It ends as it began, back to the misty mountains, only this time the word *Jamaica* in bold font is tagged in the final shot. This final scene announces the brand, that is, Jamaica as brand authentic. We know this because the word *Jamaica* is literally and figuratively stamped across this primordial-looking landscape, not unlike a nametag or a label. It proclaims an identity or character that invites a reading of Jamaica as pre-discovered and therefore untouched. This depiction recalls Pratt's (2007) discussion of the "imperial eye" that informs a lot of travel writing emanating from Europe and America about postcolonial spaces. Such writing, according to Pratt, relies on certain imperial codes that derive from Europe's dependency on others to "know itself"—that is, Europe's obsession with binary representations of place and space that perennially casts them in the role of civilized versus uncivilized, developed versus underdeveloped, enlightened versus ignorant, and so on. In her observations Pratt noted how time and again travel writings have produced a "Eurocentred form of global of 'planetary' consciousness" (2007, 4): "From time to time as I read, I glimpsed the ongoing ways empire was coded by those in whose lives it intervened—coded in ceremony, sculpture and painting, in dance, parody, philosophy and history; in expressions unwitnessed, suppressed, lost or simply overlaid with repetition and unreality" (5). Pratt's commentary is very much applicable in capturing the ways in which Jamaica's identity as a tourist destination is being constructed through the JTB commercials included in this study. The camera's gaze becomes an imperial eye, as Pratt suggests, that frames Jamaica according to a colonial, pre-discovery imagination.

Denotatively, one can surmise that Jamaica is presented as a place that has many natural beautiful attractions that tourists may find nowhere else, hence making their experience an authentic one, given that they have come to the source. However, connotatively, the idea of authenticity rings far less innocent. According to Barthes (1961), connotation is the second-order sign that operates at the level of myth. It is therefore ideological and decidedly political in nature. In the case of the JTB commercials examined here, the myth of authenticity is packed with a host of colonial references that invite the view of Jamaica as a primitive place waiting to be discovered. In the "One Love" campaign commercial, the theme of discovery is alluded to in several ways. First, the iconic use of aerial shots to depict the countryside invokes the idea of a virginal landscape being gazed upon from afar by an explorer. Based on the history of the Caribbean, we are alerted to the fact that such scenes are very much reminiscent of the points of European conquest and colonization. The colonial style veranda as well as expedition clothing worn by the lone male character in the commercial, who is captured surveying the land from afar, only adds to the sense of European exploration and subsequent domination of places like Jamaica.

The theme of discovery is rampant throughout the JTB's commercial campaigns, with one campaign even titled "Discover Jamaica" (1975–84). In a commercial titled "Come to Jamaica," the opening scene is of an unoccupied beach in a spot along the coastline that looks pristine. It is a secluded alcove with the natural vegetation coming right up to the narrow patch of white sand beach that has waves rolling in. This opening scene alone insinuates the notion of discovery on multiple levels. First, denotatively, the tourist, as it states in the ad campaign, is invited to come and discover Jamaica by finding this "secluded" area along the coast. In other words, the tourist is being invited to be an explorer and, in so doing, may happen upon uninhabited spots such as the beach depicted in the commercial.

Connotatively, however, the sign of the beach has a decidedly colonial echo. As previously stated, such themes about authenticity and discovery hark back to the colonial relation and history shared by imperial Britain and Jamaica. It is a setting that marks the margins/origins of empire, the point of conquest and domination as well as the existence and placement of the other. As the project of imperialism culminates in the domination, classification, and universal commodification of all space under the aegis of the metropolitan center (Said 1993), the reiteration of the colonial power in Jamaica's tourism advertising is troubling. Despite the fact that Jamaica obtained national independence in 1962, it is quite alarming that the colonial ethos is so strident in JTB commercials, even fifty years later. In retaining these sensibilities, the JTB's branding efforts give way to and maintain the geopolitical and postimperial significance of the former colonizer, even to the point of naturalizing it through its depictions of the island in its commercials. However, as Barthes's understanding of mythology allows us to recognize: "What we accept as being 'natural' is in fact an illusory reality constructed in order to mask the real structures of power obtaining in society . . . We inhabit a world of signs which support existing power structures and which purport to be natural . . . The role of the mythologist, as Barthes sees it, is to expose these signs as the artificial constructs that they are, to reveal their workings and show that what appears to be natural is, in fact, determined by history" (Moramollu 2016, 456–57).

Historically, a colonial space was often conceived as a passive space, and not surprisingly, Jamaica and Jamaicans are usually presented as such in the JTB commercials examined for the study. There is a perennial sense of waiting and being waited upon that pervades the commercials. Jamaica is waiting to be discovered, waiting for the tourist to come, and once they arrive, they can expect to be served, not unlike how colonial elites were once waited upon. The servitude of the locals becomes part of the authentic experience tourists can expect when they visit. Wilkes articulates this very well when she similarly observes how black bodies are predominantly packaged for consumption in Caribbean tourism advertisements. As she notes, images, such as the ones found in JTB commercials, "reveal the way in which the consumption of black labor in the Caribbean is sold as luxury; these are the reminders of successful colonial projects" (Wilkes 2016, 9).

In addition to presenting Jamaica as naturally colonial, the JTB commercials scrutinized here also deny the island modernity in their depictions of brand authentic. Here the idea of authenticity is predicated on the idea of the primitive, meaning aboriginal or indigenous, and therefore authentic. Jamaica is presented as a peasant landscape with the commercials' focus on the countryside or the use of the rural-scape as a microcosm of the entire country. As such, the island is imagined as a backward place where locals transport themselves on unsaddled donkeys or are engaging in subsistence occupational activities. Such a depiction of contemporary Jamaica is at odds with real life wherein the country, especially among the middle and upper-middle classes, has all the trappings of modernity, inclusive of decent physical infrastructure; thriving business districts in places such as capital city, Kingston; modern transportation, particularly in the cities; and a well-developed and active democracy and political system. Nonetheless, this de-contemporizing of the island "lays bare the process of constructing 'the primitive' as the necessary complement to modernity" (Desmond 1999, 466). It is a necessary way of "nativizing" the landscape and people in order to maintain the dichotomy of modern and primitive. Such oversimplified depictions of Jamaica and its inhabitants robs the country of its social, cultural, and political complexities and renders it a space in need of paternalism. They also make it easier to trade this image as a cultural production on the global market to sell Jamaican tourism and to make the precarious brand of authenticity credible, given its resurrection of all things colonial.

The JTB's, and therefore the Jamaican state's, active creation of this brand of authenticity begs reflection on the role of postcolonial subjects in perpetuating such troubling representations. There seems to be an emphasis on shaping the identities and cultural values of the local space through the creation of a particular perception that favors colonialism. Since such creations are guided by the belief systems, behavioral norms, and lifestyles of the creators, in this case the Jamaican government and elites, the implications are that there is a certain self-exploitation, or "pimping," occurring.[2] This re-creation—or more precisely, backward remodeling—of Jamaica's national identity from an independent and self-governing state to a colonial one has economic currency that benefits the creators of this identity who trade this brand as a cultural reality in the global media marketplace. This is clearly an insidious ideology that falsely represents the contemporary realities of Jamaica and its citizens, who are often ill used by the policies created by local elites and, more broadly, by the ethos of neoliberal free market systems that create harsh living conditions that affect their daily living.

Brand Magical

"Come to Jamaica and feel all right" is a signature line running through many of the JTB's commercials. It is a phrase that references the renowned Bob Marley song "One Love" and has been one of the most powerful signifiers of "magic" in the JTB commercials, especially those running from the mid-1980s onward. The song is the JTB's anthem for announcing Jamaica as a land that is problem free. The song, just like its famous singer and author, is iconic and is a global signifier of ideas such as peace, unity, and equality. Denotatively, the phrase's allusion to Bob Marley's song paints a picture of Jamaica as a friendly place. In fact, in one of the commercials the narrator describes Jamaicans as naturally friendly. There is also an allusion to Jamaica's national motto, "Out of Many One People," coined post–national independence to be inclusive of the Chinese, Indian, and Middle Eastern immigrants as well as remaining European whites who had historical roots in Jamaica. The notions of unity and inclusivity espoused through the commercials' intimation to the national motto as well as Bob Marley's song are noble ideals that tourists may undoubtedly find attractive and that might encourage them to think of Jamaica a place where there are indeed no problems, a place where everything and everyone "feel all right," a place that is in fact magical.

A poignant rebuttal of this conceptualization of tourist destinations such as Jamaica as magical comes from the activism of a group of local fisherwomen in Kerala, India. The women gagged themselves in protest against the use of the word *magical* to describe their community by Beatles star Sir Paul McCartney, who, upon a visit to Kerala, described his tour of the state accordingly (Desmond 2008). The women were drawing attention to the fact that there was nothing magical about the negative impacts that tourism was having on their local livelihoods and community. As reported in the *National Catholic Reporter*, "the women's front and their associates, the Kerala Independent Fishworkers Federation, say that the construction and the resorts are eroding the fragile coastal environment and denying fisherfolk access to the sea and their livelihood."

A recent documentary, *Resisting Coastal Invasion*, directed by the award-winning filmmaker K. P. Sasi, shows how resorts take prime beaches away from fisherfolk. One scene, for instance, shows a barbed wire fence blocking an entire fisherfolk neighborhood from the sea. Peter, one of the protesting residents featured in the documentary, said that besides denying access to the sea, the resorts eliminate space fisherfolk use for fish drying, selling their catch, and socialization. Another, Magline, says "resorts take away our space to dry fish and mingle in privacy and the places men use to mend and dry nets, park boats and relax," Magline said. "Tourism often brings people right into our backyards, where women work, wash and bathe."

Clearly, the idea that Kerala is magical is perhaps more in the eye of the tourist and those responsible for constructing the myth. Not unlike the protesting residents of Kerala, many local Jamaicans who reside and earn a living in popular tourist areas are concerned about the disenfranchisement that often results from the unrelenting creep of the tourism industry into their communities. In an ethnographic study of issues related to tourism sustainability in Jamaica, Johnson (2014) makes the observation that many of the local residents encountered seemed to occupy the periphery of a largely profitable industry that mostly disrupted rather than contributed to their livelihoods. This sentiment is painfully captured in field notes included in the published study: "These people occupy a space at the periphery of the all-inclusives. The space between resorts, on the beach, where they spend their days waiting for brief opportunities to get in on the immense profitability of tourism here in Negril. They don't have jobs as guards, entertainment staff, housekeepers, bartenders or servers that would allow them to legally occupy spaces within the lines. So they wait outside the lines" (Johnson 2014, 950).

As Johnson's study illustrates, the experiences of many local Jamaicans in relation to tourism are far from magical. In fact, they seem to benefit the least, if at all, from the immense revenue generated by the local, natural resources the industry uses to generate such profits. Johnson references this issue when she notes "tourism in Jamaica has clearly generated a great deal of revenue. However, the utilization of tourism as a way to provide sustainable support to the economy has had a problematic impact on the island. According to a 2008 IMF [International Monetary Fund] report, economic growth in Jamaica has not been correlated with increases in the tourism sector (International Monetary Fund 2008)" (Johnson 2014, 952). This is mostly because a significant number of hotels and other tourism-related activities are owned or controlled by foreign investors, an issue that points to the influence of foreign capital on the industry. There are also clear environmental costs attached to the growth of the tourism industry, most of which locals have to bear: "The promotion of tourism in the country has corresponded with the neglect of local residents regarding environmental and health concerns that directly impact the population. The environmental burdens of tourism in Jamaica include the removal of coral reefs and wetlands, along with increased water usage and solid waste, and water pollution in resort areas" (Johnson 2014, 953).

There are ethical implications related to the sociocultural and economic price that many locals have to pay for this magic. Clearly, many problems are associated with the magic of tourism, especially where local actors are disenfranchised by its activities. Piccard sees the relationship between tourism and magic as defined by two realms, one that relates to "the psychological 'material' experiences of the specific sites that seem to have seductive powers over tourists" and the other "to representations of the 'magic' of tropical islands which are merely texts used to create social aspirations associated with certain places" (2013, 32). However, apart from alluding to the historical resilience of associating tropical spaces such as Jamaica with magic, Piccard's account of what he sees as the link between tourism and the idea of magic is largely uncritical, given that he seems to naturalize this connection. There is the assumption that tropical places are naturally "seductive" because the experiences tourists will have in such places are "material." In this context material experiences are elemental, if not magical. They are experiences that the tourist should expect. Textual representations, such as the JTB commercials, per Piccard's view, also contribute to this naturalizing process. They are the conduits of expectations through which the tourist first encounters tropical magic. Therefore, when a potential visitor comes across a text such as a JTB commercial, the line between reality and fiction has already been blurred. The text only reveals the magic of the production process, the myth of place and space sold as reality. It has been rare to find in the literature critical accounts of the representation of tropical spaces with magic.

The idea of Jamaica as a magical place is further buttressed by another powerful linguistic marker that pervades the JTB commercial campaigns, that is, Jamaica as paradise. Indeed, "Jamaica Paradise" was the title of one of the JTB's very first commercials in its inaugural campaign "Come to Jamaica" (1955–63). In the commercial children are seen frolicking in various acts of play and, more important, are heard describing how Jamaica is paradise to them. In relating how climbing the famous tourist attraction Dunn's River Falls makes her feel, one child says, "It feels like I'm in a bubble bath." Another, describing a scene where children are frolicking in the ocean, says, "Sometimes the sea is so soft, it feels like a mattress." Finally, at the end of the commercial, the omniscient narrator sums it all up by saying: "For children, Jamaica is kind of a paradise. But you know, even when you grow up, it's so easy to feel like a child again here." From the outset the JTB established the motif of paradise as a branding mechanism to sell Jamaica to tourists and has consistently used it as an overarching trope in its campaigns, even in more recent times, when the idea of paradise as magic seems as potent as ever. In one of the commercials from its most recent campaign, "Home of All Right" (2012), the narrator describes Jamaica in fantasy-like terms: "There's something in the people, there's something in the sand, there's something in the air, there's something in the water, there's something in the night. It's called all right and it's something you can only find here, Jamaica, home of all right." Again, we are presented with an inexorable idea of paradise in this commercial, in the invocation of a place where everything is intrinsically "all right." Everything is also magical, signified by the amorphous but titillating "something" that is never named but left to the imagination. The word *something* therefore becomes a metaphor for magic, and its repetition in the commercial becomes an incantation of sorts, potentially conjuring all genera of caprices in the mind's eye of the tourist.

However, a second-level reading of the JTB's use of language to evoke paradise and magic reveal the myth of the sign. As Barthes lets us know, myth relies on two semiological systems, one of which is linguistic. In this system, which Barthes refers to as the "language-object," it is the language and the modes of representations that are assimilated to it that "myth gets hold of in order to build its own system" (1972, 100). This is a system of representations that reproduces signs, such as "paradise," in ways that are de-historized and therefore predominantly ideological in nature. This is the very essence of myth; that is, "it transforms history into Nature." In presenting Jamaica as naturally paradisiacal and magical, the JTB's commercial campaigns are engaging in mythical speech that distorts the historical and contemporary realities of the country. Because "myth hides nothing and flaunts nothing . . . myth is neither a lie nor a confession: it is an inflection" (Barthes 1972, 116). What this means is that myths are active constructions of human beings and so must be read as the political propositions of their creators.

Once again, this line of reasoning ultimately leads one to question the role of the local power structure in perpetuating images of Jamaica that obscure its historical realities as well as its contemporary complexities. Given that the JTB is a state agency, the mythologies contained in its commercial campaigns can be interpreted as state-sponsored distortions. Actively creating misrepresentations of one's own nation-state, especially on the capitalist global stage, seems inimical to the political and economic will to self-determination that most governments strive for. What, then, underscores the intentional creation of a brand identity that undermines that very project? A better understanding may be gained by looking at how myths operate in the first place. Linguistically, myths produce depoliticized speech, which allows certain shifts and transformations in realty to occur. Read this way, the rhetoric of the JTB may therefore be less about the intentions of the state as a national body and more about the objectives of individual state actors who may have specific agendas. Barthes makes it clear that "myths serve the dominant class" (Roy 1998). They do so by "mystifying and obscuring their origins and thus their political or social dimension" (para. 18).

Conceivably, Jamaica's political elites, while not directly benefiting in any obvious material way from promoting myths of magic and paradise or even authenticity, meet an objective in maintaining the status quo.

Certain values about Jamaica in terms of social hierarchy and class become naturalized to and unquestioned by both tourists and the laborers who work in the local tourism industry. Thus, an understanding of myths and how they function helps us to appreciate that "what causes mythical speech to be uttered is perfectly explicit, but is immediately frozen into something natural; it is not read as a motive, but as a reason" (Barthes 1972, 116). The reason for branding Jamaica in the ways it has been through the JTB commercials is clear: to market the island as a preferred tourism destination so that the state may gain revenue. What is less clear are the motives that, through careful reading, appear to be the maintenance of the social and political status quo.

The author agrees with Wilkes that "it is difficult to accept representations of Jamaica which suggests that it is a simple enduring 'paradise'" (2016, 24). Or those that invoke a colonial narrative that repackages Jamaica's colonial history "of racialized slave labor [and makes it] available to global audiences" as a commodity (23). It is not enough to rationalize these promulgations as purely external, meaning that these are paternalistic identities being imposed on countries from the Global South by neocolonialists from the Global North. As suggested in the preceding discussion, in the context of the JTB commercials analyzed here, any neocolonialism that may be at play in constructing such problematic images of Jamaica is largely homegrown. The international brand of Jamaica that is projected by the JTB does little to improve the esteem of the country as a modern, self-governing democracy.

Unfortunately, the nature of the JTB's branding efforts via its commercial campaigns have changed very little over the past fifty years, if at all. Utilizing Barthes's critical framework of the rhetoric of the image leads one to that conclusion. While the aesthetics of the commercials, meaning production values related to sound, lighting, and editing, may have evolved over time, the thematic concerns have not. The brand consistently relies on colonial and, more recently, neocolonial imaginings to establish its identity. The brand, through its invocation of magic and authenticity, invites external consumption of Jamaica and Jamaicans, not unlike the consumption that occurred through colonialism. The fact that an impressive amount of the money, approximately 40 percent (Johnson 2014), generated via tourism is repatriated to foreign hotel owners who reside outside the country speaks to that point. From a critical perspective the myth therefore continues, despite the modern "feel" of the commercials. The smiling, happy faces of the "local" residents that are sometimes depicted mask the harsh realities of the economic and cultural exploitation that is part and parcel of the tourism industry.

The JTB should perhaps strive to establish a vision of Jamaica that is more nuanced, multidimensional, and accurate. The national brand should not be reduced to myth, bearing in mind that national identities cannot be reduced to a single element (Buarque 2015), such as "authentic" or "magical." It should instead "be seen as a complex construct composed of interrelated components such as ethnic, cultural, territorial, economic, and political factors that signify bonds of solidarity among members of communities united by shared memories, myths and traditions" (Smith, qtd. in Buarque 2015). Given the ideological motivations that may be at play in relying on age-old stereotypes to construct Jamaica's tourism brand, there may be little incentive to reform it. After all, the brand has been intact for over fifty years. Notwithstanding, one wonders how much longer these romantic notions of authenticity and magic will prevail in an era of intensified competition for tourists, especially in the Caribbean, from players such as Cuba, whose tourism market is set to expand with its newly negotiated relations with the United States, and other global powers.

NOTES

1. Visual images and narration were coded discretely. This is because images and their meanings are contingent upon the verbal aspects of a text; that is to say, the verbal is constantly reinforcing the visual (Barthes 1977).
2. Please see chap. 3 of this volume for further discussion of the idea of "pimping" as a central trope of Jamaica's brand as a tourist destination.

3

Women of "Paradise"

Tourism Discourses and the Lived Realities of
Jamaican Women in the United States

Kamille Gentles-Peart

Tourism is a major part of Jamaica's global identity. The island's warm
climate, beaches, and beautiful landscape beckon over two million visitors
per year from all over the world to its shores. In 2014, according to the
Jamaica Tourist Board (JTB), over three million visitors came to Jamaica.
The economic benefits of tourism to Jamaica are unquestionable. It is a
mainstay of the Jamaican economy. Each year the sector posts the highest
levels of foreign exchange receipts, approximately US$2 billion. Resorts and
hotels, restaurants, street vendors, and farmers all benefit from the foreign
dollars garnered by tourism. Moreover, it is the second largest employer
in the island, with thousands of Jamaicans working directly or indirectly
in tourism (Martin 2013). It is therefore no wonder that the nation, led
by the JTB, places a lot of focus on building and promoting a destination
brand, constructing an image of beautiful beaches, lush landscapes, and
perennial sunshine—"paradise"—that will attract visitors to its shores.

However, while the intent of the tourism brand may be to attract tourists
to Jamaica, the image of the island that is constructed by this discourse
also has implications for how Jamaicans are perceived, particularly when
they go abroad. The brand and accompanying media campaigns project a
specific image of Jamaica and its people into its tourism markets (which
are predominantly white, Anglo societies). These images often become the
dominant narrative of the island that frames how Jamaica and Jamaicans

are viewed and influences how they are treated when they immigrate to these locations. In other words, when Jamaicans move to places such as the United States—which is one of Jamaica's most important suppliers of tourists and thus a main target for the JTB campaigns—Jamaicans come in direct contact with the idea of their homeland as paradise and have to live with the implications of being the natives of paradise. This chapter examines the impact of discourses of paradise on the lives of Jamaican women living abroad. Specifically, I interrogate how the discourses attendant to the tourism brand influence and shape the diasporic experiences of first- and second-generation Jamaican women in the United States.

Tourism and Controlling Images

Tourism, or destination, marketing is a deliberate attempt to develop positive attitudes toward a destination and hopefully shape tourist behavior. Hence, tourism foregrounds, highlights, and romanticizes select qualities and attributes of a nation in an attempt to attract visitors. This project of attraction relies heavily on disseminating particular ideologies and images of the country that help to shape consumers' or prospective tourists' attitudes toward the featured destination. Literature suggests that tourism marketing may be able to construct positive identities and images for nations, particularly developing countries that are often collapsed into a singular category and are associated with poverty, poor governance, and dysfunction (Lepp and Harris 2008). Indeed, the tourism industry in Jamaica has managed to construct and maintain a parallel narrative and image of paradise for the nation, in spite of Jamaica's global reputation for violence, homophobia, and corruption (as Hume Johnson articulates in chapter 1).

Yet the images of a nation created by tourism and the marketing used to promote it are problematic. Tourism marketing has a storytelling function that can cultivate specific, often stereotypical views of nations and the people who inhabit them; the practice thus promotes what Patricia Hill Collins refers to as "controlling images." According to Collins, controlling images are socially constructed conceptions of African American women designed by dominant groups to justify the policing, controlling, and containment of black women. In this way these mythologies are essential to maintaining "intersecting oppressions of race, class, gender, and sexuality." Collins says: "As part of a generalized ideology of domination, stereotypical images of Black womanhood take on special meaning. Because the authority to define societal values is a major instrument of power, elite groups, in exercising power, manipulate ideas about Black womanhood. They do so by exploiting already existing symbols, or creating new ones" (2000, 69).

An infamous long-standing controlling image is that of the "mammy" figure. This epitome of the faithful, obedient domestic servant was created to justify black women's exploitation as domestic slaves and restrict them to domestic service. Another controlling image is that of the "Jezebel," the sexually aggressive black woman figure that was (and still is) used to position all black women as sexually deviant and available, provide ideological justification for sexual assaults on their bodies, and feed discourses of their high (uncontrollable) fertility. The "strong black woman" is another controlling image that reifies black women as indomitable and undaunted by oppressive systems and therefore trivializes and obscures the structural issues of racism and sexism that black women face (Beauboeuf-Lafontant 2003).

These symbolic representations have systemic, far-reaching consequences. They are tenacious in their ability to cultivate tendencies and outlooks toward black women and ultimately serve to prop up power structures (Rose 1994; Carby 1994; Emerson 2002; Brown Givens and Monahan 2005). The impact of controlling images is evident in how black women are treated in their everyday lives. For example, Dorothy Roberts (1995) demonstrates how popular mythologies (or controlling images) that construct black women as undeserving mothers (such as the image of the welfare queen and Jezebel) serve to legitimize government control of black women's reproductive lives, including forced sterilization and the disproportionate removal of black children from their black mothers. Similarly, Kimberlé Crenshaw (1995) also suggests that dominant conceptions of black women as the embodiment of "nontraditional" feminine behavior (as normalized by the Sapphire and Jezebel figures) create discrimination against black women who are raped. Because of perceptions of deviant sexuality, black women are less likely to be viewed sympathetically, their rapists (black or white) are less likely to be convicted and, when convicted, receive less jail time than the rapists of white women.

Controlling images are also significant in influencing how black women perceive themselves and can impact their identity and self-image. For instance, these controlling images can foster a form of "double consciousness." According to W. E. B. Du Bois, black people in America are "gifted with second-sight . . . a sense of always looking at one's self through the eyes of others, of measuring one's soul by the tape of a world that looks on in amused contempt and pity" (1903, 9). This double consciousness creates "contradictions of double aims . . . that seek to satisfy two unreconciled ideals" (2). In other words, black people hold the desire to maintain, nurture, and speak to the ideas, truths, and consciousness of their communities but are simultaneously cognizant that the white world disparages, ridicules, and tries to stamp out blackness.

Controlling images, when internalized, can also foster practices that are detrimental to black women's well-being. The strong black woman trope, for example, has been internalized by many black women, making it difficult for them to seek and receive help. Tamara Beauboeuf-Lafontant (2003) and Cheryl Townsend Gilkes (2000) also argue that the presumption of strength and deviance in black women pushes them to develop compulsive overeating and obesity that goes unnoticed or unacknowledged by them and others. Meri Nana-Ama Danquah (1998) similarly discusses how the strength attributed to black women obscures their ability to talk about and seek treatment for depression.

While Collins speaks specifically about African American women in the United States, the concept of controlling images and their effects can also be applied to images of "third world" women that are circulated through tourism marketing. Analogous to the white supremacist images of black women in the United States, images and ideologies reflected in and projected through tourism campaigns are embedded within particular historical and ideological power structures that reinforce white colonialist ideas about the third world, it peoples generally, and women in particular.

First, the images and discourses mobilized by destination marketing of third world nations is consumer driven; that is, they respond to the needs, desires, and fantasies of (largely white) consumers and reflect an idea that is designed to coincide with and confirm the ideologies and images that already exist about a particular nation. In fact, third world destination marketing often originates in and targets populations in Europe and the United States. As a result, the majority of third word destination marketing is created and distributed by "First World promoters who are economically motivated to sell a particular brand of fantasy to a First World market" (Echtner and Prasad 2003, 661). Marketing campaigns originating from the "tourist" nation also respond to these "first world" fantasies and aim to give back to prospective consumers what they already expect of the country and its people. In other words, regardless of the origin, tourism marketing for third world countries packages and sells back to visitors (and their citizens) preexisting conceptions of the land, the culture, and the people of the destination. In this way destination marketing helps to foster a lifetime of imagery that consumers have naturally, or organically, absorbed about the destination—the country, state, or region (Kerrigan, Shivanandan, and Hede 2012).

In the context of Jamaica the controlling image being fostered is the myth of "present paradise" (Echtner and Prasad 2003, 672). In this construction paradise is a place to which one can escape from industry, modernity, and productivity; it encompasses the idea of a world untainted by the drudgery of modern life. The mythology of paradise has a long history, created by travel narratives that present the Caribbean as exotic. As Nickesia Gordon argues in chapter 2, this imagery connotes great physical beauty but also unproductivity and backwardness and serves to de-historicize and "nativize" the country. These writings and marketing strategies construct the islands as spaces that offer great vacation destinations but not much else. Their peoples are seen as warm and hardworking but incapable of innovativeness and avant-gardism (Echtner and Prasad 2003). According to prevailing discourses, therefore, while Jamaica is able to reinvigorate tourists and visitors, it does not have much to offer to projects of modernity.

Furthermore, the mythology of paradise also models the racial, gender, and sexual hierarchies of the plantation system established during slavery and colonial rule (Nixon 2015; Strachan 2002). Ideas of paradise are constructed through the colonial white male gaze that positions so-called paradise nations as economically, politically, and culturally dependent, objects of desire for conquest that are populated by inferior, exploitable "dark-skinned natives" (particularly women). As Angelique Nixon reminds us, discourses of paradise are never neutral or innocuous, as they are "inherently racialized, gendered and sexualized because of and through the histories of colonialism" (2015, 3). By presenting the island as paradise (woman) tamed and as the playgrounds of white young beautiful couples with local women only appearing as servers (Dann 1996; Morgan and Pritchard 1999; Echtner 2002), tourism marketing cultivates the idea of Jamaica as a space to be used and exploited by white visitors; it promotes the ecological, cultural, and social colonization of Jamaica and reinforces European/U.S. white male supremacy over the nations and their peoples (Nixon 2015). Ideas of paradise are therefore extensions of "European colonial expeditions, encouraged by the 'world-organising principle' of racism and European dominance in the global economy, that accentuate the racialised boundaries between 'Black' and 'white' societies" (Leed 1991, 273). Therefore, tourism marketing of Jamaica plays to the fantasies of first world consumers, resulting in the cultivation of imperialist, racist, gendered stereotypes that exist in the ideologies of the West (Echtner 2002; Echtner and Prasad 2003).

Moreover, these synthetic, selective, politically motivated (controlling) images presented in destination marketing for Jamaica can cultivate certain attitudes and practices. Images and ideologies propagated by tourism marketing campaigns play significant roles in projecting and disseminating these colonial discourses globally, including among Jamaican diasporic women. The display of these ideologies in media forces Jamaican people abroad to view themselves through the prism of white male Eurocentric society and interpellate them to perform the roles created for them in these narratives. These images can help to cultivate a double consciousness ("second-sight") for Jamaican people, particularly women, living outside of Jamaica: they value their Jamaican heritage, but they exist in a diasporic space that nurtures and upholds white male colonialist discourses that exoticize, debase, and ostracize that culture.

To be clear, tourism marketing related to Jamaica is not the only factor that contributes to Jamaican people's experience and identity abroad. As Gartner and Shen (1992) suggests, images of nations are formed organically and inorganically, through mediated and unmediated means. However, these controlling images do work with other existing narratives and ideologies to create a "symbolic environment" that fosters, upholds, and normalizes ethnocentrism and racism toward Jamaicans. According to George Gerbner, mass media (institutions that mass produce and distribute messages) have certain types of objectives and create "symbolic environments" that cultivate (support, sustain, and nourish) certain types of "collective consciousness" (1970, 69; Morgan and Shanahan 2010, 339). Gerbner insists that people's overall viewing experience (across genres) has the ability to shape audiences' perception of reality and reinforce ideologies. Based on this theory, the controlling images mobilized in tourism marketing for Jamaica reinforce hegemonic ideas of the nation, contribute to the stereotyping of the Jamaican population, particularly women, and therefore influence the experiences of Jamaican women, not only at home but also abroad. When Jamaican women move to places such as the United States, they enter a "collective consciousness" that positions their homelands as paradise and them as women of paradise.

Black Jamaican Women in the United States

Migration has been a perennial feature of the Jamaican existence. In spite of the issue of brain drain and other concerns associated with the departure of citizens, outward migration is not seen as a problem from the Jamaican perspective but is regarded as an institutionalized strategy for economic betterment (Chaney 1987). Women have been, and continue to be, significant players and participants in migration from Jamaica to the United States. They were a substantial part of the first wave of black migration in the early 1900s and have been credited with the development and maintenance of black Caribbean communities in the United States. Although their ties to and responsibility for families made migration more complicated for them than for their male counterparts, they were often the first ones in a family to migrate and subsequently facilitate the emigration of others. Furthermore, more so than their male counterparts, who were perceived as more likely to "run off" with American women, Jamaican immigrant women were expected and trusted to send remittances and goods to help care for the family left behind. In this sense, then, they were expected to be in constant contact with their homelands, a practice that has facilitated the construction and maintenance of transnational ties (Watkins-Owens 2001).

Black Jamaican women today continue to be the most likely to emigrate from their homeland, a decision made possible by the continued practice of child fostering and network migration. Their migration to the United States also remains very strategic and goal oriented, many of them coming to the United States to secure economic betterment for themselves and their families. They also continue to send money and barrels of American goods to their families in their homeland, fostering connections to their culture and creating transnational subjectivities that complicate complete acculturation and assimilation into the U.S. culture. Black Jamaican women (historically and contemporarily) clearly bear the responsibility for the economic support of their families in the United States as well as on the island, a responsibility that also falls to second-generation immigrant women. Consequently, their diasporic experiences are centered around economic success in the United States. In fact, both first- and second-generation black Jamaican women embrace the idea of industriousness, hard work, and productivity—having a job—as a significant aspect of black Jamaican women's diasporic identity (Gentles-Peart 2014). In other words, their success as immigrants is measured by their ability to earn money.

However, black Jamaican women living in the United States do not exist in an ideological vacuum; there are several intersecting factors that limit their access to gainful employment and social mobility. These women function within interlocking axes of race, gender, and national identity, systems that create complicated "outsider within" positions (Collins 1998). As raced and gendered bodies, they necessarily contend with the dominance of white male ideologies in the United States. In addition, as women from or with heritage in the Global South, they also have to wrestle with imperialist and

Eurocentric American ideologies. Their experiences are thus shaped by the multiplicative effect of being black women from a developing country. These ideas are reinforced by Jamaica's tourism brand and marketing campaigns, its global image as paradise. As the people who are most likely to emigrate and therefore whose lives are most likely to be impacted by the tourism brand when they are abroad, I center my research on working- and lower-middle-class Jamaican black women in the United States.

The analysis that follows is based on data gathered from focus groups and interviews conducted between 2006 and 2014 with first- and second-generation Jamaican women living in the United States (about twenty in all). I recruited participants primarily from New York City, which houses one of the largest Jamaican diasporic communities in the world. The initial participants were recruited through vouching figures (Weiss 1994, 34)—that is, friends, relatives, and associates with access to a variety of Jamaican women in New York City—who recommended and solicited their black Jamaican friends, associates, and business clients for the project. Subsequent participants were recruited through a "snowball sampling" technique, a chain referral system that entails asking respondents to refer other participants for the research study, thus enabling access to diverse sections of the community.

The narratives from the participants are supplemented with information from my own experiences within the Jamaican diasporic community in New York City. As an immigrant black women from Jamaica, I spent over five years in a major black Caribbean enclave in New York City, where I interacted with and observed Jamaican family members, friends, and colleagues at social gatherings, hair salons, restaurants, and in classrooms. While being Jamaican and moving among Jamaican communities does not automatically make me an authority on this group, my position provided the opportunity for informal observation of cultural traditions and texts and afforded a level of access to Jamaican women's stories and cultural practices that may not have been granted to researchers of other cultural backgrounds.

Both first- and second-generation participants of the study are working- and middle-class women between the ages of nineteen and fifty-five. All have completed at least a high school education, and some have completed or are pursuing college degrees and technical or professional training. Most of the women reside in communities with a prominently Anglophone Caribbean presence and have social networks comprised predominantly of black Caribbean people. Furthermore, many of the participants still have relatives and friends "back home" with whom they keep in contact via the telephone and the internet or to whom they send remittances in the form of money and material goods. The women themselves visit Jamaica with varying levels of frequency, but most have no desire to relocate permanently to the island. All of the participants self-identify as black Jamaican women and are socially positioned as black because of physical features such as their skin color and hair texture.

Paradise and Cultural Discrimination

A major impact of Jamaica's reputation as a tourist destination is economic and social discrimination for the women in general. One of the first things that one notices about low- and middle-income Jamaican women in the United States is that they, at least for a time, work as low-paid childcare workers, domestic helpers, and low-tier health care workers, such as health aides and nursing home assistants (Mose Brown 2011). This concentration of Jamaican women in the personal and professional service industries can be attributed to two main social factors: U.S. immigration policies that provide visas for these women to work in the service fields;[1] and the women following the path of family and friends who have successfully found employment in those fields. However, both of these reasons are predicated on the ideology that Jamaican women are good for service, a rearticulation of black women's slave status in white supremacist imagination; the white colonial image and reputation of black Jamaican women as being built for servitude (the perennial slave) facilitates their entrance into the service sector (as opposed to more white-collar, lucrative fields) and forms the basis for U.S. immigration policies. The slave image of black Jamaicans circulating in the United States—coupled with other factors such as education level—influences the women's participation in the American economy and arguably affects their chances to gain economic mobility. For example, as

Nickesia Gordon discusses in chapter 2, the commercials of the JTB are replete with imagery and rhetoric of Jamaica and Jamaicans being ready and available to service the mostly white visitors who come to the island with a "perennial sense of . . . being waited upon." In other words, Jamaican women's concentration in the service sector is influenced by constructions of black Jamaican women as the backdrop to visitors' magical vacations, the ones doing the waiting on and servicing of visitors to paradise, the workers who ensure that all needs of tourists are met—with a smile.

Furthermore, black Jamaican women's cultural heritage exacerbates their treatment in social settings. The women who work as childcare workers and nannies describe interactions with white American employers in which they are routinely ignored and disregarded and made to feel invisible by their white employers. They talk about feeling infantilized by their employers, who try to control and manage their schedules and who habitually intrude and make demands on their time and lives—again re-creating the master-slave relationship in which black women are expected to always be available for/to their employers. Their personal lives are of no significance or import, and therefore their lives revolve around those of their employers. One participant, Donna, says: "They will look right through you like you transparent or something . . . Like even when they would call the house . . . some of them would not choose to give me a message, and tell me if I could hang up and they'll call back and let the answering machine pick up, or if they calling out something for me, they want me to repeat."

Women in other sectors of the U.S. workforce have also shared numerous accounts of experiences with black and white American colleagues who perceive them as culturally and intellectually inferior because they are from or have heritage in Jamaica. They have to deal with questions and comments that imply that they are simple-minded and unsophisticated and not very useful in contexts that require creativity and original thought. The women's skills and education are therefore devalued and undermined because of their heritage, which results in downward mobility, having to do demeaning jobs, and settling for lesser living standards. Moreover, a common theme among the women who attended primary and secondary educational institutions in the United States is of being "held back" or being placed in a lower grade when they entered American schools because of the perceived inferiority of the education they had received on the island.

These women's experiences and treatment in the United States reveal that many Americans believe that Jamaican women are uneducated and inferior and should occupy positions of vassalage. This construction of black Jamaican women as good at service (which is replete in Jamaica's paradise marketing) helps to uphold a white colonialist system that marginalizes them. Their image as predominantly service workers—the help, the utility workers—tracks them into low-paying service jobs and limits the money they can make and send to Jamaica. Therefore, while Jamaican culture and products are taken up and adopted around the world (as discussed in chapter 7), low- and middle-income black Jamaican women continue to be excluded from many spaces.

Paradise and Double Consciousness

In addition to cultural discrimination, paradise discourses also cultivate double consciousness in second-generation women (women born in the United States to Jamaican parents). As Gordon shows in chapter 2, Jamaica's paradise image that is promoted in the country's tourism marketing cultivates the idea of the "primitive," the "peasant," and the "nativistic." Such "third world" branding of Jamaica fosters in second-generation women an ambivalent relationship with the country, which is characterized by dissonance and constant negotiations with popular images of Jamaica. More precisely, while second-generation women proudly claim a Jamaican identity, they also internalize, articulate, and negotiate ideas and images of Jamaica as socially, politically, and economically underdeveloped and primitive. In their everyday lives they consciously make decisions regarding their self-expression and identity performance that illustrate their struggles with being women of paradise.

These women's self-identity as Jamaicans is evident. Specifically, they claim legal (American) citizenship and cultural (black Caribbean) nationhood, challenging ideas of homogeneous nationalisms and monolithic nation-states. They have American passports but firmly establish themselves within Jamaican and Jamaican diasporic culture. Seila aptly captures the group's relationship to the United States and Jamaica when she says, "I know I was born [in the United States], but I am Jamaican in the blood." The women highlight and take pride in many aspects popularly associated with Jamaican culture and experience, such as the emphasis on education, good food, great dancers, communal living, and a good work ethic. They recount much evidence to this effect—parents who insist on children going to college; relatives who work long hours for years, sending monthly remittances to care for family in Jamaica; and children raised to respect authority.[2]

Nevertheless, they concurrently articulate their struggles with negative ideas associated with Jamaica's conception as paradise, indicating that their identities are not as cohesive and unproblematic as they appear. First, the women's second-sight and unease with being Jamaican women in the United States is evident in their selective concealment of their Jamaican heritage. In other words, while the women overwhelmingly embrace a Jamaican identity, there are specific moments when they actively hide visible markers of their connection to Jamaica. For example, some of the women discuss the unease they feel in the United States when their heritage is salient and on display through their accents. They learn from an early age that the Jamaican accent is incongruous with good (American) education and spaces of leadership. Mide describes how her teachers would constantly send notes to her parents recommending that she see a speech therapist to correct the Jamaican (and Spanish) accent she had developed. Another respondent, Debbie, explains how her schoolmates (at a predominantly black institution) mocked her as she delivered a speech as a candidate for student council president, a prestigious leadership position: "I was saying the reasons why they should vote for me and I had a really strong accent. So one of the kids, my other classmate, was saying, 'Why is she talking like that? What is she saying? I can't understand her.' They started laughing . . . I took a moment and walked outside of the class-room . . . I just wanted to get myself together." She eventually returned to the classroom and completed her speech (and was voted in as student council president), but she realized in that moment that her identity and the external cultural markers of being Jamaican could be read negatively in contexts of leadership in the United States and may not be good for her image. The same participant also confesses to having not taken "hardcore" Jamaican food to school for lunch to avoid the exoticizing gaze of her fellow students, who perceived that food as "gross" and abnormal. For these reasons she feels as if she was wearing a mask; she could not and still cannot be her full self in American schools and now on her job.

Other women also understand this reality; they recognize that performances and expressions that readily identify them as Jamaican undermine and undo their professional and intellectual capital, and so they take steps to conceal them. Shamia admits: "If someone asks me, I say I'm Jamaican . . . but just for purposes like in school and stuff like that, I talk regular or American . . . I try so hard to hide [my accent]. Especially public speaking or speaking to my classmates—I try to hide just because I feel weird when it comes out when I'm trying to say a speech or something . . . Like out of place, people are not going to understand." Her response exemplifies the angst-filled duality that many of the participants express: she does not deny being Jamaican, but she believes that her Jamaican accent draws attention to her "otherness" in ways that detract from the substance of her knowledge. In the United States, because of Jamaica's association with "sand, sea, and sun," the Jamaican accent signifies amusement, beach, and carefree living. It does not represent professionalism and intellectualism (in the way that the British accent, e.g., connotes intelligence). Therefore, the Jamaican ethos of "no problem, mon" embodied in the accent connotes a lax approach to "serious" endeavors that the women believe works against them in the U.S. and other Western societies. In this way the women wrestle with the pride as well as the learned shame of being women of paradise when in professional, serious settings.

The women's double consciousness is also evident in how they discuss the values and standards that they associate with Jamaica. As mentioned earlier, all the women describe Jamaican culture as education centered, very disciplined, communal, and characterized by hardworking people. However, they concurrently project ideas that construct Jamaican values as regressive, oppressive, and ultimately of the third world. Patricia highlights the conservative gender roles that she thinks are still prominent in Jamaican culture: "There is so much added pressure on [Jamaican] women to have to cook, you have to clean . . . if you cannot cook, and you can't clean, you are *wutless* [worthless] . . . I don't subscribe to that . . . America allows more leeway in some of these areas." Sade implies a similar perception of Jamaicans not born and/or raised in the United States. When asked if there are any aspects of her identity that she would characterize as American, she responds: "Open-mindedness. In America everything is exposed. It's not like Jamaica, where things are not as out there as in America . . . Like affection in public, homosexual relationships."

Many participants also map the primitive ideology onto the bodies of Jamaican women, suggesting that they embody the indelicate, uncultured, and unrefined qualities associated with the third world. They describe what they believe to be Jamaican women's uncouth, unpolished fashion sense. Karen says: "I don't think Jamaicans are stylish. Their style is just not up to par with me: too many colors . . . too much accessories . . . They just look cheap . . . If I were to go to Jamaica today, they would know I'm from *fahrin* [the United States]." Similarly, Mia says: "The stereotypes that they have of Jamaican women—with the wigs and the loud hair, the colors and the fingernails and be all out there—I'm not more reserved, because I'm still just as colorful, but I think I tap into mine a different way than a Jamaican woman would who is more close to her Caribbean colors . . . the red, yellow, green, and just wearing it all [at once], and it's so vibrant and loud . . . I have the same passion, but I do it more in an American fashion-forward kind of way." Through these and other statements, these women rehearse the kind of traditionalism and unworldliness that is often ascribed to people who live in or who migrated from paradise islands. What is clear is that these women have internalized both the reality of Jamaican women's diasporic experiences and the paradise image of Jamaica that circulate in the United States. They move about with both white European/U.S. constructions of Jamaica and their personal knowledge of the diasporic lives of black Jamaican women, creating their double consciousness.

Participants also repeat discourses that pathologize Jamaica as structurally flawed and question the nation's ability to compete in and prepare its citizens for the global economy. Again, the women repeatedly describe Jamaica as a place where, among other things, the educational system is rigorous: teachers are strict and dedicated; students are focused and driven; and parents are supportive, if not obsessive, about education. However, they simultaneously construct the social structures and institutions of the nation as peculiar, bizarre, and not at all developed like those of the United States. For example, the women dismiss and undermine the Jamaican health care system. Debbie says this institution relies on "Jamaican remedies" such as bush teas and rubbing alcohol. In other words, in her conception, doctors in Jamaica rely on homeopathic, unscientific measures to treat illnesses. She goes on to say that Jamaican doctors do not receive good training in Jamaica, a direct comment on the educational system that she previously praised: "[The doctors in the United States] are better than those in Jamaica. I don't really know anything about Jamaican doctors. [The United States] is where people really come anyway to get their bachelor's and nursing stuff . . . This is where they do it." Moreover, when asked if she would consider studying for her degree in Jamaica, she said, "I don't know anything about education in Jamaica. They have universities?" She said this laughingly, but even in humor, her statement reveals the contradictions of maintaining a Jamaican identity in the United States: The general perception among Jamaicans is that Jamaicans value education and are more advanced educationally than Americans, yet Jamaica is not respected as a space to attain good, competitive erudition, particularly tertiary and skilled training. Here the double consciousness (seeing themselves through the prism of both Jamaican and Western ideologies) is brought into sharp relief; they hold, wrestle with, and negotiate competing, contradictory ideas about Jamaicans as a people and Jamaica as a space.

Overall, while the women assert a predominantly Jamaican identity, they concurrently wrestle with the "third world" conceptions associated with their heritage. The women's opinions about the culture and society of Jamaica are not necessarily based on facts about the country. Jamaica has produced many renowned scholars and professionals, including cultural theorist and activist Stuart Hall and former U.S. secretary of state

General Colin Powell, for instance. Furthermore, contrary to the women's statements, American society maintains deeply conservative approaches to gender roles.[3] Rather, the women's ideas reflect existing ideologies of the nation overall: Jamaica as outdated, Jamaica as offering little value to twenty-first-century modern spaces, Jamaica as a failed imitation of America. Specifically, the women's negative comments about Jamaica emphasize the position of Jamaica, and the Caribbean, in the global economy. It reinforces the "globalist geo-temporal politics" that positions Jamaica and its culture as lagging behind (Chow 2013, 101), in contrast to the advanced, dynamic environment of the United States. Moreover, it highlights the dependency of Jamaica on the United States. Largely due to its proximity to the United States as well as global neocolonialist policies and agendas, the Caribbean relies on the United States for information, resources, and trade. For this reason its society, industries, and cultures often reflect Euro-American perspectives and trends and thus support the cultural, social, and political interests of the more dominant nations of the world (Sheller 2003). The women's negative statements paint Jamaica, its culture, and the people who live or lived there as conservative, closed-minded, and incompetent. In contrast, the United States is constructed as professional, modern, cultured, and open-minded. This construction of Jamaica largely reflects and reinscribes white imperialist ideologies about the nation as nothing but sand, sea, and sun, an image that essentializes and exoticizes—and thereby diminishes—Jamaica and its peoples.

As is evident in their statements, the women do not only articulate and rehearse the paradise discourses associated with Jamaica; they also make efforts to disassociate themselves from these negative conceptions of Jamaica (by concealing their accents, claiming more liberal ideas, and professing better fashion sense, e.g.). In other words, to avoid being tarnished by the underdevelopment ascribed to their cultural nexus, the women align themselves with the perceived developedness of the United States to establish themselves as modern citizens of the developed world; they foreground their connection to the United States to neutralize the perceived third world pathology associated with Jamaica and Jamaican people. Therefore, the second generation's internalization of the stereotypes of Jamaica helps to preserve and perpetuate Eurocentric and racist ideas and marginalize people of their communities, including themselves. This internalization also creates fractures within the diasporic community as those of the second generation disparage and ridicule their first-generation counterparts.

The Appropriation of Paradise

Jamaica's tourism brand does not engender all negative consequences for the women, particularly those of the first generation. The women with whom I interact in my research embrace and appropriate some aspects of the paradise narrative and mold them into their own diasporic identities, adopting the images of unspoiled nature; easy, uncomplicated living; pastoral environment; and freedom from too many responsibilities into their own constructions of home and culture. In contrast to the United States (in their case New York City)—which they perceive and experience as impersonal, hectic, immoral, and impolite—they talk about Jamaica as a place where community is important, where people care for others, where children are respectful, and where there is a strong sense of morals. Through descriptions such as these, Jamaica does emerge as a virtuous paradise with leisurely, convivial environments, the manifestation of "no problem, mon," and the antithesis of the United States.

The women share many fond memories of growing up in Jamaica and of the traditions practiced there, indicating that the construction of their perceptions of home are at least partially grounded in actual experiences. However, their descriptions of life in Jamaica largely conflict with the harsh realities of living there as working-class black women, conditions that probably brought many of them to the United States in the first place, and most had no intentions of permanently relocating to Jamaica. Furthermore, as Hume Johnson highlights in chapter 1, Jamaica has many contradictions; even while it is seen as an "island paradise" for many people of the Global North, it simultaneously has a reputation for violence, homophobia, and corruption.

The women themselves openly discuss the difficulties and challenges of Jamaica, but these discussions are generally kept to within their communities. They are willing to share information about the difficulties of Jamaica with others outside of their group but only secondarily. In many instances they choose to foreground the paradise narrative that constructs Jamaica as beautiful, peaceful, warm, and far removed from life in the United States. These ideas reflect dominant tourism discourses. The women appropriate these ideologies about Jamaica and rework them into their self-expressions. When challenged to reconcile the two versions of Jamaica, Janet says: "With the crime, it is [still] paradise, because with all the natural attractions that we have, you can still relax. When you go there, sometimes you [even] forget that someone get shot behind you (*laughs*). It's so calming and tranquil there that all your worries disappear." The women are thus fully aware of the duality of Jamaica but choose to privilege the exotic images, even if they reinforce white colonialist ideas about themselves and their worth and create dissonance for their daughters. These are preferable to the other competing images of the island. Karen sums up the general attitude by saying that she does not challenge the idea of paradise that is projected about Jamaica because "very few times you gonna say [good things about Jamaica]. A lot of [Americans] will dwell on the fact that [Jamaica is violent] . . . So if they think it's paradise, let them run with it." In other words, the women seem to foreground these narratives to drown out the more negative images of Jamaica that circulate globally.

Relatedly, as I argue elsewhere, the women seem to mobilize the discourse of "paradise home" to help cope with life in the United States (Gentles-Peart 2014). When they encounter aspects of the United States that concern or displease them or make them uncomfortable, the women draw on ideas of paradise to create a superior place that they can claim as home, which allows them to disassociate from the negative circumstances they face in the United States. As Sheila says: "I guess when you are here and it's all about work and just trying to get the American Dream, you get so tired and you remember when you were back home and you didn't have to worry about all [these things]. You had a house and you didn't have to worry about paying rent and you feel like you want to go home . . . You didn't stay in your kitchen and see somebody else's bathroom and stuff like that. I guess that's where the paradise come in because we dream of going back home." Her statement shows that the discourse of paradise home is an explicit challenge to the downward mobility, hardships, and indignities that she and others face in New York City. These narratives enable the women to adapt to and cope with their new social positions in the United States. In essence, while the discourse of paradise constrains their inclusion into American society, it also provides a strategy that helps these immigrant women survive in America. The mythology of paradise aids in the formation of more positive narratives of themselves and their homeland, demonstrating that far from being victims, the women actively employ dominant discourses for their own purposes (Gentles-Peart 2014).

Both the first- and second-generation women actively engage with the discourses that constitute the tourism narrative of Jamaica but with different results. The second-generation women create distance between themselves and the uncomplimentary ideas about Jamaica fostered by the paradise brand. As self-described American-born Jamaicans, their liminal existence between Jamaica and the United States facilitates this kind of maneuverability, the flexibility to move between these cultural spaces in ways that are personally favorable and beneficial. On the other hand, the first-generation women foreground the more agreeable (though still ideologically problematic) aspects of the tourism brand to undercut their own marginalization.

The tourism identity of Jamaica is not only about creating an image for an abstract entity; it also involves creating the image of the people. This global tourism brand that Jamaica constructs—or that is constructed for it—is projected onto the people. In many ways Jamaica's tourism identity constructs a narrative—often the only narrative—about the Jamaican people. So, the existing identity of Jamaica as an "island paradise" has implications for how Jamaicans are perceived and treated, particularly when they go overseas. When they move abroad, Jamaicans come in direct contact with ideologies circulated in tourism marketing that furnish the basis for their ethnic and racial subjectivity and provide rules on how they should be treated. Ideas of Jamaicans, specifically women, as built for service that circulates in these campaigns, contributes to the tracking (and trapping) of Jamaican women into the low-paying health care and service sectors of the United States.

Discourses of paradise help to reinforce a new form of imperialism that doubly marginalizes Jamaican women in the United States on the basis of their race and national heritage. In the context of dominant American society, their social and cultural capital—education and class privileges, for example—are nullified and erased as these women routinely encounter paradise ideologies that label them as intellectually inferior, socially unsophisticated, and culturally backward. Ultimately, they are perceived as poor, dependent, and unprogressive, different from and inferior to their (black and white) American counterparts.

These ideas may also be internalized, creating psychological and cultural dissonance. The statements of second-generation Jamaican women living in the United States illustrate that they actively struggle with being Jamaican in the context of the United States at least partially because they have internalized tourism discourses of Jamaica that position the country as underdeveloped and of the so-called third world; the women simultaneously occupy two levels of awareness: they know what it means to be black Jamaican women (the values and mores, including the emphasis on education, discipline, and hard work), but they are also cognizant of the white colonial discourses that "other" and marginalize their community. Their simultaneous embracing and rejection of Jamaican and American ontologies is indicative of their double consciousness.

Ironically, this conception of Jamaica as pathologically undeveloped may have been cultivated by the first generation's own construction and projection of Jamaica to subsequent generations. The latter construct and disseminate narratives about the goodness of the Caribbean but also frequently discuss the problematic aspects of the islands: the economic hardships and high inflation, the "slackness" (informality) of business practices, the corrupt politicians, and the ineffective social systems. These characteristics often emerge in intragroup discussions about the island in which the first generation, whose members remain deeply invested in their homelands, criticize their homelands. They share many of their criticisms directly with members of the second generation, often to emphasize how relatively "easy" their lives are in the United States and to highlight the hardships their parents endured. Undoubtedly, it is also likely that the second-generation women learned these perceptions of Jamaica through its persistent representation as paradise in American and Jamaican media.

Jamaica relies on its diaspora and expatriates to support the nation at several levels. In the absence of investors, they are called upon to funnel money into the nation's economy. They are encouraged to help care for their poorer relatives and communities and thus assume some of the responsibilities of the national social service systems. They are expected to be ambassadors of Jamaica to the world, to help project a good image to the world and create goodwill toward the country. However, the images of servitude, backwardness, and carefreeness that Jamaica's tourism campaigns construct about its people precedes its emigrants, contributing to their denigration and disempowerment in foreign, particularly Western, spaces. Before Jamaicans even enter a country, ideologies about their intelligence, abilities, and value to that society already track them along predetermined, low-paying, subservient paths.

Jamaican authorities need to recognize the role of its insistent tourism brand in reinforcing negative ideas about its population, particularly black Jamaicans. This must begin with confronting the obvious unequal positioning of its black population in the nation's actual and projected identity. In reality black Jamaicans continue to occupy lower social and economic positions than their brown and white counterparts and continue to be constructed as only good for service. This reality of the black Jamaican experience makes a mockery of the "Out of Many One People" national motto, which presents the nation as a multiracial society built on equality, and negatively shapes the lives of black Jamaicans—at home and abroad.

NOTES

All names used throughout the chapter are pseudonyms.

1. In 1965 the United States implemented yet another reform to its immigration policies, catalyzing an era of West Indian migration that differed from other periods in history because of the volume of people who immigrated and the

ensuing racial and political conflict into which they entered. On October 3, 1965, President Lyndon Johnson signed the Hart-Celler Immigration Bill, which phased out the national origins quota system established in 1921. The new legislature valued family reunification and needed skills, rather than immigrants' country of birth, supposedly allowing equal access to all peoples regardless of nationality (Center for Immigration Studies 1995). The recruitment of workers centered on procuring two forms of labor—agricultural for the sugar fields and professional—created a community of skilled as well as unskilled and poor constituents (Portes and Grosfoguel 1994). Jamaicans and other people from the English-speaking Caribbean were attractive to U.S. industries because they spoke English, making them good for service jobs. In addition, these immigrants were perceived as coming from places that produced skilled workers, such as nurses, who were needed in the United States. The poor, rural farmers of the English-speaking Caribbean could also be recruited to work in sugar fields.

2. For a full discussion of black Caribbean women's diasporic identity in the United States, see Gentles-Peart 2014.

3. The literature on gender inequality in the United States is vast. On female sexuality in Jamaica, e.g., see Boyce-Davies 2004; and Cooper 2005.

4

Brand Jamaica and the Economic Cost of Homophobia

Initiating a Conversation

Anna Kasafi Perkins

Jamaica is a brand in itself. Its colours are very distinguishable, and the ideas that come to mind when you hear the word "Jamaica" are very clear, and very widely shared.

—JACQUELINE CHARLES, "Brand Jamaica: Copyrighted"

The boycotts and concert cancellations affected the income of artistes immensely while the international media coverage of Jamaican homophobia had a very negative effect on the country's international reputation, which was explosive, because one of the country's main sources of income is tourism.

—PATRICK HELBER, "Between 'Murder Music' and 'Gay Propaganda'"

"Jamaica as a brand is one of the most recognised globally" (Myers 2014). That means that almost everyone in the world has heard of Jamaica, and this knowledge is accompanied by images, ideas, associations, emotional content; much of this brand is romanticized, stereotyped, and decontextualized and often assumes a life of its own (see Steffen Mussche-Johansen and Hume Johnson's discussion in chap. 7). Some would argue that Jamaica in the global imaginary far outstrips its size or sociopolitical and economic significance. Indeed, Jamaica has been branded explicitly and implicitly through various mechanisms, which have contributed to this larger-than-life status (Mussche 2008). Jamaica's positive global brand recognition has the potential to generate substantial economic benefits for the country, with an economic value of between US$33 billion and US$35 billion (Myers 2014).

However, there are numerous threats to earnings from "Brand Jamaica," including the lack of capacity of the island to effectively monitor and protect the brand from exploitation by some in the global marketplace. It can be argued that among the threats to earnings from Brand Jamaica is the presence of a persistent negative "rival brand image," which serves to undermine its more positive global image and the island's potential earnings from it (Johnson 2014). One aspect of this negative branding is the perception of high levels of homophobia and the concomitant violations of the human rights of gender minorities in the country; this perception has led to Jamaica being called "the most homophobic nation in the world" (although other countries, such as Nigeria and Uganda, regularly vie for the title). Yet Jamaica's branding as the most homophobic nation on earth has not been sufficiently countenanced as a significant source of lost earnings for the country by the Jamaican authorities or in scholarship. Concern with the negative financial impact of international perceptions of Jamaica's excessive homophobic violence is captured anecdotally in a Facebook conversation quoted on August 17, 2013, by social commentator Annie Paul in her blog, *Active Voice*, after the mob murder of Jamaican transvestite Dwayne Jones. Part of the exchange is reproduced here, typos and misspellings included:

> Greta Mellerson: You see de now Dean Strachan, people reading this [story about Dwayne Jones being murdered for cross-dressing] would believe it and don't have somebody like you fe straighten out de story! Now this is coming from yahoo (USA), that means lots of people maybe cancelling their trips to the island because of this, that means less $. So it could be a political move! thanks for straightening out dis story ya!

> Dean Strachan: the story has been all over the place, but the government dont think it is important enogh to deal with it before it start affect the revinues. then they wiill spend millions to mop up it

Dwayne Jones had been murdered by a mob of people in what was arguably a "hate crime" (*Jamaica Observer* 2013c). No one was ever brought to justice for his killing, and the story made international headlines as another frightening example of Jamaica's extreme homophobia. As Hume Johnson discusses in chapter 1, the presence of a negative brand as a result of violent crime, breaches of human rights, and perceived high levels of homophobia can have a large impact on Jamaica's socioeconomic development and even undermine the achievements from its positive image. This calls for direct responses at the level of policy makers and other leaders in Jamaican society.

This contribution aims to start a conversation on the impact that the perception of Jamaica as highly homophobic may be having on earnings from Brand Jamaica. It draws from a piece of unpublished research, "The Economic Cost of Homophobia in Jamaica: An Exploration," to which I contributed, which establishes that homophobia has significant negative effects, first, at the micro level, that is, on the lives of individual Jamaicans, who are victims of stigma and discrimination and, as a result, are able to live less productive lives. At the same time their productive contribution to the nation is lost or significantly lessened because of their drastically reduced contribution. Second, and more important for this conversation, Jamaica, having been branded as a homophobic nation, has suffered from serious reputational damage, resulting in lost earnings, thereby further limiting growth in an already moribund economic space.

The measures for the losses accruing from such perceptions of homophobia are difficult and complex to calculate. It is possible, however, to arrive at proxy measurements that *indicate* the scope of the losses due to reputational damage. Using local and international popular culture developments in and responses to Jamaican dancehall music, I will show that there have been measurable losses from the negative effects to its brand in the area of so-called murder music, as Jamaican dancehall music has been labeled. Negative attitudes toward gender minorities, especially gay men, in dancehall has elicited various international boycotts (Helber 2015). Much anecdotal evidence is available concerning the direct losses to individual dancehall performers, who are barred from earning a livelihood on the regional and international stage, and these losses accrue to the Jamaican economy both directly and indirectly. Similarly, the earnings that could be garnered from a more welcoming attitude to diverse tourists, including those with the "pink dollar" (spending in gay communities), are significant and can be approximated. The losses from these two segments will be deployed as proxies for the reputational costs being incurred due to perceptions of the country as one where people display extreme homophobia. First, I provide some insights into nation branding and why a brand holds such premium here.

Brand Premium and Nation Branding

For most Jamaicans "Brand Jamaica is everything distinctively and creatively Jamaican: from Blue Mountain coffee and Bob Marley, to reggae and Rastafarianism to herbs and seasonings" (Charles 2009, n.p.). The brand provides a value premium that Jamaica realizes from its recognizable name as compared to other countries. According to Simon Anholt, who coined the term *nation brand*, "Countries have images, and those national images are as important to the prospects of those countries as brand images are to corporations . . . Countries with a powerful and positive image find that everything they do . . . is easier and cheaper" (qtd. in Charles 2009, n.p.). To this end, many nations engage in a process of nation branding, which Kaneva defines as "a compendium of discourses and practices aimed at reconstituting nationhood through marketing and branding paradigms" (2011, 118). As such, nation branding seeks to reconstitute a nation on two levels: ideology and praxis, whereby the meaning and experience of nationhood is transformed in several ways.

Such a definition of *nation branding* assumes that branding is an internal process and takes account of the power of a nation to reconstitute its own nationhood by its own efforts; it seems to take little account of the extrinsic processes by which nations are branded. National identity is thus seen as an asset to be managed and deployed by experts in tactical and strategic ways. This discussion does not explore the formal process of nation branding per se but, rather, addresses a "brand" as an identifiable image or symbolic narrative that is attached to a country. At the same time, it acknowledges the technical-economic value and impact of such identity, reputation, and symbolic narratives on the livelihood of the nation.

Among the multiple symbolic narratives (brands) associated with Jamaica are:

Sand, sun, sea, and sex—the idea that the country is a tourist haven.

Caribbean paradise, including the popular slogan that at one time was used to market Jamaica—"Jamaica no problem."

Reggae capital of the world and home of reggae icon Bob Marley and Rastafari, encapsulated in the phrase *Roots Rock Reggae*.

Track and field, with Jamaica seen as the sprinting capital of the world—the "sprint factory," as it affectionately labeled.

Jamaica's Blue Mountain coffee.

Jamaican rum—Jamaica is home to several world-class rum brands, including the Appleton label, perennial winner of international competitions.

Murder capital of the world ("sand, sun, and savagery," according to a headline in the British newspaper *the Independent*). Jamaica has consistently been in the top ten countries for per capita homicides over the last two decades.

Most homophobic place in the world premised on songs in the popular culture that condemn homosexuality, such as popular entertainer Buju Banton's "Boom Bye Bye."

The final two narratives are aspects of the negative rival brand identified by Hume Johnson in chapter 1 as undermining Jamaica's socioeconomic progress. The peculiar branding of Jamaica as "the most violently homophobic place on earth," given to Jamaica by gay rights activist Peter Tatchell (2004), is often overlooked or dismissed in the discussions on national development. Attempts continue to be made to play up the positive dimensions of Jamaica without regard for and recognition of the need to address the so-called rival brands (JAMPRO 2016).

Jamaica's Homophobic Brand

The negative image of Jamaica with regard to gay rights and other aspects of human rights is widespread. In terms of the cold hard facts, the 2017–18 Amnesty International *Country Report—Jamaica* details the "rights of lesbian, gay, bisexual, transgender and intersex [LGBTI] people":

Consensual sex between men remained criminalized. LGBTI organizations continued to report attacks, harassment and threats against individuals based on their real or perceived sexual orientation, which were not fully and promptly investigated.

On 14 June [2014] a mob attacked a young man at a shopping mall in the town of May Pen because he was allegedly seen putting on lipstick. There was no police investigation into the incident.

In August, Javed Jaghai, a member of the Jamaica Forum of Lesbians, All-Sexuals and Gays [J-FLAG], discontinued the constitutional challenge he had filed in February 2013 against laws criminalizing sex between men, following the receipt of threats against him and his family.

A "conscience vote" by MPs on legislation criminalizing consensual same-sex relations, which the government announced would be held before April, did not take place. (https://www.amnesty.org/en/countries /americas/jamaica/report-jamaica/)

A global development firm states the problem plainly: "In the Western hemisphere, Jamaican vigilantes harass gay people as the police often watch and turn a blind eye, even as the prime minister Portia Simpson-Miller hollowly promises a vote conscience on the country's 'buggery law'" (Bassiouni Group 2014). Indeed, former Jamaican prime minister Portia Simpson-Miller, when confronted by gay rights activists in New York, responded angrily. Her angry reaction serves to deepen the perception of state inactivity and tacit support for the mistreatment of LGBTQ individuals (Brown 2015). Another prominent example of the unprogressive stance of the Jamaican state to gay rights is a June 2016 incident in which the country's attorney general, Marlene Malahoo-Forte, created an international media outcry when she tweeted that the U.S. embassy flying the rainbow flag at half-mast following the murder of forty-nine people in an Orlando gay bar was disrespectful of Jamaican laws. In the wake of Orlando many U.S. embassies around the world flew the rainbow flag in solidarity with the victims of the mass shooting. The government of Jamaica was alone in criticizing this act of solidarity (Jørgensen 2016).

Moreover, Jamaica also maintains anti-gay laws. The buggery law, for example, which criminalizes anal sex, particularly between men, has been interpreted in the Jamaican justice system and among the general population as outlawing homosexuality. It carries a maximum prison sentence of up to ten years with hard labor. "Furthermore, the laws' ambiguity fuels homophobia in Jamaica, and the courts often interpret them as a legal justification for their own bigotry. Further, over seventy per cent of Jamaicans support the retention of these laws" (Boxill et al. 2012). "Jamaica's structural violence has driven many LGBT+ Jamaicans to seek asylum in the United States, Canada, and the United Kingdom" (Jørgensen 2016).

For these reasons Jamaica is consistently in the "persecuting" category of the Global Barometer of Gay Rights (GBGR), which "provides a measurement tool to systematically quantify the degree to which countries are human rights protecting or persecuting of sexual minorities" (Dicklitch-Nelson and Tov n.d.). In a study of Jamaica's GBGR over a fifteen-year period (2000–2015), Dicklitch-Nelson and Tov determined that the score increased from 17 percent from 2000 to 2013 to 21 percent in 2014 to 24 percent in 2015, which earns Jamaica a grade of F, putting it consistently in the worst category on the scale. Interestingly, the category in which Jamaica's score showed improvement was in gay rights advocacy, with the growth of civil society groups such as J-FLAG and Caribbean Vulnerable Communities (CVC). In spite of this, "the state of gay rights in Jamaica continues to be dismal and state persecution and societal hatred towards gays will likely continue unless drastic policy actions are taken" (Dicklitch-Nelson and Tov n.d., 19).

Jamaica's international brand as homophobic was sealed in a 2014 *Newsweek* article in which Max Strasser listed Jamaica as one of the "twelve most homophobic nations" in the world. Although there was no formal ranking, Jamaica was seventh on the list, preceded by Nigeria, Uganda, Zimbabwe, Saudi Arabia, India, and Honduras. In describing Jamaica's homophobic state, Strasser notes, "Sex between men is illegal, hate crimes are alarmingly common and the government seems reluctant to protect gays from violence" (2014, n.p.). The list does seem somewhat arbitrary as even a nation without anti-gay legislation such as Lithuania is included. India, with its recent high court reinstatement of colonial era anti-gay laws, which is under challenge, is also included.

It is not surprising that Jamaica makes this list, given its strong and sustained anti-gay stance. Yet designating Jamaica the "most" homophobic suggests exceptionality, which is difficult to sustain or substantiate. Gutzmore (2004) cautions that Jamaica's treatment of homosexuals, in many key respects, is very much in keeping with similar discriminatory practices worldwide. As studies such as Wilets (2011) and Smith and Kosobucki (2011) point out, Jamaica, other Caribbean, and many African nations carry forward "the norms and rules regarding homosexuality emerging from plantation societies that began with English laws and culture" (Smith and Kosobucki 2011, 1). Kirby argues that "these laws have passed their use by date and have been repealed by the older members of the Commonwealth, from whose culture they were exported to the new, and remain the unlovely legacy of the Empire" (2009, 2).

This is not to deny the homophobic nature of Jamaican society. Gutzmore makes the point that in certain clear respects Jamaica is "demonstrably exceptional" in its treatment of homosexuals and homosexuality—not in the area that people expect, that is, "the proven brutality and physical and psychological violence of its homophobia." Gutzmore states that "the exceptionality of Jamaican homophobia is at the expressive level within both secular and religious popular culture" (2004, 124). LGBTQ activist Angeline Jackson concurs with Gutzmore's assessment, saying, "Our culture is this melting pot of religion, culture, music and misogyny . . . All four of them just combine to give us this unique Jamaican homophobia" (qtd. in Lavers 2014, n.p.).

Indeed, one of the few, if perhaps the only, points of concurrence between dancehall culture and religious popular culture in Jamaica is around the question of homosexuality. Cowell (2011) finds that the public behavior of dancehall artistes is firmly rooted in public attitudes as well as in the beliefs and attitudes of top-ranking members of church and state. Added into the mix, of course, is the highly politicized nature of the issue of homosexuality and the buggery law in Jamaica, which is very different from the experience, for example, of The Bahamas (Gaskins 2013).

Jamaica is far from a rights-protective or rights-respecting society for sexual minorities. But what is the direct impact of being labeled the most homophobic nation? I answer by looking at the economic fallout for Jamaica as evidenced by international responses to dancehall music and tourism.

The Economic Cost of "Murder Music"

Much anecdotal evidence is available concerning the direct losses to Jamaica as a result of its homophobic branding, especially in the area of music. Jamaica and Jamaican products have been the target of various boycotts in Europe, Canada, and the United States over the years. In 2009, for example, Michael Petrelis started a "Boycott Jamaica" campaign to pressure the Jamaican government and private sector to provide more protection for gay rights. The campaign targeted Jamaica and Jamaican products, encouraging Americans to boycott Jamaica as a vacation destination and not buy products such as Red Stripe beer. At the historic Stonewall Inn in New York, which is a heritage site for the LGBTQ liberation movement, there was symbolic dumping of Jamaican rum down the sewers. Jamaican products were removed from the sales of Stonewall Inn and other similar establishments (Tatchell 2009). The campaign even adopted a logo resembling the logo of Jamaica's world-famous beer, Red Stripe.

The targeting of Red Stripe, though misguided, aimed to attack a primary and globally known Jamaican commodity. Products originating from a country carry the brand of the nation as consumers' emotional attachment (or lack thereof) to a place redounds to products from that place (see Mussche-Johansen and Johnson's discussion in chapter 5). Ironically, Red Stripe itself had been at the forefront of a corporate movement to withdraw support from entertainers who endorse violence and/or bash homosexuals. Red Stripe withdrew its support from live shows, where artistes spewed anti-gay-vitriol, sponsoring education programs for artistes instead.

Another area of loss was to dancehall music itself. Since the early 1990s various groups, both locally and internationally, have protested against the homophobia in Jamaican dancehall music. Kohlings and Lilly, for example, mark the shift in perception of the message of reggae music to 2004 in Germany, where it was reduced to the expression of "hate music" (2013, 3). Buju Banton's "Boom Bye Bye," which advocates the shooting and killing of gay men, was perhaps the epicenter of the protest, which gained momentum and culminated in the "Stop Murder Music" campaign led by such groups as OutRage, at whose helm was Britain's Peter Tatchell, a well-known gay rights activist. The campaign focused on the violence against gay people that was espoused by dancehall music in particular. The homophobia projected by the music reflected the cultural opprobrium against homo-sexuality, as discussed earlier. Kohlings and Lilly note that "this campaign coincided with the commercial peak reggae and dancehall had been enjoy-ing, a peak which had both been on the verge of establishing themselves as permanent features of the urban pop culture scene [in Europe] . . . At that time Jamaican artistes were touring Europe like never before" (2013, 10).

Major artistes were the targets of this campaign. Locally based or lesser-known artistes were less impacted by the campaign. The campaign against so-called murder music led to the banning and cancellation of international shows of many major artistes, including Beenie Man, Sizzla, Capleton, and Bounty Killa, who, being world-famous stars, make most of their earning from tours and international performances, not just sales of music. Ele-phant Man and Vybz Kartel were excluded from the British MOBO Awards (BBCCaribbean.com 2004). Radio stations were pressured to take these artistes off their playlists. In Germany, among the various actions initiated against dancehall artistes was the placing of certain artistes on the "Index of Youth-Harming Media." This meant that their recordings could not be sold or advertised in places that those under eighteen years old had access to, including the internet. It also meant the complete disposal of these recordings, and many chain stores got rid of the entire catalog of certain artistes' music or even that of their recording company. In 2010 Guldner presented detailed research on these banned recordings (see Kohlings and Lilly 2013). At the time thirty-five reggae albums had been placed on the index, including those by Bounty Killa, Elephant Man, Sizzla, and Vybz Kartel and compilations such as *Reggae Gold* and *Strictly the Best*.

The economic fallout was great. In December 2004 Tatchell estimated the loss to these singers, promoters, and venues to be around five million pounds (Petridis 2004). Rosie Swash, three years later, estimated losses to Beenie Man, Sizzla, and Capleton at 2.5 million pounds (2007). Kohlings and Lilly (2013) estimated that losses to Beenie Man, Sizzla, and Capleton amounted to four million euros in 2004. Over a ten-year period the earnings lost to these entertainers alone would have been in the hundreds of millions. These losses would have had a multiplier effect on the entire local music industry and, ultimately, the local economy.

The losses to the Jamaican economy as a result of the Stop Murder Music campaign were computed by Nicardo McInnis. Using the figure presented by Tatchell, which only captures the European experience, McInnis argues that it is highly likely that this figure is an underestimate, given that several other artistes apart from those named would have also been affected. McInnis, nonetheless, used it as a base to estimate the annual losses to the Jamaican music industry. McInnis makes clear that it is important to note that his own estimates are themselves underestimates, having been based on a figure that may already be an underestimation.

ESTIMATED LOSSES TO THE JAMAICA MUSIC INDUSTRY
DUE TO "STOP MURDER MUSIC" CAMPAIGN, 2002–12

Year	Gross savings (% of GDP)	Multiplier	Losses to music industry ($Ja)	Nominal multiplier effect on GDP ($Ja)	Real multiplier effect on GDP (base year = 2012)
2002	15.95	6.27	129,277,778	810,528,533	23,952,739
2003	17.85	5.60	147,118,111	824,002,794	22,089,015
2004	20.71	4.83	167,273,292	807,844,494	19,080,419
2005	15.18	6.59	188,349,727	1,240,819,555	25,464,375
2006	33.98	2.94	199,085,662	585,960,404	11,088,820
2007	15.53	6.44	232,532,053	1,497,388,950	25,920,126
2008	6.26	15.96	271,597,438	4,335,984,701	61,509,706
2009	12.93	7.73	299,300,376	2,314,043,875	29,951,220
2010	13.40	7.46	334,318,520	2,494,786,530	28,673,744
2011	8.41	11.89	354,377,632	4,213,676,265	45,038,542
2012	8.24	12.13	382,727,842	4,643,287,224	46,432,872

Source: Centre for Leadership and Governance 2015 (used with permission).

As the table details, the loss to the Jamaican economy over a ten-year period, from 2002 to 2012, was significant. The average percentage loss to GDP was 0.22 percent each year. This totaled Ja$155,364 million (over Ja$1.55 billion) in constant 2012 dollars over ten years. These estimates, of course, would be significantly increased with the inclusion of figures from the Americas, Africa, Japan, and other parts of the world. Such losses are indeed nothing short of a recession (Badgett et al. 1998). Such losses must be taken seriously in a country that has suffered anemic growth over the last three decades and has moved to position its music and entertainment industries as drivers of economic growth and Brand Jamaica.

Generally speaking, since its launch in 2004 the Stop Murder Music campaign has been reasonably successful in reducing the production, distribution, and performance of homophobic dancehall music. It brought the negative effects of dancehall's homophobia on Jamaica's international reputation to the attention of the Jamaican nation. It generated much discussion among Jamaicans and members of the Jamaican diaspora (Helber 2015). By targeting the eight major artistes known for violent homophobic lyrics, it caused them significant loss in earnings. Four of the eight artistes chose to sign the Reggae Compassionate Act contract (RCA), in which they renounced their homophobic songs and agreed not to promote or perform any songs that would incite violence toward the LGBTQ community. This did not stop these same artistes from performing their anti-gay songs locally and at some international venues. Sizzla, for example, shortly after signing the RCA contract in 2007, went on European tour and performed many times his anti-gay anthem "Nah Apologize" without saying the word *battyman* but allowing the crowd to fill it in for him (SoulRebels.org n.d.). Of course, the campaign had a negligible effect on homophobic sentiments within Jamaica. Nonetheless, its success indicates that financial pressure can play a major role in effecting change with regard to protecting the human rights of homosexuals in Jamaica. Yet one of the biggest earners for Jamaica is in the tourism industry. It is here that Jamaica's homophobic brand may cause the greatest damage.

Homophobia and Tourism

Tourism is a major foreign exchange earner for Jamaica. Globally, the LGBTQ community has had a positive and growing impact on tourism. The LGBTQ vacation market is estimated at US$140 billion annually (Tomlinson 2013). Community Marketing and Insights, in its *22nd Annual LGBTQ Travel Survey Report* (2017), noted that Americans in the LGBTQ community are active international travelers. Seventy-seven percent of LGBTQ participants in the survey reported having a valid passport (compared to 36% of the general U.S. population). Significantly, among these passport holders, 53 percent used their passport in the past year to travel to another country. When asked about concerns when selecting an international travel destination, participants expressed mostly safety-related concerns as an LGBTQ individual as well as a foreigner. Political environment in the destination also has an influence on selection. Notably, concerns such as language, natural disasters, and currency rates were not significant barriers to LGBTQ international travel. Only 6 percent of the respondents had a negative travel experience related to their LGBTQ identity. When selecting an international destination, the respondents cited scenic or natural beauty as the top destination attribute (60%), followed by LGBTQ friendliness (45%). The top two international destinations among those surveyed were Canada and Mexico, regardless of gender.

In 2014 Caribbean and Latin American countries such as The Bahamas, Barbados, and Cuba were listed among the top ten countries for LGBTQ vacationers (Silvera 2014). The powerful lesbian and gay magazine the *Advocate*, in July 1999, compiled a special report on "Gay Travel." In a cover story by David Kirby, the author described the gay person's love of travel but said that the welcome mat was not laid out for them in many places, including Central America and the Caribbean. Kirby referenced a series of highly publicized "ugly" events featuring the Cayman Islands, The Bahamas, Belize, and Jamaica. All of these places are described as where religious conservatives, who oppose homosexuality, live.

Gay individuals, in the incidents, recalled having felt threatened and in danger. Jamaica was described, at that time, as emerging as a danger spot for homosexual tourists, with travelers returning and reporting having felt uncomfortable and even in danger. What was described as a rising tide of intolerance and what was deemed Jamaica's lack of willingness to grant human rights to gays and lesbians living in and visiting the country led the International Lesbian and Gay Travel Association (ILGTA) to condemn the country. Furthermore, Jamaica has been accused by ILGTA of being a leader in the emerging homophobia affecting the Caribbean region. In its spring 1999 newsletter the ILGTA said it was prepared to warn its members not to spend their tourist dollars in Jamaica. And many sites and newsletters have warned LGBTQ people against vacationing in Jamaica.

In 2014 a story in the *New York Times* detailed the experience of the writer Steven McElroy from when he landed at the airport in Montego Bay until he and his partner decided to leave the Royal Decameron hotel a few days early because they felt unsafe. It is noteworthy that upon calling Angelica Daza, the sales director of the Royal Decameron, McElroy was told: "We are not gay-friendly because our hotel is a family resort . . . Don't take that response as if we discriminate . . . We don't discriminate against gays." When McElroy detailed his experience and asked if employees were expected to treat every guest equally, she bluntly told him that "she cannot control how the staff might feel." "Everybody is free to express what they think," she said. McElroy closed his article by telling of his next vacation plans—to Argentina.

Not much has changed since that time, even as the Jamaican government makes conciliatory noises about being "opposed to discrimination or violence against persons whatever their sexual orientation" (Avery 2017). *Spartacus International Gay Guide* has been compiling its gay travel index since 2013. The 2017 "Spartacus Gay Travel Index" ranks 194 countries from best to worst when it comes to safety for and a positive attitude toward LGBTQ persons. Using fourteen categories, the index "reflects both the legal provisions as well as the social conditions that homosexuals in the respective countries are confronted with." In an article for a travel website in 2017, Sullivan and Hegenauer lament that in over seventy countries in the world homosexuality is still a punishable offense. They caution that "the LGBT community at large still needs to be on their guard when travelling in many other parts of the world, where such public displays would be unthinkable or even downright dangerous." This includes Jamaica, which in 2017 shared 183th place on the index with nations like Russia, Afghanistan, Cameroon, and Libya.

Hospitality Jamaica, a publication of the Gleaner Company, has called upon the tourism sector to innovate and evolve in challenging economic times. The idea of the "gaycation" was discussed and recommended to the Jamaican tourism market. The LGBTQ market was recommended as a new group for Jamaica to go after, especially as other Caribbean islands are marketing themselves and their businesses as gay owned, gay operated, and/or gay friendly (Evans 2009). Indeed, Dominica and St. Lucia welcome gay tourists despite the presence of anti-buggery statutes. Curaçao has organized its first national gay pride parade and, as such, has become a more welcoming space. In the case of Jamaica, as LGBT activist and attorney-at-law Maurice Tomlinson tells it: "I have personally been contacted by travel agents who indicated that when guests request Jamaican holiday packages, they actively dissuade them. A sad fact is that there is an unofficial boycott of Jamaican tourism in place as a result of our infamous homophobia. We are just not willing to accept this fact or to do anything about it" (2013, n.p.).

There have been attempts to manage negative perceptions. In November 2017 Minister of Tourism Edmund Bartlett asserted in a statement in eTurboNews that "LGBT travelers should feel relaxed traveling to Jamaica . . . It's 'tourism for all' in our country, regardless of gender, religion, handicap, or sexual orientation" (Avery 2017). This remark has been met with understandable skepticism. In 2018 celebrity fashion designer and LGBTQ activist Dexter Pottinger was murdered in his home (*Jamaica Observer* 2018), same-sex intimacy remains criminalized, and anti-gay violence appears endemic.

Toward Further Conversation

There is no question that Brand Jamaica has continued to be negatively impacted by the island's reputation for extreme levels of homophobia. The greatest loss is economic, especially when the figures for losses from proxy measurements such as losses to dancehall and "pink" tourism are totted up. Jamaican authorities and citizens need to get past the lie that the economy is not affected by negative perceptions of the country as the most violently homophobic place in the world. When hundreds of otherwise productive youth are sidelined, left uneducated, and treated as outcasts merely for being gay, the taxpayers must pay for the lost productivity and provide their support. Similarly, when investments and tourism are reduced because of the country's stance on gays, Jamaicans must pay for the resulting joblessness and the currency devaluation (see White 2014, n.p.). Homophobia hurts the nation's bottom line. Perhaps that is the place for Jamaica to start the conversation on addressing the country's informal brand of homophobia and Brand Jamaica.

5

An (Un)easy Sell

Rebrandings of Jamaica in Marlon James's *A Brief History of Seven Killings* and Its French and Spanish Translations

Laëtitia Saint-Loubert

> Smell carries the memory of sound and there's that as well. Reggae, smooth and sexy but also brutal and spare like super poor and super pure delta blues. From this stew of pimento, gunshot blood, running water and sweet Rhythms comes the Singer, a sound in the air but also a living breathing sufferah who is always where he's from no matter where he's at.
>
> —MARLON JAMES, *A Brief History of Seven Killings*

Mainstream Caribbean literature circulating on a global scale is often marketed and packaged as an exotic and regional brand, "Brand Caribbean," in order to appeal to international readers. Caribbean literature therefore holds a specific position within the international literary market and the study of global cultural traffic, whereas Caribbean writers maintain complex and ambivalent relationships with mass culture as a site of representation for the various locales and polyphonic cultures they stem from. When it comes to Jamaica and its international image, it seems that the country remains chiefly known as the birthplace of reggae music, Bob Marley, Rastafarians, and Usain Bolt, among other cultural references, and is mostly celebrated for its touristic image based on a "sun, sand, and sea" model. It is as such that "Brand Jamaica" appears to be received abroad, partly due to an "official" national endorsement dating back to the 1960s: "The 'official' expression of Jamaican identity endorsed by the government, and upon which it has relied since independence in 1962 is an exotic island paradise of beautiful beaches, tropical weather, friendly, laid back people and Reggae providing a musical backdrop. This ready-made, unchanged, fixed Jamaican identity was manufactured over time through ideology and global mediated discourses that feature the islands of the Caribbean as exotic places; as paradise where the so-called natives are not only laid back, but seen to be poor, under-educated and under-employed" (Johnson 2014, 204).

In response to the situation, this chapter seeks to investigate the extent to which literary fiction marketed for various global audiences and in different languages can generate more complex representations of Jamaica than the tourism brand the country is often limited to. Focusing on Marlon James's *A Brief History of Seven Killings*, I will start by investigating how the novel originally offers a potentially (but still problematic) rebranding of Jamaica for Anglophone readers. By downplaying the postcard picture of his native country and relocating reggae music and its most world-famous representative within a highly politicized, complex (trans)national setting, James invites his readers to actively immerse themselves in a representation of Jamaica that stands at a great remove from its Edenic image.

If James's novel, which received the 2015 Man Booker Prize, could at first appear as an easy sell for the European book market, as it benefited from translations into several languages in the wake of its international recognition, it can nonetheless hardly be defined as an easy read, whether considered in English or in its subsequent translations.[1] This chapter will investigate how James's initial rebranding of Jamaica's complex identity can in turn be translated for Hispanophone and Francophone readers. How is the author's original rebranding of Jamaica in *A Brief History* carried across by Javier Calvo and Wendy Guerra in the Spanish translation or by Valérie Malfoy in the French edition? Are the expectations that those consumers might have of Jamaica anticipated in a similar fashion as they were by James for Anglophone—yet not necessarily Caribbean, let alone Jamaican—readers? Do the translations further challenge the simplistic postcard picture of Jamaica, as is the case in James's original, or do they fall back into some patterns of exoticization that limit Brand Jamaica to a fixed identity? With these interrogations in mind, I argue in what follows that the global, translational circulation of the novel calls for a reflection on our own practices of consumption of Jamaica as well as on the ethical dimension that needs to be taken into account when addressing the production and subsequent marketization of any nation brand.

Nation Branding, Authenticity, and Translation

This contribution is going to explore the concept of nation branding from a dual perspective—that of cultural studies, by examining the relationship between nation branding and the issues of authenticity, representation, and cultural commodification, on the one hand, and that of translation theory, on the other hand. Drawing from scholarship that has insisted on the importance of "truthfulness" and "authenticity" in the fashioning of nation brands (Dinnie 2016; Aronczyk 2013), truthfulness consists of bringing to the fore "existing values of the national culture rather than the fabrication of a false promise" (Dinnie 2016, 7). It is therefore closely connected with the idea of giving a legitimate, true-to-life representation of a given country, whereby some of its core, essential values are represented in such a way that they seem real to Jamaicans themselves or anybody familiar with Jamaican culture. In a section on "Treating Nations as Brands," Keith Dinnie notes the "importance of truthfulness when constructing the nation brand" and asserts, in relation to F. Gilmore's work on Spain and its self-promotion, that what should prevail over stereotypes in successful nation branding "is amplification of the existing values of the national culture rather than the fabrication of a false promise" (2016, 7).

Yet as has been shown by cultural critic Dean MacCannell and nation branding specialist Melissa Aronczyk, the emphasis has been instead on the notion of a "staged authenticity," the intentional construction of local cultures by writers to satisfy Western audiences who seek "authentic cultural artefacts."[2] Interestingly, Russell Cobb links this quest for authenticity in the Western world with the question of profitability. He observes, for instance, that "authentic cultural artefacts are often appreciated as such in an inverted correlation to its value in the marketplace in Western capitalism, such that a monetary value on something becomes a taint to its authenticity." In other words, "to create an aura of authenticity in the age of digital reproduction, an object or a text must seem not only irreproducible, original, but also uncorrupted by Western capitalism, even though these very objects rely on the marketplace for dissemination" (Cobb 2014, 5).

Furthermore, in the context of Brand Jamaica, Melissa Aronczyk insists more specifically on linking it to a "creative industry" that is depoliticized, as Paul Gilroy also suggests in connection with Bob Marley's international image (2005). Brand Jamaica would thus aim "to generate economic value in spheres of activity that were more likely to be seen by the international community as apolitical and therefore unproblematic and nonthreatening (and by the domestic community as unifying)" (Aronczyk 2013, 152). In sum, to effectively "stage authenticity" in ways that are palatable to Western consumers, Jamaica has to be presented in noncommercialized, depoliticized, simplified ways.

Brand Jamaica is hardly turned into an easily sellable, simplified item for global audiences, however, in James's novel. The novel not only redefines the sun, sand, and sea tourism model often associated with Caribbean islands (Pattullo 2005; Strachan 2002), but it also repoliticizes Brand Jamaica and the figure of Bob Marley ("the Singer"). This chapter questions the underlying notion of cultural commodification in relation to nation branding and global publishing (Aronczyk 2013; Maccarrone-Eaglen 2009); further, it investigates authenticity as a cultural construction, a "paradox" fabricated for external consumers so that they feel they have access to a real, complex Jamaica, as opposed to an exoticized, simplified version of the country (Cobb 2014).

When it comes to the translational strategies used to transpose James's complex rebranding of Jamaica, Lawrence Venuti's (1995) conceptual framework proves useful to shed light on the strategies deployed by the translators to market the text as specifically "Jamaican" or "Caribbean" for their targeted audiences. The notions of "foreignization" and "domestication" in particular allow us to explore the different marketing thrusts perceptible in the French and Spanish translations of the novel. In his study of the translator's invisibility in the North American book market,

Venuti argues that domesticating tendencies correspond to an ethnocentric approach to translation, as they tend to smooth out any preexisting difference encountered in the original. The aim in domesticating a text is to make it seem as transparent as possible so that it can be easily consumed by the reader. Conversely, foreignizing the text consists in (re)introducing linguistic variations that were present in the original and can, to varying degrees, "alienate the domestic language." To Venuti foreignizing the translated text not only consists in bringing to the fore the authentic difference of the original; it is first and foremost about adopting "an ethical stance that recognizes the asymmetrical relations in any translation project" (1995, 11).

Following Venuti's approach, this contribution shows how the French and Spanish translations of *A Brief History* partake in both strategies of domestication and foreignization. Yet this study departs from Venuti in his aim to oppose the two strategies, as it insists instead on the complementarity of the two approaches in their attempts to translate a "plausible" Brand Jamaica.[3] Altogether, looking at nation branding from a translational perspective allows us to gain insight on the role of translators as cultural brokers (Tymoczko 2010; Cordingley 2013), and it lets us see whether core representations of national identity and cultural values are immutable or can be rebranded when recontextualized for varying global audiences, across cultures and languages.

A Brief History of Seven Killings tells the story of the failed assassination attempt of the Singer—Bob Marley, doubtless, although his name never appears once in the novel. Initially set in 1970s Jamaica, it follows the lives of thirteen different narrators who are all connected, one way or another, to the assassination attempt, starting with gang members from the rival communities of Copenhagen City and the Eight Lanes, the fictitious garrison communities of West Kingston. From the beginning of the novel, the two political parties of the time, the People's National Party (PNP) and the Jamaica Labour Party (JLP), are shown as the forces actually pulling the ropes behind the dons who run the gangs. But the novel also explores the aftermath of the assassination attempt beyond Jamaica and establishes connections between the involvement of the United States on the island, through its CIA operatives trying to destabilize the then left-wing government, and the presence of Jamaicans in 1980s New York as well as their role in the drug wars there. Within this entangled narrative web, the Singer is presented as one of the many characters caught in the politics of the time—along with many other well-known political and anonymous figures. This feature of the novel allows James to offer a (re)politicized and potentially problematic rebranding of Jamaica, in which acts of un-naming and renaming contribute to restoring a complex identity for the country. Here the notion of cultural authenticity will be analyzed to see whether it contributes to creating a more "truthful" Brand Jamaica.

Manufacturing "Real" Jamaica for Global Readers: Strategies of Un-Naming and Renaming

When taking into consideration the global circulation and consumer orientation of the novel, whether in translation or in its original version, it is essential to remember that *A Brief History* does not address itself primarily to Caribbean—or Jamaican—readers. In fact, most Caribbean writers of international fame could be said to circulate "back" to the region only once they have achieved a certain degree of visibility and international recognition. This is a crucial point about Caribbean literature, as it entails a marketing of the region in such a way that it appeals first to external audiences. Therefore, these authors have to engage directly with the staged authenticity expected in presenting their nations' brand. This might even be more so the case with Marlon James, whose global success has turned him into a national asset for Jamaica.[4] James, who lives in Minnesota, not only writes but also publishes from a distance and has adapted his novel accordingly, representing Jamaica as being distinctly recognizable as a country and—it may be argued—as a (trans)national brand in its own right.

Yet James does not provide his readers with a postcard picture of Jamaica. Quite the opposite. The blurbs on the back covers of all three versions of the novel examined here emphasize either Jamaica or Kingston, and the designs found on the front covers also either stress elements of (reggae) music, with the presence of a vinyl with the colors of the Jamaican flag in the English version or a profile of Bob Marley in the Spanish edition, or suggest local fauna, with the insertion of a tropical bird where the French text is concerned. All those elements are easily identifiable by readers as Brand Jamaica. Yet within the text itself, James focuses on the complex politics of the time, and his un-naming of Bob Marley could be said to participate in a process of reappropriation of a key Jamaican figure.

The failed assassination attempt of iconic figure Bob Marley, which took place in December 1976, lies at the core of *A Brief History*. However, Marley's name never once appears in the novel, where he is only referred to as "the Singer," suggesting perhaps that iconic figures who have become part of a neoliberal (re)appropriation of Jamaica's popular culture need to be rid of their names in order to be better recast as "genuinely" Jamaican. As Sheri-Marie Harrison (2015) argues:

> Though not a fictional character, Bob Marley is prototypically the most iconic of Caribbean figures, real and imagined. By not using his name, the novel signals an iconicity that does not rely on the specificity of naming. Today, Marley's name and iconic visage grace numerous branded products that include everything from coconut oil produced in Indonesia to children's books sold on Amazon, in a manner that epitomizes the amalgamation of national culture, corporate branding, and the neoliberal instrumentalization of national identity as intellectual property. James's simultaneous centering and ironic silencing of the Singer becomes all the more interesting when one considers the ways in which Marley has posthumously metamorphosed into a neoliberal brand.

Rather than turning Bob Marley into a marketing product, Marlon James's *A Brief History* resituates the reggae legend within the violent context of 1970s Jamaica, realities that challenge readers on several levels.

The novel's title soon appears to be misleading, as what is presented as a "brief history" is in fact a hefty volume, all the more difficult to read as it alternates among no less than thirteen different narrators, who appear in the cast of characters provided at the beginning of the book. Another challenge that the reader is faced with lies in the range of languages and idiolects that James uses, as the novel oscillates between patois, American

English, Jamaican street language and slang, CIA jargon, as well as snippets of Spanish inserted here and there. Third, numerous cultural references to Jamaican society and the geopolitical international scene of the time as well as to various musical genres are foregrounded in the novel. These features of the text can be felt as hurdles to the reading experience. On the other hand, it could well be argued that all those elements participate in creating a plausible image of Jamaica, one that the reader believes to be real rather than embellished or romanticized. They present readers with a complex picture of Jamaica that goes far beyond the staged authenticity that attract Westerners to the island.

Early on in the novel, in an exchange between Jamaican former receptionist Nina Burgess and American journalist Alex Pierce, the question of the "real" Jamaica is brought into the conversation:

—Oh. Well Jamaica is all over the news this year. And this concert. *New York Times* just did a story that the Jamaican opposition leader was shot at. From the Office of the Prime Minister, no less.

—Really? That would be news to the Prime Minister, since the opposition would have no reason to be at his office. Also that's uptown. On this very road. Nobody firing no bullets here.

—That's not what the newspaper said.

—Then it must be true then. Guess if you write shit, then you have to believe every shit you read.

—Aw come on, don't bust my balls like that. It's not like I'm some goddamn tourist. I know the real Jamaica.

—Good for you. I've lived here all my life and haven't found the real Jamaica yet. (50–51)

Interestingly, James shows in this extract that authenticity is a feature that is important to those characters who are not themselves Jamaicans, as if authenticity was created specifically for non-natives and tourists, in response to specific market demands.[5] The extract also shows that

Jamaican realities are varied and can easily be altered and manipulated when they are presented to the outside world, all the more so when information is falsified to fit certain political agendas. Instead of "cleansing" the nation and Bob Marley of political and social issues that would make them threatening or frightening or that would damage their reputations, James consistently reanchors Jamaica in the domestic and broader geopolitical context of the Cold War.

James also replaces the names of Kingston's infamous Tivoli Gardens and Matthews Lane garrison communities with Copenhagen City and the Eight Lanes. By renaming some of Kingston's most infamous sites of violence, James manages to keep the plausibility of Jamaica—as Jamaican realities are still easily decipherable under the guise of fiction, at least to readers willing to see beyond the country's postcard picture—while simultaneously decoupling violence from Jamaica. Although neither the original nor the translations explain to the reader what garrison communities represent in the context and history of Jamaica, the (fictitious) figures of Papa-Lo, don of Copenhagen City, Josey Wales, and various gang members all contribute, in their own voices, to depicting realities of entrenched violence that take place in "inner-city" communities of Jamaica. However, by giving them names of European locales, James also removes them from Jamaica. In this way James represents the realities of these communities in Jamaica but also disrupts the narrative according to which violence is exclusive and uniquely native to Jamaica. Furthermore, while his presentation of violence can be seen as reinforcing existing ideas about Jamaica as the "troubled paradise," James's reframing of European cities in the context of violence can also be read as a "defilement" of the cities and irreverence toward colonizers.

James also calls his readers' attention to the issue of cultural consumption and even goes as far as ridiculing Westerners' attempts at "educating" Jamaicans:

—Do you know what we mean by the Cold War?

—War don't have no temperature.

—What? Oh no, son. War is a term, a figure of . . . it's just a name for what's happening here. You know what? I've got something right here . . . Here look at this.

The white man take out a colouring book. When you keep playing fool with Americans you learn to expect anything, but this one throw even me off.

—A wha this?

I had it upside down because who need to flip around a cover to read the *Democracy Is for US!* title. (412)

A Brief History thus renegotiates Brand Jamaica in such a way that it ridicules stereotypical views that conceive of Jamaica as a backward island, where people are assumed to be illiterate. Instead, it invites the reader to question Western modes of representation. The following sections of the chapter will interrogate, in turn, the extent to which the French and Spanish translations of the novel mobilize the author's strategies in a similar vein so as to offer a complex rebranding of Jamaica.

Translational Rebrandings of Jamaican . . . "-Ism"

As the opening note to the Spanish translation argues, the variety of languages used in the novel participates in creating authentic testimonies, in which each witness (*cada testigo*) offers their version of events in a story that seems anchored in a specific time and place:[6]

> Unos habitan el territorio de un inglés ciertamente jamaicano, pero más o menos canónico. Otros no salen del dialecto criollo (el *patois*) usado por el pueblo llano de la isla. [. . .] Tres hablan un estadounidense genérico. ¿Cómo puede reflejarse esa variedad en una traducción? Si cada jerga «vulgar» está indeleblemente marcada por su tiempo y su espacio, ¿cómo podemos trasladarla a las volubles geografías de otro idioma? Todas las soluciones a ese viejo (e intratable) problema son, en cierto modo, artificiosas. (James 2016b, 5)

> *Some [characters] speak an English that is definitely Jamaican, but more or less standard. Others strictly speak the creole dialect known as "patwa" and used*

by the common people of the island. [. . .] Three [characters] speak mainstream American English. How can such variety be carried across in a translation? If a "dialect" is deeply anchored in its time and place, how can we transpose it to the different linguistic geographies of another language? Any answer to this old (and unsolvable) issue is, in a way, artificial.

The questions raised by the translators here on the specificity of language and the impossible task of transplanting local speech forms and dialects to different settings are crucial to Caribbean literatures circulating in translation, as they inevitably bring about the issue of representational authenticity and linguistic and cultural plausibility. What should be stressed here is that James's own version of *A Brief History* is itself a manufactured form of authenticity, that is to say, a literary artifact, inasmuch as the writer himself needs to provide his Anglophone readers—which he does not necessarily assume to be Jamaicans—with cultural and linguistic explanations from time to time. As such, James's original could be said to be a translation.

However, the use of Rastafarian language in the novel necessitates a form of "interlinear translation," in-text alterations provided for a specific term or set of words:[7] "Kimmy learning from Ras Trent to take the words English people gave her as a tool of oppression and spit them back in their face. Rastaman don't deal with negativity so oppression is now downpression even though there is no up in the word. Dedicate is livicate, I and I, well God knows what that means, but it sounds like somebody trying for their own holy trinity but forgetting the name of the third person" (James 2015, 156). Rather than adding a footnote or a glossary entry to terms such as *downpression*, *livicate*, and *I and I*, identified as authentic linguistic features of Rastafarianism, the author inserts elements that, on the one hand, attempt to present a Rastafarian philosophy of life that advocates peace and nonviolence and, on the other hand, point to the impossibility of ascribing a fixed meaning, let alone a grammatically correct form of English, to such a philosophy. Interlinear interventions such as this one allow James to present some of Jamaica's cultural specificities in a subtle, creative way that participates in challenging Brand Jamaica from within, as it were, as the author does not rely on paratext to explain or frame Jamaican-ness for North American readers.

When adapting the text to non-Anglophone audiences, the translator is similarly confronted with the task of transposing the text on a cultural level but also has to take into account the original's linguistic features (including its variants), which she or he then has to reinscribe within the expected linguistic background of the target audience. The French and Spanish translations of *A Brief History* opt for two complementary strategies—that of foreignization for the former and (relative) domestication for the latter. As a rule, *Breve historia de siete asesinatos* transplants Jamaican features to Hispanophone realities while retaining linguistic variations, as noted earlier by the two translators in their notes to the text. As the Spanish translation of the extract quoted earlier shows, the aim here is to bring the text closer to the reader rather than taking the reader to the original, more plausible foreign setting: "Kimmy está aprendiendo de Ras Trent a tomar las palabras que los ingleses les han dado como herramientas de opresión y a escupírselas a la cara. Los rastas le dan la espalda a la negatividad, o sea que «opresión» se convierte en «malapresión», aunque no exista nada llamada «buenapresión». En vez de dedicarse, dicen «vivicarse». También dicen «yo y yo», que, en fin, Dios sabrá qué significa, pero parece como si el que habla estuviera intentando montarse su propia santísima trinidad y olvidara el nombre del tercero en discordia" (James 2016b, 194). Words such as *malapresión* and *buenapresión* transpose into Spanish what *downpression* suggested in the original, namely, that negative thoughts are rejected by Rastafarians in their language ("Los rasta le dan la espalda a la negatividad"). Similarly, the Rastafarian expression *I & I* becomes *yo y yo* to make sure that any semantic ambiguity is lifted for the reader.

By contrast, the French translation tends to retain expressions in English, thereby opting for a foreignizing approach: "C'est Ras Trent qui lui a appris à s'emparer des mots légués par les Anglais, qui sont des moyens d'oppression, pour les leur recracher à la figure. Le Rastaman refusant tout ce qui est négatif, l'oppression est devenue *downpression*, même s'il n'y a pas de *up* dans ce mot. De la même façon, il évite d'utiliser des termes qui se rapprochent, même phonétiquement, du mot *dead*—ainsi, *dedication* est remplacé par *livication**. Quant à «I & I*», euh, Dieu sait ce que ça peut bien signifier, mais c'est comme si on s'était efforcé de concevoir une sainte

Trinité en oubliant le nom de la tierce personne" (James 2016a, 211–12). This strategy requires additional linguistic information that was not present in the original ("il évite d'utiliser des termes qui se rapprochent même phonétiquement, du mot *dead*") and aims to stress an authentic Jamaican culture. The use of italics in the text as well as the addition of a glossary at the end of *Brève histoire de sept meurtres*, visible in this example through the presence of asterisks, underline the alien nature of the Rasta terms and expressions for the Francophone reader, rather than blend them in the narration. In that sense it could be argued that the French translation flags the text as specifically Jamaican in a much more visible and systematic way than James did for Anglophone readers. The presence of footnotes throughout the text and the appended glossary at the end of the novel give Francophone readers the opportunity to complete and adjust their own understanding of Jamaica, generating a more complex representation of Jamaica than the tourism brand. The paratext, for example, guides the reader through the numerous musical references inserted by James, including but not limited to reggae and Bob Marley. It also establishes more distance between Jamaica and the target audience's linguistic and cultural background than the Spanish edition does, thereby showing a different marketing thrust. The French translation tends to retain more Jamaican expressions and cultural references overall, allowing the reader to familiarize him- or herself with Jamaican linguistic features for which the translator does not provide French equivalents. Where the original describes, for example, "boys and girls playing Dandy Shandy" (448), the French and Spanish versions opt for different strategies:

Des enfants jouent à «Dandy Shandy.»

Jeu similaire au ballon-chasseur, le ballon étant généralement remplacé par une vieille boîte de conserve. (James 2016a, 563)

Los niños y la niñas jugaban a tirarse y esquivar la pelota. (James 2016b, 529)

As these extracts indicate, the French reader learns about "Dandy Shandy," which is explained further down as a local ballgame in which the ball is often replaced by an old tin can, whereas the Spanish text opts for the more generic term *pelota*, which turns the typically Jamaican game into a universal recreational activity. On the one hand, the French translation could be said to challenge a touristic approach to Brand Jamaica, by signposting a cultural reference that evokes a different reality than the sun, sand, and sea model. On the other hand, the Spanish translation does altogether away with identifying Jamaican uniqueness in this particular case.

On another level it could be argued that the Spanish translation reinscribes Jamaica within the larger context of the Caribbean without limiting its references to a generalized Brand Jamaica hinted at earlier. It is worth noting, for instance, that Cuba and Cubans play an important part in the plot and are mostly pitted against the United States and American spies who have come to Jamaica to try to curb communism. In its rebranding of the novel, the Spanish translation insists on the special relationship Jamaica and Cuba had at the time ("Jamaica y Cuba son uña y carne" [James 2016b, 5]), using the proximity between the two countries, beyond their linguistic affinities, to present its strategy of Cubanization of the text:

Entre los muchos lenguajes del castellano (todos felizmente locales) hemos escogido la versión cubana de la elocuencia caribeña. No, como es obvio, por afinidad lingüística, sino por proximidad física y, sobre todo, psicológica. Casi por analogía. «Jamaica y Cuba son uña y carne», leemos, muy oportunamente, en la página 209 de este libro. Fijado el objetivo, la novelista Wendy Guerra acometió a tarea de cubanizar los pasajes pertinentes en la meticulosa traducción del no menos novelista Javier Calvo. (James 2016b, 5–6)

Among the many varieties of the Spanish language, which are all fortunately local, we opted for the Cuban variant spoken in the Hispanophone Caribbean. Not, as it may seem obvious, because of linguistic proximity, but because of geographical, and above all, psychological proximity. Almost by analogy. Page 209 of the book says rather appropriately that "Jamaica and Cuba are two peas in a pod." With this in mind, novelist Wendy Guerra undertook the task of cubanizing strategic passages of the meticulous translation carried out by her fellow novelist Javier Calvo.

The translators' task (*tarea*) is doubtlessly associated with the idea of re-Caribbeanizing James's novel, an agenda that can be confirmed, for example, in the numerous instances of consonant weakening, the deletion of intervocalic /d/ in the particle ending -*ado*, and the debuccalization of /s/ in syllable coda, which are all characteristic of Cuban and to a larger extent Caribbean Spanish.

The French translation by Valérie Malfoy similarly attempts to oralize the text, as in a passage well into the novel, in which a Jamaican woman working for an employment agency in the United States addresses another Jamaican woman, Dorcas Palmer:

You know how them girl stay, come all the way to America and still going on like them is some dutty whore from Gully. Me tired of them girl so till. Me just tell one nasty slut who was working with Miz Colthirst. Nasty slut, me say, as long as you working for this here job and living under that there roof, you better lock up that pum-pum, you understand me? Lock up the pum-pum. Of course the bitch never listen so now she pregnant. Of course Miz Colthirst have to let her go—on my recommendation of course. Can you imagine? Some little stinking bottom naigger pickney a run rapid 'round the place? On 5th Avenue? No, baba. The white people would have one of them white people things, a connniption to rahtid. (James 2015, 439)

Tu sais comment qu'elles sont, ces filles, ça vient jusqu'en Amé'ique et ça se compo'te toujou' comme une *fam de vi* du ghetto. Moi, je suis fatiguée d'ces filles-là. Moi, j'ai dit à une *vilén fam* qui t'availlait chez Miss Clothirst: *vilén fam*, tant que tu t'availles là et qu'tu vis sous ce toit, tu fe'ais bien de mett'e sous clé ce *pum-pum*, comp'is? Tu le mets sous clé. Bien sû', cette salope m'a pas écoutée alors elle a ramassé un ballot. Bien sû, miss Colthirst a dû la laisser pa'ti'–su' mon conseil bien sû'. Quoi? Un sale ma'mot qu'au'ait cou'u pa'tou dans l'appa'tement? Su' la Cinquième Avenue? Non, baba. Les Blancs qu'aient fait un de leu' t'ucs de Blancs, un *avot-man*. (James 2016a, 551)

The extract in French indicates that some Jamaican expressions have been kept from the original (e.g., *pum-pum*), while others have been translated in order for Francophone readers to phonetically make sense of a given term (*avotman*, from the verb *avorter*, to have an abortion, where the English read a more cryptic *conniption to rahtid*, e.g.).

More generally, the whole passage in translation is based on the systematic elision of *r*'s at the end of words or syllables, a controversial strategy sometimes used in French to "imitate" black speech patterns that has been labeled as "petit nègre." The passage doubtlessly establishes a distinction between blacks and whites ("The white people would have one of them white people things"), but apart from a few terms left in Jamaican patois or that "sound" Caribbean (*vilén fam*), the French translation associates Jamaican-ness with blackness rather than Caribbean-ness. In that sense the French translation can at times be said to rebrand James's *A Brief History* along ethnic lines, which creates other levels of exoticism in the text, as the strategies used in the aforementioned example evoke black characters whose speech patterns are not specifically Jamaican. This in turn introduces different modes of consumption of Jamaica that could run the risk of eliding altogether the complex realities of Jamaican dialects were there not additional paratextual references—some of which have already been discussed—to re-complexify Brand Jamaica in *Brève histoire de sept meurtres*.

Another example is when narrator Barry Diflorio, working for the CIA, asks about "jerk chicken" being served at the Burger King; he is told that this is "ghetto food," as opposed, say, to a staple dish of Jamaican cuisine (James 2015, 17). The French and Spanish translations similarly suggest to the waitress that this is ghetto food; however, they add elements to further characterize what jerk chicken is supposed to taste or look like. The Spanish erases the English expression altogether and speaks of "pollo con salsa picante jamaicana" (33), whereas the French keeps *jerk chicken* and explains within the text itself that it refers to grilled chicken that has been marinated, "du poulet mariné grillé" (36). While the glossary provided at the end of *Brève histoire de sept meurtres* explains expressions left in English within the French translation, particularly when they apply to Jamaican phrases or words kept in the text, it does not provide any entry that suggests French "equivalents" to Jamaican realities, thus avoiding any anthropological readings of Jamaica. When it does rebrand Jamaica, it does so not by limiting the country to a postcard picture but by signaling some of the country's strong identity markers, as is the case with the mention of ackee, described as a national fruit: "Fruit national de la Jamaïque, très souvent cuisiné avec de la morue salée dans un plat traditionnel" (James 2016a, 36).[8]

Valérie Malfoy's interventions on the text are certainly more visible than her Spanish counterparts', who tend to (re)incorporate Jamaican realities into a Hispanophone world rather than keeping native expressions, which often necessitates additional information for the non-Anglophone reader. Yet this is not to say that Wendy Guerra and Javier Calvo do not act as cultural brokers themselves; their strategies offer a rebranding of Jamaica that seems to retain an illusion of transparency, as they translate Jamaican words and expressions into Spanish so that they can be consumed by Hispanophone audiences. One instance, in which the English mentions a minibus "with Irie Ites painted on the side in blue, not red, green and gold,"[9] is a case in point:

Pasó el 42 y ni paró siquiera, supongo que estaba intentando llegar a su casa antes de convertirse en calabaza. El problema es que eran las seis en punto. El toque de queda empieza a las siete, pero en los barrios altos no hay policias que lo hagan cumplir. [. . .] La última guagua que pasó era una guagüita con el lema «Rastafari Irie Ites» escrito en el costado con letras azules en lugar de rojas, verdes y dorados. (James 2016b, 130)

Le bus 42 est passé sans même s'arrêter. Pressé d'arriver à destination avant de se changer en citrouille, je suppose. Sauf qu'il était dix-huit heures. Le couvre-feu, c'est à partir de dix-neuf heures, mais on est dans les beaux quartiers ici, donc pas de police pour le faire respecter. [. . .] Le dernier bus était un minibus avec *Irie Ites** peint sur son flanc en bleu—pas rouge-, vert et jaune. (James 2016a, 143)

1. Le Drapeau rasta est jaune,
vert et rouge (symbole de la
lutte pour la libération).

Irie: salutation rasta, parfois
conjugué en «Irie Ites!» (James
2016a, 850)

Here both translations indicate that *Irie Ites* is a reference to Rastafarianism, whereas the English was more cryptic; the French edition even refers to a form of greeting in Jamaica for readers who decide to turn to the glossary entry and further (re)politicizes the text with the description of the independence flag. As for the Spanish translation, it privileges the word *guagua* to designate the "bus," thereby rebranding the text as Caribbean, as suggested earlier.[10]

Un-Branding "Jamerica," Rewriting Jamaica?

Commercial brands abound in *A Brief History*. This is particularly striking when it comes to U.S. (cultural) brands that appear throughout the novel, at times taking the form of fast food restaurants, at others that of allusions to popular culture, particularly through constant references to TV programs or action movies, such as *Starsky and Hutch* or the character of Harry Callahan. All three versions of the novel therefore highlight processes of global capitalism and cultural imperialism.[11] The inclusion of these American commercial brands in the novel often shows, however, that the introduction of Brand USA is not adapted to Jamaican realities. This in turn poses the question of the validity of Brand Jamaica in Jamaica itself when it is challenged by competing brands such as Brand USA. Do the French and Spanish translations reveal similar attitudes toward global capitalism? With such interrogations in mind, this section is going to argue that *A Brief History* offers a complex rewriting of Jamaica that challenges our consumption of the country as a generalized brand and questions nation branding as a whole.

In the first section of the novel Bam-Bam, a young boy originally from the Eight Lanes, recalls the day his father was shot and how, before he himself fled the scene of murder, he took off his father's Clarks shoes to put them on, so that they would not be stolen:

> The Clarks too big and I *clupclupclup* to get over to the back of the house, with nothing outside but old railway and bush and me trip over me damn whore mother who jerk like she alive but she not. Me climb up the window and jump. The Clarks too big to run so me take them off and run through bush and broken bottle and wet shit and dry shit and fire not yet put out and the dead railway taking me out of the Eight Lanes and I run and run and hide in the macka bush until the sky go orange, then pink, then grey, and then the sun put out and moon rise fat. [. . .] I can't talk, all me can say is Clarks is good shoe, Clark is good sh . . . and the man with the gun go click and somebody shout that bloodcaat Josey Wales love fire a gun so! (James 2015, 14)

The scene shows how the narrator is proud of owning Clarks shoes, but it also reveals that they are hardly adapted to Jamaican realities. The American brand becomes a source of impediment and mockery that turns a violent, tragic moment into a scene of slapstick comedy. On a different level the introduction of North American staple foods and mainstream products on the island constitutes another form of cultural imperialism, as the following extract illustrates:

> *Two men bring guns* to the ghetto.
> One man show me how to use it.
> But they bring other things first. Corned beef and Aunt Jemima maple syrup that nobody know what to do with, and white sugar. And Kool-Aid and Pepsi and a big bag of flour and other things nobody in the ghetto can buy and even if you could, nobody would be selling it. (James 2015, 33)

It is worth noting here that even before guns are distributed to the ghetto, American food brands are what is first brought to Jamaicans, as if suggesting a more insidious form of cultural imperialism: soft power.

In the French and Spanish versions of the novel, those elements also appear in the text, reinforcing the idea of a global circulation of American food brands:

Dos tipos traen armas al gueto.	Deux hommes fourguent des armes au ghetto.
Y otro me enseña a usarlas.	Un homme m'apprend à m'en servir.
Pero primero traen otras cosas. Carne enlatada y sirope de arce de la marca Aunt Jemima que nadie tiene ni idea de cómo usar y azúcar blanco. Y Kool-Aid y Pepsi y un saco de harina y otras cosas que nadie en el gueto tiene pasta pa comprar, y aunque la tengas, tampoco te las vende nadie. (James 2016b, 52)	Mais avant ça, ils apportent d'autres choses. Du corned-beef et du sirop d'érable Aunt Jemima que personne sait vraiment à quoi ça sert, et du sucre blanc. Et du Kool-Aid et du Pepsi et de gros sacs de farine et d'autres choses que personne peut acheter dans le ghetto et que, même si on pouvait, personne en vendrait. (James 2016a, 57)

By providing Francophone and Hispanophone readers with references as detailed as in the English version, one might read into such translational strategies not only the choice to remain faithful to James's original but perhaps also the wish to widen our reflection to other (neo)colonial times and places. Both translations, for instance, keep brands such as Aunt Jemima and Kool-Aid; they do not provide the reader with French or Spanish equivalents, despite the fact that both items are not necessarily familiar to European readers.

In another example in the novel, gang members are strongly influenced by popular culture coming from the United States, but James inserts linguistic variations that subtly undermine the mainstream culture otherwise consumed by most Jamaican characters. A telling example lies in the alteration of the famous advertising slogan developed by Burger King, "Home of the Whopper," which becomes "Home of the Whamperer" when transplanted onto a Jamaican setting: "There's also a McDonald's farther down Halfway Tree Road. The logo is blue and the people who work there swear Mr. McDonald is in the back room. But I'm at King

Burger, Home of the Whamperer. Nobody here has ever heard of Burger King" (James 2015, 16).

The linguistic un-branding that the author performs in the original is echoed in the translations:

También hay un McDonald's bajando por Halfway Tree Road. Tiene un logo azul y la gente que trabaja en él jura que el señor McDonald está en la trastienda. Pero yo estoy en el «King Burger, pruebe nuestro Whamperer.» Por aquí nadie ha oído hablar nunca del Burger King. (James 2016b, 32)	Il y a aussi un McDonald's un peu plus loin sur Halfway Street Road. L'enseigne est bleue et le personnel jure que M. McDonald est dans l'arrière-boutique. Moi, je vais au King Burger. «Home of the Wham-perer.» Ici, personne n'a jamais entendu parler de Burger King. (James 2016a, 35)

Both translations keep James's linguistic alteration of the original slogan, maintaining *Whamperer*, even if the Spanish text translates the phrase "Home of the Whamperer" into "pruebe nuestro Whamperer." The original American brand is therefore further dislocated and to a certain extent discredited, while traditional Jamaican food is reinstated. However, none of the versions of the text, whether in the original or in the French or Spanish translations, explain what a "whamperer" might be, leaving the expression open for interpretation.

Altogether, excerpts such as these invite us to reflect on the marketiza-tion of culture and its asymmetrical flows of circulation. As Katja Valaskivi observes, "Mechanisms of marketization are not only transforming the ways in which national identity is performed and represented externally, but the external perception is also reflected back into the ways of identity building. This exemplifies how branding 'brings the outside in.'"[12] *A Brief History* epitomizes both the marketization of cultures and the asymmetry of this process, with its numerous references to U.S. popular culture, which seems to have become a global brand, in the Jamaican context. Yet as the French and Spanish translations have shown, the novel also manages to export its own cultural specificities, including James's own rebranding of Jamaica to

Europe. In that sense the issue of cultural imperialism seems to have been preserved in the circulation of *A Brief History*. Meanwhile, Brand Jamaica itself has retained depth and substance in the translations of the novel.

Reading James's *A Brief History* is no easy task, regardless of the language we read it in or feel most comfortable with. Using linguistic and cultural features that give readers the impression of being confronted with the real Jamaica, the novel at once interrogates our practices of cultural consumption and the global reach of certain national brands while overcoming potential translational shortcomings. Rethinking nation branding from the perspective of literary texts and their translations offers a rich course of analysis in that regard, as it underlines how cultural consumption varies across time and space but also according to the receiving culture targeted by the writer and his or her translator(s).

When it comes to *A Brief History*, the novel proves to be a product of its time and age, that is, a global novel whose translatability currency has doubtless gained from its literary recognition (through the award of the Man Booker Prize in 2015). As far as James's rebranding of Jamaica is concerned, this contribution has shown that his repoliticization of Jamaica, and more specifically of the Singer, as well as his various attempts at complicating the notion of cultural authenticity play a determining role in the reconfiguration of the country's image for external consumers. In turn both the French and Spanish translations regenerate in their own terms Brand Jamaica so as to offer a more complex representation of the country, away from the sun, sand, and sea model it is often associated with. To do so, the Spanish translation re-Caribbeanizes the text through its linguistic choices and, to some extent, smooths out Jamaican specificities to facilitate the reader's entry into the text. Conversely, the French translation opts for a more systematic foreignizing approach to the text, retaining Jamaican expressions and cultural markers in English yet providing a glossary and footnotes for the reader.

When it comes to the actual reception of *A Brief History* in the Caribbean, though, studies remain to be conducted to see the extent to which such a novel would actually circulate "back" to its country of—at least imaginary—origins. If in fact James now makes the headlines of the *Gleaner*, it remains to be seen whether *A Brief History* is going to appear on Jamaican bookshelves, let alone on school or university syllabi. On a more regional scale, it would be of particular interest to see whether the novel ultimately manages to be translated into indigenous languages of the Caribbean, thereby disrupting the centripetal routes of literary circulation that traditionally entail translations into European languages.[13] Alongside its desire for global relevance, Caribbean literature could then engage in an archipelagic dialogue aiming to reimagine and rewrite nation brands that are anything but fixed standards meant to be passively consumed.

NOTES

1. The translations that will serve as our main case studies here are *Breve historia de siete asesinatos*, trans. Javier Calvo, in collaboration with Wendy Guerra (Barcelona: Malpaso Ediciones, 2016); and *Brève histoire de sept meurtres*, trans. Valérie Malfoy (Paris: Albin Michel, 2016).

2. See MacCannell 1992, in which MacCannell argues that authenticity is a form of deceit found at the heart of the (postmodern) tourist encounter with the "ex-primitive." MacCannell talks about "Cannibal Tours."

3. I prefer *plausibility* to *authenticity* here, as it conveys the underlying idea that literature (and translation) can only sound or seem close to one interpretation of reality, rather than aiming at a flawless, essentialist rendering of it. The term further alludes to the writer's (and the translator's) intention to offer a convincing, persuasive tale to their readers, which ultimately brings out the trickster figure (rather than the traitor) in any fictitious account.

4. See West and Houlden's (2016) research project on that point.

5. The Spanish translation insists on the "authentic" rather than the "real" Jamaica: "No me trates como a un estúpido turista. Yo conozco la *auténtica* Jamaica." James 2016b, 74; emphasis mine.

6. The suffix -*ism* is repeated throughout the novel to describe how clientelist political agendas characterized the last decades of the twentieth century in Jamaica. It appears in the following context: "Louis Johnson, my little compadre in '76, got sent back to Central America, I'm guessing the School for the Americas needed some hand-holding this year. Gotta keep building that army to vanquish the forces of socialism and communism, and whatever ism washes up next week." James 2015, 317.

7. Chantal Zabus (1991) uses the expression *interlinear translation* to refer to in-text alterations provided for a specific term or set of words (171).
8. This quotation corresponds to a footnote for *aki à la morue* in the text.
9. The passage in the original version reads as follows: "Bus 42 drove past and didn't even stop, trying to get home before turning back into a pumpkin, I suppose. Except it was six o'clock. The curfew started at seven, but this was uptown so there wasn't any police around to enforce it. [. . .] The last bus was a minibus with Irie Ites painted on the side in blue, not red, green and gold." James 2015, 99.
10. *Guagua* is used throughout the Hispanophone Caribbean and reminds us of Puerto Rican writer Luis Rafael Sánchez's *La guagua aérea*.
11. Sheri-Marie Harrison defines *cultural imperialism* as "economic subordination and cultural suppression" (2017, 93).
12. Valaskivi 2016, 102.
13. "The case of inter-Caribbean language translation is off the beaten track of language pairs, where the match usually is from Caribbean language into Euro-centre languages." See Tomei 2016, 113.

6

Brand Kingston

Reimagining Jamaica's Capital City

Hume Johnson

Faced with the effects of globalization, cities all over the world find themselves in fierce competition with each other for foreign and local investment, tourists, visitors, and residents. In this new reality brand reputation is critical and urgent. Cities are busy trying to differentiate themselves and assert their individuality in pursuit of various economic, sociocultural, and political objectives. In order to assert its own cultural clout, the government of Jamaica in 2015 successfully lobbied the United Nations Educational, Scientific and Cultural Organization (UNESCO) for its capital city, Kingston, to be designated as a "Creative City of Music." This classification positions Kingston among the world's top "creative cities" at the front line of innovation and creativity and offers it a means to sustainable urban development (*Jamaica Observer* 2015; UNESCO 2017). Likewise, in 2018, the government of Jamaica, again, successfully petitioned UNESCO, to formally recognize the cultural value of Jamaica's reggae music by placing it on the list of the world's "intangible cultural heritage." Reggae's inclusion means that UNESCO sees Jamaican reggae as a cultural treasure which deserves protection and preservation (Hassan 2018).

The success of Jamaica's appeal for global recognition for creativity in music is hardly a surprise. From the 1960s and 1970s Kingston provided the backdrop for Jamaica's triumphant explosion as a major player in world music and culture as Jamaican popular music—ska, rocksteady, and later reggae—catapulted into the global mainstream. Reggae's iconic emissary was the Rastafarian singer Bob Marley, who drew on his early social milieu of Kingston's inner-city community of Trench Town to disseminate powerful messages of love, peace, equality, and justice that resonated with oppressed peoples on every continent (Horan 2012).

Yet like many cities of the Global South, the context for this creative cultural explosion was a troubled city, characterized as a dangerous and chaotic place blighted by violent crime, urban decay, poverty, and underdevelopment. Kingston, undoubtedly, has had a varied history and suffers from a contradictory image. But is Kingston just a "woefully underrated and misunderstood metropolis" (Dreisinger 2014)? The city appears to be experiencing a spectacular cultural resurgence that would lend fresh and positive perceptions of itself as a cultural mecca and a modern cosmopolitan city of the future. Could this give city authorities new impetus to establish Jamaica's first city brand, "Brand Kingston"? In other words, can Jamaica leverage and reimagine its capital city as the "creative capital" the UN designation envisions? Can Kingston's cultural credentials help to undermine its historically unfavorable image and bolster the island's effort to achieve economic prosperity and reposition "Brand Jamaica"?

Drawing on available theoretical literature (local and foreign data) and my own empirical analysis of Kingston's complex characteristics, this chapter explores the complicated brand image and reputation of Jamaica's capital city and asks whether Jamaican authorities can help to reconcile them by capitalizing on the city's creative capital. Specifically, I discuss the various aspects of Kingston's culture that can be leveraged and submit that global recognition for Kingston as one of the world's creative cities is an opportunity for Jamaican authorities to reimagine the city and fundamentally alter its image from dangerous to benign and to design a new future for the capital city based on its creative economy, urban regeneration, and good governance. The chapter specifically proposes what a (reimagined) Kingston city brand might look like, drawing on aspects of the city's identity; its cognitive, cultural, geographical, and other attributes; what takes place in the city; current and future marketing strategies; as well as policy decisions and actions of the government. As a point of departure, I explore theories on city branding, why a focus on cities is seen to be important to a nation's overall image and reputation, and why branding a city ought to mean more than superficial marketing and promotion but must include attention to governance and other aspects of urban redevelopment and revitalization.

Cities as Brands

Fifty-four percent of the world's population now lives in cities. This number is predicted to rise by 66 percent by 2050. With more than half of the world's population now living in urban areas, cities are crucially important, becoming critical drivers for global economic growth and prosperity (Trujillo and Parilla 2016). Cities are now a huge part of how we imagine the modern nation-state, leading to a fundamental shift from the nation-state to cities as centers of global competition and cooperation (Mostashari, Arnold, Mansouri, and Finger 2011; Pillai 2017). Cities are also obliged to aggressively compete against other global population centers and position themselves as attractive for tourism, business investment, and skilled labor as well as for cultural and sporting events, international conventions, institutions, and even film locations. Cities have thus become integral pillars in building strong, competitive nation brands. They are now an inevitable aspect of a country's ambition and agenda, especially a nation's economic development strategy as well as a major part of urban strategies and tourism marketing. In fact, one can now speak of the city as a brand and hence of *city branding*.

The idea that a city can transmogrify into a brand has gained enormous traction among scholars and practitioners in recent years. To fully grasp the idea of city branding, it is important to talk, more generally, of place branding. Place branding is "the management of place image through strategic innovation and coordinated economic, commercial, social, cultural and government policy" (Anholt 2007). Place branding is also seen as a strategic process for developing a *long-term vision* for a place that is relevant and compelling to key audiences. The brand of a place ultimately shapes positive perceptions of it, so place image tends to occupy a central role not just in place research but also in the plethora of efforts and initiatives to brand places. It is important here to grasp the relationship between a city's brand and a city's image.

An image "is the result of various, different and often conflicting messages sent by the city and formed in the mind of each individual receiver of these messages separately" (Kavaratzis 2004). In short, people encounter places through perceptions and images. The image of a city is hence largely developed by experience—that of the people who are inhabitants of the city as well as outsiders. It is their own awareness and conception of the city, its quality and what they associate with the name of the city. Kotler et al. (1993) explains that the image of a place is the sum of beliefs, ideas, and impressions that people have toward a certain place; that is, the sum of all the characteristics that come to mind when one thinks of a place— *cognitive* (what one knows about a place), *affective* (how one feels about a certain place), and *evaluative* (how one evaluates a place and its residents). It is now accepted that the image of a country, city, or tourist destination influences our interactions with the place, whether we wish to live or work there, visit the place, do business there, or even buy products manufactured there (Boulding 1956; Elizur 1987). Some scholars even posit that place image is so powerful that in many cases it appears to have assumed more importance than the reality of the place (Avraham and Ketter 2013; Morgan and Pritchard 1998).

Place branding scholars agree that a place's image can be positive, attractive, negative, and weak (as in the case of peripheral places that are not very well-known); mixed (when the image contains negative and positive features); and contradictory (when the place has a favorable image among one population and a negative one among another). Place images can also be classified as rich or poor: A rich image means that we know a lot about the place, usually from different sources; a poor image is when we know very little about the place and what we do know comes from one source of information. Some places are plagued by stereotypical images—simplified attitudes or beliefs about a place that are not examined thoroughly or are difficult to change. The notion is that once a stereotype is formed, it is very difficult to change since much effort is required to make the target population amenable to a new and different image (Avraham and Ketter 2013; Kotler et al. 1993; Elizur 1987).

For Moghaddam "a brand is the foundation that helps to make a place desirable as a business location, visitor destination or a place to call home. A successful brand is therefore one that generally creates a powerful and unique image for the city" (2013, 121). This is because place branding campaigns rest on the notion that through the use of public relations and advertising campaigns (logos, slogans, visual imagery, and a strategic communication plan), one can turn an existing image into a better one. In fact, Avraham and Ketter maintain that effective campaigns usually engage in in-depth research to measure and analyze the current image of a place (and variables that affect it) in order to determine what campaigns might work best, arguing that "places with a negative public image must focus their efforts on changing it, while places with a very weak image must focus on gaining awareness and then creating a public image" (2008, 19).

Place experts and marketers believe that successful branding can turn a city into a place where people want to live, work, and visit. A strong identity, they agree, is vital if a city is vying with other places for attention in tourism and business or is relaunching an area after a regeneration initiative. The city brand has become one of the most valuable and tangible assets of the city, not just because it can give the city a good image but because it can create a new set of values by which the city abides (Moghaddam et al., 2013; Salman 2008). In other words, building or rebuilding a city and making it a place where people can genuinely live, raise families, work, and visit requires more than a dash of paint and snazzy marketing slogans. So, what exactly is city branding, and what does it take to make a successfully branded city?

"Branding" the City: A Theoretical Overview

Extant scholarship on city branding reveals that in order for a city to be a good brand, it must possess defining and distinctive characteristics that can readily be identified. These include, inter alia, the city's appearance, history, cultural attractions, demographics, economics, and governance; people's experiences with and perceptions of the city; what the city stands for; and what kind of people inhabit the city as well as consensus on the city's identity and core values among stakeholders, including city authorities and the public (Moghaddam 2013; Pfefferkorn-Winfield 2005; Kavaratzis 2004). Based on these characteristics, among the essential factors in successful city branding is attention to the city's image—the sum of beliefs, ideas, and impressions that people hold about a place as well as all the characteristics that come to mind when one thinks of the place, including its appearance and physical characteristics, its attractions and amenities, and how people feel about the place and how they feel being there.

In addition, "everything a city consists of, everything that takes place in the city and is done by the city, communicates messages about the city's image" (Kavaratzis 2004, 7). This communication is taking place at three levels—primary, secondary, and tertiary. At the primary level communicative messages are not the main goal; that is, the communication is not intentional, but the *city landscape, infrastructure, behavior, and structure* have communicative effects. Secondary communication, on the other hand, is intentional communication and in this sense would be manifested in established marketing practices, while tertiary communication is word-of-mouth communication (e.g., about the city) by the mass media.

In this regard, to establish a successful city brand, place branding experts suggest that city administrators first undertake a "strategic examination of trends in the social and economic environments; determine where the opportunities, skills, resources and capabilities lie within the city; what core values, attitudes, behaviors and characteristics have enabled the city to achieve these; and then figure out what combination of these provides an appeal to different groups" (Middleton 2011, 15). In other words, an *integrated brand communication strategy* should be developed and executed, including a brand position based on the city's core values, attitudes, behaviors, and characteristics. City administrators must then decide which blend of skills, resources, and assets can be expressed and promoted. Middleton (2011) maintains that failing to engage an integrated approach to the city's brand communication and avoiding an active city branding process altogether weakens the brand. Effective city branding therefore includes image building and perception management (including tangible attention to city appearance, urban development, and governance) as well as proactive marketing and promotional practices.

In addition, there is a third requirement for a successfully branded city: the importance of the resident-stakeholder in shaping a city's brand. Scholars such as Insch (2011) and Biel (1993) argue that residents are critical participants in the cocreation of a credible and enduring city brand. While city authorities cannot realistically satisfy the demands and desires of all who live there, residents are instrumental in building a city brand as they live and breathe the city's brand identity. For Insch: "Residents' attitude and attachment to the city where they live, work and play can influence the perceptions of tourists and visitors through their recommendations and complaints. Residents' skills, talents and entrepreneurial drive also contribute to the city's and region's growth and prosperity. In these and other ways, residents can add value to the brand equity of the city in which they live" (2011, 8).

Biel puts it well when he asserts that cities depend on their residents for economic, social, cultural, and environmental vibrancy (1993). Maintaining a diverse, skilled, and satisfied residential population is thus vital for a city since residents' disenchantment could trigger a vicious downward spiral. Biel argues that low levels of resident satisfaction are also negatively perceived by potential business migrants, who assess residents' well-being and satisfaction compared to rival locations. In addition to "hard" factors—human resources, infrastructure, transportation, education, and training opportunities—quality of life is evaluated by company executives, management, and their families in making a decision to relocate and invest. The ultimate goal of resident involvement is therefore to engender loyalty and create a preference for the city among the segments it serves. Some of the most visible and salient groups with an interest or stake in the city are business owners, investors, not-for-profit organizations, residents, students, special interest groups, tourists, and visitors. The brand strategy for a city must thus resonate and appeal to both outsiders and residents.

Current City Branding Models

The ultimate goal of city branding is therefore to create an attractive place to live, work, study, play, and do business. In order to raise awareness about and enhance the appeal of their cities, many urban authorities around the world have begun to embrace the notion of branding as part of city marketing and urban development. For example, one can readily point to many cities across the world associated with positive images: Paris is associated with romance, Milan with style, New York with energy, Tokyo with modernity, and Barcelona with culture. It is these images that play a crucial role in people's decision to live, work, raise families, do business, or visit there. Yet we do not come to our perceptions of these cities by accident. Their images have been deliberately constructed. Kavaratzis (2004) asserts that people make sense of places or construct places in their minds through three processes: the first via proactive interventions such as planning and urban design; the second through the ways they or others use specific places; and the third through the ways in which places are represented in popular culture—in films, novels, paintings, and news reports. As such, for Kavaratzis the first step of the branding of a city is for city authorities to find this important quality and make it more tangible and distinct.

For many developed countries and new emerging economies, building smart, powerful cities with tangible, distinct identities—and letting the world know about them via city branding strategies—is already old news. New York was one of the first cities to develop a formal branding strategy. In the decades prior to gaining its fantastical image as the place to be, New York was a feared city. In the mid-1970s crime was at its highest level in history. The streets were filthy, a heroin and cocaine epidemic had gripped the city, and many neighborhoods had fallen into disrepair. Its image was in tatters, visitors were staying away out of fear, corporations were relocating, and residents found little to love about their own city. New York desperately needed something to change. The now famous "I Love New York" slogan and its iconic logo, I ♥ NY, was part of a new campaign to encourage tourism and rebuild the image of New York City. Broadway theater, restaurants, and nightlife were promoted as part of the culture of the city and the great outdoors for the rest of the state. More significantly was the work of city government to clean up the city and crack down on crime to make way for New York's recovery, featuring a booming tourism industry, a financial hub, and a cultural mecca (D'Cruz 2016; Chan 2008; Place Brand Observer 2018).

In Europe cities such as Dublin, Stockholm, Berlin, Barcelona, and Prague have also been reinventing themselves, launching dynamic marketing campaigns to reposition themselves in the international marketplace. Dublin's 2015 "Breath of Fresh Air" campaign, for example, encouraged visitors to look beyond the city center and see Dublin as a coastal city with mountains and sea and experience a vibrant population, dynamic personality, evolving culture, and openness (Conghaile 2015). Since Barcelona hosted the 1992 Olympics, the city became an international success, having anchored itself as the home to big business (large publishing, pharmaceutical, and manufacturing industries) and one of the world's dominant football clubs and a cultural hot spot, attracting some thirty-two million people in 2016 alone (Stothard 2017). This is while Prague is busy strengthening its reputation as a tourist and conference destination, enticing visitors to get caught up in the feelings and experiences of this capital city through its "Pure Emotion" campaign.

In Asia, China is spending trillions to build cities such as Beijing and Shenzhen into "megacities." These large Chinese cities are designed to play an important role in the globalization of China. Despite being the political and cultural center of China, the overall strategic goal is for Beijing to become, by 2050, a world city—a global center for education, health, culture, and technology, providing sophisticated technology, first-class infrastructure, and human capital. Shenzhen is branding itself as a research and development center and an innovative and creative hub as well as a leader in internet innovation, telecom technology, and communication networks (Sevin and Bjorner 2015). In 2014 India's new prime minister, Narendra Modi, campaigned on a platform of economic development and good governance, promising Indian urban redevelopment, the creation of "new age cities," and a new era of Indian achievement in the world (CNN 2014). Across Africa cities such as Cape Town and Johannesburg, Nairobi and Lagos, are reimagining their urban cities as "smart cities" focused on innovation, commerce, and culture (Giles 2018). Indeed, building smart cities is now all the rage. Smart cities are premised on the idea of municipalities taking a proactive, technology-driven approach to urbanization. Smart cities essentially focus on workability, livability, and sustainability by adopting smart technologies to optimize all of the functions of the city. In this regard a smart city would call upon information and communication technologies to increase efficiency, share information with the public, and improve the quality of government services and the welfare of citizens (Rouse 2018).

But what of Caribbean islands such as Jamaica that already possess a globally recognized symbolic culture? Although the capital city of Kingston and other urban centers across Jamaica (Montego Bay, Ocho Rios, and Spanish Town) have had moments of flourish and show potential to explode into thriving urban centers, city branding has yet to take root in Jamaica in the way it has in other parts of the world. In other words, no formal city branding project currently exists in Jamaica. Among its fourteen parishes, none has sought to establish a "parish brand" or yet emerged as a potential player in the larger efforts undertaken by the authorities to promote the brand that is Jamaica. As noted, the city brand has become one of the most valuable and tangible assets of a country brand, with more and more city authorities launching campaigns to create distinctive identities for their cities, build positive perceptions, and attract tourism and investment. If Jamaica is to reframe its identity and the way the nation formally projects itself in the world, moving from a largely destination tourism model to one that fully acknowledges and promotes other aspects of its identity, city branding is a way to go. In this sense a focus on Kingston is an appropriate starting point.

It is important to reiterate here that for any city to be a good brand, it must possess readily identifiable defining and distinctive characteristics such as city appearance, history, culture, economy, and governance as well as account for people's beliefs and impressions about it. The city brand also needs to have a strong sense among all stakeholders about what the city stands for and therefore what it wishes to draw upon and communicate about itself to target groups. How does Jamaica's capital city stack up against these criteria, and what can city authorities do to build Kingston's brand and improve the prospects for this Caribbean city? These are salient questions, the answers to which can only be fully gleaned by looking more closely at the existing brand image of Kingston, including the history of the city and some of the variables that have come to define it.

Kingston: History and Defining Characteristics

As Jamaica's capital city, Kingston is the island's economic and political center and principal seaport, boasting a natural harbor, the seventh largest in the world. In terms of geography Kingston is located on the southeastern coast of the island, in the county of Surrey, and is protected by the Palisadoes, a long sandpit that connects the former naval town of Port Royal and the Norman Manley International Airport to the rest of the island. The city is the smallest of the island's fourteen parishes but the most populous. Yet in order to fully grasp and come to terms with the brand image and complex identity of Kingston, it is the city's history that tells the most compelling story.

From its earliest beginnings Kingston was a city "born of 'wickedness' and disaster" (Mann 2016), having been formally established as a refuge for survivors of a massive earthquake and tsunami that devastated Port Royal, on June 7, 1692. Up until that year, Port Royal was the unofficial capital of Jamaica and one of the busiest and wealthiest ports in the West Indies. An important commercial center for trade in slaves, sugar, and logwood, Port Royal was controlled by English buccaneers and was home to dangerous pirates operating in the Caribbean Sea, among them the renowned privateer Henry Morgan, who plundered the Spanish colonies for the British king. The city quickly developed a reputation as a place of drunkenness, excess, and debauchery and became known as the "wickedest city on earth" and the "Sodom of the New World." The earthquake and tsunami—seen by many then as retribution by God—caused much of the city to sink below sea level, killing more than two thousand people. By the late eighteenth century Port Royal was largely abandoned, and much of the sea trade had moved to Kingston. Following the reorganization of Jamaica after 1865, the colonial authorities formally relocated Jamaica's capital from Spanish Town to Kingston (Mann 2016).

In terms of economic activity, infrastructural development, and population, Kingston developed at a phenomenal rate in the 1900s, emerging as the center of trade and commerce. It is noteworthy that in 1933 the parishes of Kingston and St. Andrew were joined to provide better administrative management to each. Together they constitute the Kingston and St. Andrew

Corporate Area (JIS News). In the early postindependence period retail was the outstanding feature of the city's economy. This was reflected in the growth of suburban shopping plazas and later a burgeoning informal sector of street vending and small-scale entrepreneurship. As the city's economy grew, Jamaicans moved from rural villages into Kingston to seek employment, resulting in a population explosion. From 1960 to 1970, for example, the population of Kingston increased from 376,000 to over 500,000 (Clarke 1971). Today Kingston is bursting at its seams, with a population of over 900,000. Overcrowding and high unemployment placed enormous pressure on the economic resources and social facilities of the city.

This growth in the city's economy resulted in the rapid expansion of the residential area but in a way that emphasized "social and spatial segregation" (Clarke 1971). Those of a higher socioeconomic status and ethnic group retreated to the elite enclaves and gated communities in Kingston and upper St. Andrew, popularly referred to as "Uptown," and those of the so-called underclass (largely black) were relegated to the low-lying shantytowns of Downtown Kingston. Urban scholars such as Norton refer to this development as the making of "two Kingstons" (1978). The obvious consequence has been marginality and exclusion of a significant segment of the population, reflected in the emergence of squatter settlements and slum communities alongside all the deprivations and degradation that characterize this way of life (Clarke 2006; Portes, Dore-Cabral, and Landolt 1997).

Kingston at this time was also becoming a hotbed of political protests, warfare, and mushrooming crime. A "rude boy" culture had taken root in the 1960s as warring gangs, known for their violent and antisocial behavior, faced off with each other for scarce resources in the tense political geographies of Kingston. In the 1970s a bloody political civil war between the island's two main political parties—the Jamaica Labor Party (JLP) and the People's National Party (PNP)—played out in Kingston's inner cities. From the 1980s onward, as a new world economic order took hold in the world, crime mushroomed in Kingston (and throughout the island), driven by the international drug trade. Gang warfare deepened, and Jamaica saw the emergence of local warlords and rogues, called "dons," who assumed leadership of local communities, called "garrisons" (Johnson 2008).

This situation created an uncivil social fabric in Kingston, reflected in crime in communities; violent behavior in public places; vandalism of public property; corruption, obscenity, and violence in the media; corruption in public life; and indiscipline in schools and sporting activities. Noted Jamaican political scholar Carl Stone remarked that all this was a reflection of the serious breakdown in the norms, values, and attitudes that shaped Jamaican society (1992). He argued that while social institutions such as the family, church, and community were more important to the society's core values in rural nineteenth-century Jamaica, in the postwar, urbanized Jamaica the workplace and school and the mass media (including dancehall and reggae music as well as social media), have assumed ascendancy in shaping the society's values (Stone 1992; Johnson 2011). Indeed, the core values and norms shaping life in Kingston and the wider Jamaica are being reflected in the popular culture—in the violent music of some of the top acts of the day and even in globally acclaimed films such as *The Harder They Come*, starring reggae superstar Jimmy Cliff, who played a gun-slinging "bad boy" character creating havoc within Kingston's inner cities. Other more recent films such as *Dancehall Queen* and *Shottas* also replicate the turbulence and violence of Kingston.

Toward a Brand for Kingston: Current Perceptions

It is almost a truism that Jamaica has a problematic image. From its early history Kingston has been known for danger and tumult—a hotbed of social unrest, political warfare, mushrooming crime, massive social inequities, impoverishment, and a generally uncivil environment. No formal research has yet been done on people's perceptions of and experiences with Kingston, but based on informal polls carried out by this author on social media, media reportage, and anecdotal evidence, we can get a sense of people's beliefs, impressions, and ideas about Kingston. International perceptions of Kingston are anchored in the notion that Kingston is the "murder capital of the world," having ranked consistently among the top ten cities with the highest murder rates in the world (Mead and Blason 2014; UNODC 2013) and thus it is a city to be feared.

Jamaica has been grappling with a spiraling murder rate over the last three decades. Despite a downward trend in murders after the 2010 state of emergency, Jamaica's homicide rate continues to climb, rising to 1,192 in 2015 (45 per 100,000) and 1,610 by 2017 (56 per 100,000). This astonishing murder rate is the toughest challenge that Jamaican authorities face in any branding of Kingston. The association with danger is echoed by human rights organizations such as Human Rights Watch, which speaks of Jamaica's unchecked homophobic violence, including discriminatory laws and inadequate police protection for those in the island's LGBTQ community, with the bulk of such violence taking place in the capital, Kingston (Human Rights Watch 2014). Further, the U.S. Department of State maintains a warning to its citizens visiting Jamaica to avoid Kingston and other urban centers after dark. This is while the popular tourist site Trip Advisor consistently warns tourists visiting Jamaica of the "danger in paradise," with Kingston being the most risky. Indeed, one posting boasts a glaring headline, "Don't Go! Dangerous!" Place branding specialist and writer Samantha North (2015) writes in London's *CityMetric* magazine: "When I told people where I was going [Jamaica], 'It's not safe there' was a common response. This wasn't a one-off remark from an overprotective relative—it was a recurring theme. It was almost as if they expected me to get robbed the instant I set foot in Norman Manley Airport."

This reputation of unsafety menaces Brand Kingston, fueling negative perceptions of Kingston (and Jamaica in general) as a "dangerous paradise," so to speak. It also undermines the confidence of local and foreign investors hoping to do business in the city; renders the city unattractive to overseas residents and students as a place to work, live, raise families, and study; and robs it of its economic viability. In a 2014 interview outgoing vice chancellor of the University of the West Indies, E. Nigel Harris, admitted that the "perceptions regarding the state of crime and violence in the country" have caused a "general problem with attracting academics and students" (qtd. in North 2015). In addition, in a 2014 report the World Bank estimated that the direct cost of crime to Jamaica was J$61 billion, or 4 percent of the country's gross domestic product (GDP), measured in terms of potential losses in investment and in human capital from skilled migration. According to the World Bank, crime also affects people's propensity to save and invest in Jamaica (Blackford 2017).

Kingston struggles to overcome this torrid history and conflicted image. For better or worse, this is Kingston's existing brand and the most dominant perceptions that circulate about the city; these are deeply entrenched negative ideas and beliefs that may be difficult to change. Most place brand practitioners and scholars accept that once a stereotype is formed, it is very difficult to change since much effort is required to make the target population amenable to a new and different image. Yet in reality, Kingston's image contains both negative and positive features and is in an enviable position of being highly familiar to a lot of people (i.e., it has a popular or rich image). Kingston can therefore build on its positive features and undermine unfavorable perceptions of the city. City authorities have to foreground the positive aspects of Kingston and reinforce the idea that the city is more than a singular narrative of crime and violence and underdevelopment. By enacting a formal city branding strategy, they can showcase the city's many positive aspects and its possibilities. It is important to note some efforts are under way that lends a more favorable image to Kingston, but these are yet to be part of a cohesive city branding program. In other words, the city's image, including negative stereotypes, can only change via a deliberate Brand Kingston project.

Branding Kingston: The "Creative City"

Caribbean authorities largely accept that the economic future of the region itself rests on the cultural industries and creative sectors—music, visual and performing arts, fashion, design, craft, culinary arts, sports, advertising, leisure software, architecture, video games, with linkages to subsectors such as merchandise, public relations, marketing, photography, online/mobile services, web development, heritage, and tourism services (Patterson 2014). Regional governments also understand the incalculable value of the creative economy. UNESCO and United Nations Conference on Trade and Development (UNCTAD) figures suggest a market value of the creative economy as US$1.6 trillion. Further, the World Economic

Forum reported that in 2015 the world's creative and cultural industries generated US$2.2 billion in revenue, or 3 percent of the world's GDP.

It is within this creative space that Jamaica, which is considered the creative hub of the Caribbean, has a competitive advantage. Jamaica has earned its place in world culture. For the last seventy years Kingston has been a melting pot of cultures and a true creative capital in the Northern hemisphere. As early as the 1930s, Kingston became the focal point for the emergence of Rastafarianism as the world's newest religion. Rastas drew their philosophy from famed black activist, and national hero of Jamaica, Marcus Garvey, who promoted pride in black identity, black economic empowerment, and the repatriation of black people to Africa, which he saw as the motherland. In postcolonial Jamaica, Rastafari culture was both a profound cultural and political statement. Its symbolisms—dreadlock hairstyles; the signature colors red, green, and gold; and smoking of weed (marijuana) as a religious sacrament—took hold among the subaltern classes in Jamaica (Chevannes 1995). This powerful subculture was to remain localized, and ostracized, until the 1960s, when the global civil rights and black power movements coincided with the explosion of Jamaican music on the world stage.

From the 1960s and 1970s Kingston provided the backdrop for Jamaica's triumphant rise as a major player in world music and culture. Thanks to the rising popularity of the "Sound System" in Kingston's inner cities and the likes of musicians King Tubby and Lee "Scratch" Perry, dub became an art form and made its way into world culture (McCleod 2014). Jamaican popular music as a whole—ska, rocksteady, and later reggae—quickly catapulted into the global mainstream. Reggae's iconic emissary was Bob Marley. Marley drew on his early social milieu in Kingston's inner-city community of Trench Town to raise awareness about racial and social justice through socially conscious "message music," which resonated with oppressed peoples everywhere during the global civil rights movement (Aïnouche 2012). Marley, himself a Rastafarian, not only popularized reggae worldwide but, by adopting his country's indigenous religion and its culture, helped to globalize Rastafari and Rasta symbolisms and deepen its acceptance as a lifestyle (Mussche 2008). Jamaican dancehall music, a reggae offspring birthed in the 1980s, also had its roots in Kingston's inner cities and also quickly became part of the urban music landscape around the world.

Today the island is in the throes of a magnificent cultural and creative renaissance, and capital city Kingston is, once more, at the heart of this glorious cultural resurgence. Kingston, undeniably, has cultural clout. However, having received the acclaim from the UNESCO as a "Creative City of Music" in 2015, Kingston is yet to truly actuate its cultural credentials. I submit that this is Kingston's "creative moment"—an opportunity for Jamaican authorities to, quite literally, bank on its creative, cultural brand and build an authentic and successful city brand for Kingston, based on its creative economy.

Kingston's Creative Moment: The Arts

Kingston boasts vibrant and energetic arts and culture scenes featuring a boundless collective of artists of every genre and a pulsating nightlife featuring a plethora of live reggae festivals and dancehall music events that cater to an energetic youth culture. A new, young crop of reggae artistes— among them the twenty-somethings Protoje, Chronixx, Jesse Royal, and Kabaka Pyramid—are busy "repopularizing the [roots reggae] genre in a wave that has been called "reggae revival" (Aguirre 2015). It is a fact that dancehall music—featuring artists such as Vybz Kartel, Popcaan, Sean Paul, and Shaggy—has dominated contemporary Jamaican music culture, with a cultic following among the youth. Yet there is renewed interest in the roots reggae movement begun by Bob Marley back in the 1970s. This is thanks to "legit" roots reggae festivals such as Rebel Salute—a two-night outdoor festival that adheres strictly to Rastafarian principles, with a prohibition on alcohol and meat at the venue and that has for decades given platform to the classic reggae genre and tries to maintain its relevance in the modern music market (Aguirre 2015). As the home of reggae, events like these bring multitudes of tourists to the island and, for those who travel to Kingston, showcase the vitality of the city, adding to the range of entertainment available even for the business traveler.

Jamaica's capital city is also emerging as a fashion capital, having developed a successful fashion and beauty industry via the city's main modeling agencies, Pulse International and Saint International. Together these agencies churn out some of the world's tops models and highlight designers who are on the cutting edge of fashion. An indication of Kingston's clout in fashion is the large number of Jamaican models signed to top agencies around the world and gracing the cover of some of international fashion's elite magazines (Okwodu 2015). In addition, of remarkable note is London Fashion Week's 2014 ode to Kingston's rude boy subculture with an exhibition at Somerset House featuring what they called "rude boy fashion." The "Return to Rude Boy" exhibition seized upon the children of the ska music scene of the 1960s to re-create and "re-present" the rude boy culture not as merely deviant but as a modern, cool, desirable lifestyle, influencing music, fashion, art, technology, and business. According to a *Washington Post* blog, this rude boy cool has deepened in contemporary England so much so that *rude boy* is not a term associated with one sect (Kingston's gun-toting bad boys) but an all-encompassing style and attitude belonging to those males and females that are some of today's leading creatives and entrepreneurs and who are projecting their individuality through "rude fashion" (Crowder 2014). Of course, there are obvious problems with this cultural appropriation, such as the romanticization of life in inner-city Jamaica and the adoption and decontextualization of Jamaican history. Admittedly, however, it also signals a greater recognition of Jamaica's contributions to global fashion.

Jamaican creatives are also making films and documentaries like never before. They are deploying social media and numerous film festivals to share their creations, telling Jamaican stories and, in so doing, showcasing the multitudes of other stories about the island in general and Kingston in particular, and essentially changing the dynamic of Caribbean representation. Many of these young artists are educated in the Kingston-based Edna Manley College of the Visual and Performing Arts, one of the Caribbean's top institutions dedicated to the pursuit of creative careers. Aguirre, writing for *Vogue* magazine, calls it the "Juilliard of Jamaica" (2015). The college graduates exceptional visual and performing artistes, such as popular millennial musicians Raging Fyah, C Sharp, and

Blu Print. Cultural commentator and the school's marketing executive Coleen Douglas asserts that the college is a creative hub in Kingston and has played a major role in "improving the aesthetic sensibilities and the value of arts and culture in the society." She argues, however, that the institution needs to push the boundaries in the arts by ensuring its course offerings are current and groundbreaking (Douglas 2018). For example, new innovations in the creative sector, such as animation and gaming, are needed. In order to truly fulfill its role as part of the United Nations' creative city network and contribute to Kingston's consolidation of its brand as a creative city of the future, Douglas maintains that there is urgent need for funding to support the upgrading and modernizing of facilities at Edna Manley College and carrying out critical research in the Jamaican creative sectors.

Kingston's "Creative Moment": Historical and Other Attractions

Kingston has a powerful history and heritage that has yet to be fully showcased, communicated, and explored for its potential economic return from inbound tourism. Famous landmarks and attractions litter the city, such as the Bob Marley Museum housed in the iconic reggae singer's former home; the famous colonial mansion Devon House, which was voted by *National Geographic* as the place selling the best ice cream in the world; Hope Botanical Gardens, which showcases the island's flora and fauna; the Blue Mountains, the island's coffee-growing region with trails and waterfalls; the University of the West Indies; and Kingston Harbor—the seventh largest natural harbor in the world as well as the former naval city of Port Royal. The multitude of heritage site and attractions available in Kingston illustrate its enormous pull and vast potential as a creative, cultural city. The government of Jamaica and city administrators must act urgently to develop Port Royal into an established attraction. The once famous city, pivotal to the global trade in slaves, wars of conquest between the English and the Spanish, and privateering and piracy for nearly two centuries and steeped in the history of the city of Kingston, suffers gross neglect. Successive Jamaican governments have paid lip service to this project (Hall 2018). The redevelopment of Port Royal needs to be fast-tracked and incorporated into an active city branding process, not as a piecemeal project but as part of a larger redevelopment of Kingston.

Also located in Downtown Kingston are a raft of institutions and monuments that reflect the city's rich heritage. These include the National Heroes Park, the National War Memorial, the Gleaner Company, the Jewish Synagogue, Jamaica's Parliament (called "Gordon House," after national hero George William Gordon), the Jamaica National Heritage Trust, the famous intersection at Parade, the Ward Theatre, the Norman Manley statue, the Coke Methodist Church, St. Williams Grant Park, the Kingston Parish Church, the statue of national hero Alexander Bustamante, King Street, the Supreme Court, the National Library (aka Institute of Jamaica and the National Gallery), as well as the Bank of Jamaica and the Africa-Caribbean Institute (VisitJamaica.com).

It is worth noting that the Jamaica Tourist Board, the island's tourism agency, lists these attractions on its website as part of what it calls a "Downtown Kingston Heritage Walking Tour." Yet this is not a formal, guided tour but what one might call a "suggested tour," where visitors are advised to hire a local person to accompany them on the suggested route to see these monuments and sites or otherwise sightsee in a motor vehicle. In recent times an increasing number of tour operators are taking tourists from the walled resorts in the tourist hot spots of Montego Bay and Ocho Rios to explore Kingston. The Jamaica Tourist Board recorded more than 750,000 "stopover" visits to Kingston in 2017, writes Canadian journalist Kate Chappell, noting that tourist arrivals in Kingston are up 11 percent over the past five years. While that number is only a fourth of the 3.1 million–plus stopover visits recorded at popular Montego Bay, for many onlookers this marks a decisive shift (Chappell 2018). A new modern highway infrastructure makes access to Kingston from Montego Bay easier; there is ongoing expansion of the capital's port to accommodate cruise ships; and the positioning of Kingston as a Logistics Hub to facilitate increased trade between international markets, specifically business opportunities through an expanded Panama Canal (Collinder 2018), offers a unique opportunity for Kingston to deliberately and strategically promote its cultural credentials and assets. This is an opportunity to establish real avenues for inbound tourism, including formal educational tours and sightseeing.

At the time of writing, a placemaking project dubbed Kingston Creative was launched, with the objective of developing an art district in Downtown Kingston. The project is designed to create space for the city's artisans, artists, and creative entrepreneurs to exhibit their arts and crafts and for the public to experience art in the streets of Downtown Kingston. Art walks, performances, and painting of murals are some of the events already underway. Kingston Creative is an important development that communicates and reinforces the city's foundational place as the creative capital of the Caribbean. Founder Andrea Dempster-Chung, asserts that the overarching goal is to empower entrepreneurs to create economic and social value, gain access to global markets, and have a positive impact on their local communities (Small 2018; Loop Jamaica 2018). Yet projects of this nature do more. Kingston's historical attractions and places of interest provide a unique opportunity to create a distinctive identity for the city, to reimagine and recast Kingston as a city that stands for creativity and culture, and reconnect the people to their city's history, culture, and community.

It is noteworthy, however, that while the city's notable attractions and monuments are incredibly important to Kingston's cultural identity, many have gone into disrepair and are badly in need of restoration. Downtown Kingston, in general, remains largely unappealing and unwelcome to visitors. The various, buildings, statues, monuments, and attractions in the city are sites that hold the story of the place, of the people who live and have lived there, their narratives and experiences. Old monuments need to be restored, and new ones ought to be unveiled that tell the story of the Jamaican people and Jamaican civilization, past and present. These are aspects of Kingston that are distinctive and identifiable and are cultural resources and assets that can be called upon to communicate and brand the city. A city such as Kingston is not just physical matter. It is an urban actor with a personality and a story that ought to be allowed to play its role in defining the life and core value of the city.

Kingston's "Creative Moment": Sports

Sports has always played an important role in Jamaican identity, and Kingston is the seat of the island's sporting identity. Kingston is home to the Jamaican national stadium and a host of sporting events, including year round-marathons, premier league and schoolboy football, net ball, boxing, athletics, and cricket. Indeed, CHAMPS—the very popular High School Boys and Girls Athletic Championships—is the breeding ground for the country's successful sprinters; and Test cricket games featuring the West Indies team or regional 20/20 competitions are extremely popular and attract thousands of visitors to the city. Noted sports commentator Carole Beckford argues for Jamaica to maximize its potential as a sports tourism destination, focusing on beach volleyball and other events and leading the way in training other Caribbean athletes (2017). Sport tourism is anchored on the premise of people traveling to a destination to watch or participate in sports, including World Games, International Test series, mass participation events, player testimonials, group tours, sporting events, and exhibitions. Sports tourism is said to be the fastest-growing sector in world tourism, generating some US$450 billion annually (Eapen 2014). Jamaica has the opportunity to leverage its multiple local sports events, instead of relying on mega events, and establish a niche in the sports tourism sector in sports such as sprinting, in which it has dominance. Athletics, particularly sprinting, is steeped in Jamaican sports history—from the legends of the 1948 London Olympics, Herb McKenley, Arthur Wint, and Donald Quarrie, to the athletics revolution of the modern era led by Usain Bolt, Shelly-Ann Fraser-Pryce, and others (Franklyn 2009). Beckford also stresses the importance of the branding of sports and also the branding of individual athletes (2017). Jamaica's inspiring record in athletics and its world-famous athletes offer a unique opportunity to establish a sports museum of the caliber of the United States' sports halls of fame that tells the story of the island's achievements in world sport and as a means to play up the positive narratives about the city of Kingston.

Kingston's "Creative Moment": Gastronomy

A city branding strategy for Kingston must include a focus on gastronomy. Food is central to Jamaican culture, and Kingston boasts a vibrant "foodie culture" replete with restaurants, cafés, and street food as well as a variety of food festivals and food awards. An increasing variety of Jamaican foods has also achieved global recognition, such as the country's national dish, ackee and saltfish, which was voted the second best national dish in the world by *National Geographic* in 2011. Jerk chicken and Jamaican meat pies, called "patties," are also internationally known, the latter thanks to immigrant entrepreneurs such as Lowell Hawthorne, whose Golden Krust chain of Jamaican restaurants has been introducing America to Jamaican food for decades. Jamaican patties are now even a part of the lunch menu in the New York City school system (Oliver 2017). Food is a viable aspect of marketing a city, whether its local restaurants, bars, distilleries, or local markets. In fact, tourists often travel to experience the food culture of other nations. In 2017, for example, I had a memorable gastronomy tour of Colombian cuisine in Bogotá.

The Jamaican government has been historically slow to reach beyond its laser-like focus on a "sun, sand, and sea" tourism-centric nation branding model. It's announcement in early 2018 of a renewed focus on gastronomy and a desire to reap earnings from the US$150 billion global gastronomy industry is welcome news. Minister of Tourism Edmund Bartlett argues, "As competition between destinations increases, it will be cultural heritage, entertainment offerings and the unique local and regional intangibles like food and cuisine that will make the difference" (qtd. in Davis 2018). The island's first gastronomy center was opened at Kingston's Devon House. There is also a Blue Mountain Culinary Tour, where visitors can learn about the coffee-growing process, while the island's oldest distillery, Appleton Estates, will be upgraded to expand the "rum experience." It is important, however, that Jamaican gastronomy includes an appreciation of the culinary practices of "ordinary" Jamaicans. For example, the popular Coronation Market, located in Downtown Kingston, frequented by a wide cross section of locals on Saturdays as well as jerk chicken—grilled on old barrel drum containers (called "pan chicken") and sold on street corners on the weekends—are steeped in the popular culture of the city. Pan chicken has also become a key sector for developing budding small-scale entrepreneurs and is already a favorite when enticing tourists to sample the country's food heritage (*Jamaica Gleaner* 2012). Gastronomy cannot be positioned solely as an elite activity but has to be inclusive of all the elements of Jamaican food culture that are embraced by Jamaican citizens.

This is what building a creative city and a creative economy is about—a city that can attract tourists but also help to deepen global knowledge and understanding of the city. Kingston is without question a bustling metropolis, outfitted with a cosmopolitan culture, a vibrant city lifestyle, globally renowned and monumental cultural movements in reggae and Rastafari, churches, educational institutions, as well as sundry festivals, galleries, museums, and artifacts dedicated to Jamaica's rich heritage. The government, through the Jamaica Promotions Agency (JAMPRO), the Jamaica Tourist Board, and the Ministry of Culture, lends support to many events that define life in the city. However, these efforts are piecemeal and episodic and not part of a cohesive city branding strategy or program.

Media organizations such as the Gleaner Company have also been proactive in aspects of city branding. In 2017 the *Jamaica Gleaner*, for example, held its successful "Capture Kingston" photography competition. In over seven hundred submissions, city dwellers looked at their city through their own lenses, capturing the people, history, and infrastructure from their perspectives. Life in a city is an intensely visual process, and so these visual representations of the city are crucial (Dodman 2003). They show how Kingston is experienced by different socioeconomic sectors and how inhabitants of Kingston imagine their city. Photography competitions of this kind can also serve to undermine the idea that only violent things happen in Kingston. This kind of local knowledge is needed to make informed decisions about marketing and branding strategies for Kingston. City branding is a powerful strategic tool and a conscious and deliberate effort that can help to build a positive reputation for Kingston and reshape popular perceptions of the city. To use it successfully, however, as I posited earlier, will require city administrators to adopt a formal city branding strategy and an integrated approach to communicating and branding the city, involving the consensus of all stakeholders.

"Creative Kingston": Inclusivity and Citizen Participation

A reimagined Kingston as a creative, global, new age city of the future cannot and should not happen without the full participation of Jamaican citizens. The planning process ought to assume a bottom-up, collaborative approach. In 2018, in an open letter to city authorities (including mayor of Kingston Delroy Williams, member of Parliament Delroy Chuck, the Social Development Commission, the National Environment and Planning Agency, the Town and Country Planning Department, and the Urban Development Corporation), residents of the middle-class community of Barbican in St. Andrew protested the new infrastructure developments that they claim were taking place in their area without their consultation or even prior notification. The residents expressed concerns about the construction of hotel and business properties in the residential area and the traffic congestion, upsurge of crime, and potentially negative impact on the aesthetics of the area that it could create. In the letter the residents of Barbican demanded to have a voice in the discussions taking place about their community (*Jamaica Observer* 2018c).

The Barbican example is indicative of the citizens' rejection of elite, top-down approaches to urbanization and development in Jamaica. City leaders must crowd-source ideas from citizens about how they imagine their own cities and towns. Urban planning has to be participatory, involving a diversity of opinion, and fundamentally people centered. Kingstonians must feel engaged in shaping their city. Branding Kingston is not just about improving the infrastructure and marketing the city's cultural credentials but must also include improving people's relationships to one another and their sense of who they are and how they fit into their society. Being a society plagued by massive inequalities, this is a welcome social order for Jamaica.

Kingston's Urban Moment: Quality Governance

Quality governance is imperative and fundamental to the success of any city branding project. It is important to remember that branding is not a cure-all to mask a city's problems. In fact, good governance—manifested in low levels of crime and reliable transportation, sewerage, public power, and water supply as well as other aspects—is seen to be essential to a successful city branding project. For developing countries with social and economic challenges, city branding has to assume a sort of "governance-centric" approach. To be a successful city brand, for example, Kingston administrators must urgently address some of the major problems created by industrialization. Downtown Kingston, in particular, still faces some of the common challenges confronting many cities of the developing world—traffic congestion, solid waste management, water supply, public health, sanitation, and environmental issues as well as unregulated and uncontrolled informal trading, uncivil behaviors, and unchecked criminality. To undermine the perception of Kingston as "the murder capital of the world" and for people to feel safe visiting, living in, working in, and exploring Kingston, the monster of crime must be controlled. The police services must be resourced, and the police must establish relationships with civic groups and engage citizens in their communities, launching informational campaigns that rebuild trust. The institutional systems used to collect information, which allow for participation in the criminal justice system, has to be improved so citizens can feel confident about participating in crime fighting by reporting crimes. Meantime, citizens are obliged to uphold and foster civil values in their own silos and spheres of influence.

A creative city expecting an increased influx of tourists also requires a consistent water supply and electricity, good infrastructure, roads, and reliable transportation. If a city's infrastructure is old and decaying, it renders the city unattractive, unsafe, and not a great place to live. Furthermore, few investors will find incentives to set up businesses in a city with a deteriorating infrastructure. This in turn deepens poverty and joblessness for the people who already reside there. Despite heavy investment of resources in elite areas such as the New Kingston business district and shopping plazas around Constant Spring, Liguanea, and Manor Park, change of government administrations and priorities have managed to recalibrate the pace of development of Downtown Kingston. Infrastructure expansion can help to restore social and cultural vitality to this part of the city as well as bring economic prosperity.

At the time of this writing, new infrastructure developments and upgrades to existing infrastructure were being proposed by the government of Jamaica under a "Downtown Kingston Redevelopment Project." These include the Musson's West Kingston Business Park; Coronation Market; Kingston Lifestyles Plaza; Railway Station Museum projects; a microbrewery, restaurant, and beer garden; B&D Trawling Seafood Market; the Major WaterFront Entertainment Park; the Culture Hub Social Enterprise in Trench Town; and the Pan-Jam Boutique Hotel and Business Centre (Patterson 2017). It is important to remember that while these exciting additions to the city are welcome and will create employment and spur the economy, to be effective they must become part of a larger and active Brand Kingston strategy.

At the same time, the development of national parks ought to be part of the government of Jamaica's active agenda for Kingston, not just paying lip service to it. In addition to Hope Botanical Gardens and Emancipation Park located in the city's middle-class neighborhoods, there is a need for more green spaces throughout the city. Dodman (2003) notes that green spaces in urban areas provide aesthetic, recreational, and sociological functions in community life and are critical to the well-being of citizens. Chicago-based social activist and artist Theaster Gates puts it well when he says, "Beauty is a basic service" (2015).

With regard to transportation, a crucial aspect of quality city governance, Kingston's road network and public transportation have seen marked improvements with the building of large bus parks at city hubs such as Half Way Tree and Downtown Kingston as well as the registration and regulation of route taxis that ply routes across the metropolis (*Star Newspaper* 2015). Yet major deficits in public transportation remain, which must be addressed if the city is to open itself to increased tourist visitors and business opportunities. In addition, an efficient health care system and medical facilities that are well serviced and maintained as well as medical authorities able to control and manage public health issues such as outbreaks of diseases and deliver health care to Jamaica's citizens and to visitors, is fundamental to branding Kingston as a city of the future.

To bolster their economic competitiveness and attract tourism, many cities across the developed and developing world have launched extensive marketing and promotions campaigns to showcase their culture, attractions, historical sites, and leisure activities; in short, they are taking measures to brand their cities as great places to live, visit, go to school, work, raise families, and conduct business. This is Kingston's urban moment—an opportunity to design a new future for Kingston as part of a larger restoration and city branding project that will foster a powerful, distinctive image that makes Kingston desirable as a business location, tourist destination, and place to call home. Although city branding is not yet part of its Vision 2030 plan or any formal economic development model, Jamaican authorities, nevertheless, see Kingston as integral to the nation's relationship with the rest of the world and as a pivot point as the country accelerates its integration into the global economy.

It is for this reason that reshaping and reimagining Jamaica's capital city, Kingston (as well as other major urban centers and towns), is inevitable and necessary. In other words, Kingston must reinvent itself and establish a new paradigm for the city based on the opportunities, skills, resources, and capabilities that lie within the city and the core values, attitudes, behaviors, and characteristics that have enabled the city to achieve these benefits. City authorities have finally begun to invest in the urban infrastructure as a means to economic prosperity in an otherwise moribund economic space. As the economic center of the island—home to the island's large manufacturing corporations, small- and medium-sized businesses, entrepreneurship, and a massive informal economy of petty traders and itinerant traders—Kingston has always been defined and constructed in the public imagination as a place of business. The rise of business hotels (the Marriott Courtyard, the Spanish Court, and others under construction at the time of writing) and a new generation of smart, tech-savvy millennial entrepreneurs and innovators establishing and inhabiting a plethora of successful startups in Kingston are good indicators for some that the city is making progress in this regard (North 2015).

Yet in order to truly harness the benefits of urbanization and reconcile the image of the city, which is complex, the government of Jamaica must derive a philosophy upon which they wish to develop and restore Kingston so it can become central to the brand that is Jamaica. City authorities, in tandem with stakeholders (investors, civic groups, and members of the community), must forge a consensus on what kind of city they wish Kingston to be and what a future city of Kingston looks like in terms of livability, workability, and sustainability. In short, how might Kingston project itself to the world?

Based on the evidence presented in this chapter, it is clear that Kingston possesses strong capabilities, resources, and skills embedded in the extraordinary talents of its inhabitants and the broad range of opportunities to be exploited. But above all, Brand Kingston is a cultural mecca. Designated by UNESCO as a Creative City of Music and among an elite global group of creative cities, Kingston is obliged to embark on a proactive process of city branding in order to truly arrive at, and live up to, this creative city status. City administrators already know that they must redevelop Kingston, especially Downtown Kingston, as part of their effort to revive the economic prospects for the city. However, they must imagine Kingston as a whole, paying close attention to its distinctive identity and core values, that is, what the city stands for, which is a modern cosmopolitan city of the future anchored in a creative economy—a city of music, dance, and drama; fashion and design; sports; and gastronomy—whose success will be spurred by the creative talents of its people.

There is now consensus that you can reawaken cities by using culture and ignite participation and a sense of ownership of the place by including citizens as stakeholder-participants in the branding of the city. If Kingstonians are to own their city, they must feel like equal participants in its development. Encouraging this kind of consciousness among residents of Kingston about their city is crucial because it creates a sense of collaboration, connectedness, and community among the various sectors of the city, as opposed to the prevailing elite, top-down approach to city development.

To engage a process of city branding, Kingston authorities must also understand how those who inhabit the city as well as outsiders perceive the place, based on their experience of Kingston. At present there is a dearth of formal research on perceptions of the city. City authorities should aim to discover what people currently associate with Kingston.

Do people find it to be clean, beautiful, and safe? Does it have a wide variety of cultural attractions? Are tourist services of a high standard? Are Kingstonians warm and welcoming? Is Kingston a fun place to hang out in? Is it easy to get around using public transportation? If the city has a problem with its image among local and overseas populations, as Kingston undeniably does, local authorities must decide how to confront the findings and determine which marketing strategy should be employed to reverse negative associations and bolster positive ones.

Meanwhile, to earn a good, solid, and positive reputation, Kingston city authorities ought to see city branding not just from a marketing and public relations perspective (i.e., as more than snazzy slogans and superficial branding) but from one that is fundamentally governance-centric or policy driven. In other words, quality governance must be the platform upon which developing cities such as Kingston build a successful city brand. To do this, city authorities must continue to find new ways to continue to develop and reimagine Kingston, including adopting smart city initiatives that will improve city management—from traffic management, transport services, energy conservation, and efficiency to public safety and public health (e.g., improved sanitation and waste removal). So, rather than ad hoc infrastructure improvements, city administrators must take a holistic approach to city development, establish specific projects to fulfill this agenda, and set benchmarks to assess whether the city is delivering a decent quality of life and a clean and sustainable environment. In short, Kingston's reputation ultimately cannot be constructed; it has to be earned.

7

Hold On to What You Got

Intellectual Property and Jamaican Symbols and Culture

Steffen Mussche-Johansen and Hume Johnson

Despite having one of the world's most recognizable symbolic cultures, Jamaica has been reluctant to see the potential economic value of its own cultural symbols. Popular Jamaican entertainer Shaggy opines on some pertinent issues with regard to copyright and intellectual property (IP) governance in Jamaica:

> For me copyright law in Jamaica is extremely important. I mean, it is what you could call our "pension," which is what we have been lacking within the reggae fraternity in my opinion. You know, the first time that a copyright law was implemented in Jamaica was around 1993. For an island that survives off its music and its culture, it should have been long before. When I look at so many great artists from Jamaica whose recordings are owned by other people, and probably licensed out by other people, and they get nothing for it, well, that saddens me. For the government to set in place certain laws that protect these artists and create our pension—that's the best we could ask for. (Qtd. in March 2007)

Although Jamaica's copyright law has now been in effect for some twenty-five years, Jamaica still has a long way to go in implementing adequate and pragmatically effective IP rights governance and protection—in short, in protecting "Brand Jamaica."

The purpose of the chapter is twofold. First, it examines Jamaica's symbolic narrative. On the one hand, Jamaica is the home of Bob Marley, reggae, and Rastafarianism as well as a tropical sultry island dream boasting sun, sand, and sea. On the other hand, Jamaica is also associated with violent crime and virulent homophobia. (This dialectic is discussed by Hume Johnson in chapter 1 in this volume.) Based on the romanticized and socially constructed notion that Jamaicans are dreadlocked and laze on the beach under a coconut tree smoking ganja while listening to reggae music, Jamaican symbols and cultural expressions have been misappropriated and may have their meanings diluted, devalued, or associated with unwarranted (and unsolicited) connotations. This discussion argues that the somewhat dichotomous and stereotyped cultural representations of Jamaica may in fact be an external, discursive reading of prominent internal Jamaican cultural cues in a manner detached from their original signifiers. Second, based on the narrative placement of Jamaica, the chapter looks at the economic and judicial viability of a more structured and proactive approach to IP governance. Looking at Jamaica's strong name yet apparent inability to transform it into real revenue, the chapter discusses how Jamaica could greatly improve its strategic position vis-à-vis more structured governance of its cultural products and intangible resources.

We suggest that Jamaica may be able to reclaim moral, economic, and judicial ownership of its own symbols and narrative through adequate intellectual property rights' protection and proactive deployment of identity politics. In other words, we believe that Jamaican stakeholders can better ensure that Jamaican cultural and symbolic expressions are appropriated and projected in a manner that serves Jamaican interests and the Jamaican people as a whole. Of course, it is important to bear in mind that while IP governance is a powerful tool that can potentially empower Jamaica in this realm, the judicial intricacies of IP can also provide challenges regarding the full protection of the symbols under discussion. Many of the Jamaican symbols can be subject to scrutiny, but our focus will be on the Jamaican flag and to a lesser extent the Rastafarian colors.

Realities of Jamaica's Symbolic Culture

Jamaica's symbolic culture—the manifestation of the people's identity and their culture—is undoubtedly strong and holds a distinct status, which makes it difficult to associate Jamaican products and symbols with any arbitrary nation or brand. The Jamaican symbolic portfolio—the symbols that have been associated with Jamaica and Jamaican culture—include the Jamaican national flag and its colors (black, green, and gold) and the colors associated with Rastafari (red, green, and gold). It is the flag that has the most direct and undeviating symbolic link to the nation. On July 13, 1962, just under a month before gaining independence, the new Jamaican flag was unveiled for the first time, replacing the colonial predecessor, the British Union Jack. The Jamaican flag consists of the colors black, green, and gold. The colors were chosen to acknowledge and highlight the character and aspirations of the nation: green represents the lush green vegetation, the nation's agricultural richness, and hope for the future; gold represents the year-round sunlight and the country's natural wealth; black symbolizes the majority Afro-Jamaican population and the strength and creativity of the Jamaican people. On visiting Jamaica, one is readily exposed to the flag: wall paintings depicting the flag with *Proud to Be Jamaican* superimposed on it, people wearing green or yellow T-shirts depicting the flag, Jamaican flags as bumper stickers, the flag in earrings, the flag on slippers; wherever the Jamaican flag can be displayed, it is displayed. This panoply of the flag connotes a passion for the nation, its culture, and its heritage, and this zeal for things Jamaican is, arguably, one of the defining factors of the Jamaican people.

However, Jamaica is concurrently a case in which its flag, to some degree, has taken on its own life. The flag stands for Jamaica, but it also signifies something more; for Jamaicans it connotes positive values, vibrancy, creativity, and bold energy; for many around the world it represents notions of a troubled paradise. The potential effect of this dual meaning is that the Jamaican flag takes on a physiognomy or a character in its own right. Examples of this phenomenon are DuPont's trademark of *nylon* and IBM's trademark of PC (personal computer). In both examples the sign becomes synonymous with products of a certain category. While this is the result of successful branding, it also means that the signifier loses association with the specific product and it is to a greater degree up to the interpreter to project his or her meaning onto the sign.

In this way the Jamaican flag and other recognizable symbols of the nation are hyper-visible internationally but not exclusively mobilized by Jamaica. Therefore, it is not unusual to find Jamaica's national flag and its colors being used in other spaces outside of the nation and on bodies and products that are unrelated to the island. One example is the 2013 American Volkswagen Super Bowl commercial that explicitly draws on Jamaican cultural aesthetics (language, accent, and music) to market a car with no real connection to Jamaicans and the nation. Another case specifically related to the flag is with the German appliance company, Saturn, in its 2013 advertisement. In the ad the Jamaican flag—displayed in a German coffee shop with no discernible connection to the island—is inadvertently set on fire and taken outside, where (white) men stomp on it, trying to put the fire out. The company claims that it is meant to be "tongue-in-cheek" (Gilpin 2013). The commercial was ultimately withdrawn by the company after there were protests against its use of images depicting the burning of the Jamaican flag.

These and other incidents speak to the larger issue of how non-Jamaican companies and other entities often appropriate Jamaican symbolic cultural artifacts (such as the flag) in ways that align with their own agendas and reinforce their own ideas and narratives about the country and its people. This misappropriation and co-optation of Jamaica's symbols largely contributes to the narrative and metaphorical dilution of the sign. Ramello (2006) discusses *dilution by tarnishment* as the phenomena whereby stakeholders other than the rightful owner of a symbol produce goods of inferior quality that diminish the overall value of the brand or symbol (555). This major issue of trademark and IP governance at large relates to the corruption of symbols and describes the process whereby the symbolic value is diminished and has its original meaning altered. Ries and Ries (2002) puts it bluntly: "The easiest way to destroy a brand is to put its name on everything" (49). The implication of this process for Jamaica would be that the Jamaican flag, and to some degree the Ethiopian colors associated with the Rastafarian movement and reggae, is overly commercialized by stakeholders with little or no regard for the long-term viability and existence of the Jamaican brand and its cultural referents.

Jamaican symbolic culture is also threatened by symbolic *unbundling*, in which the sign gradually detaches itself from the original signifier (Ramello 2006). As discussed earlier, the counterfeiting of Jamaican products—understood here as products that, by chain of association, purport to be Jamaican by displaying symbols associated with the nation while not actually being authorized by or meaningfully related to Jamaica—is prevalent. Ramello (2006) asserts that when this practice is nondeceptive in nature, that is, customers are able to tell the legitimate products from the illegitimate ones, it may potentially be welfare enhancing. The question, then, is: Has this phenomenon been detrimental or advantageous in Jamaica's case? Both answers can be argued. While on the one hand the widespread counterfeiting of products, most notably in Asian markets, depicting the Jamaican flag has brought fame and recognition to Jamaica, Jamaican stakeholders exert no directive guideline over the message embodied in the symbol. Lash and Lury (2007) argues that cultural entities, like the Jamaican symbolic portfolio, take on a dynamic of its own. While on the one hand adding value, in the economic sense, this appropriation can also result in the cheapening of symbolic and cultural entities, in the signifying sense, and their detachment from their original signifiers. In the global culture industry, which is one of the spaces in which Jamaica's symbols operate, products and symbolic expressions are distributed as much by accident as by intention (Lash and Lury 2007). In this liminal space subliminal meanings are communicated, and the cultural entities themselves become inevitably modified over a range of environments. This is where symbolic logics become ambiguous and market mechanisms and branding principles become relevant—the symbols are commodified.

Jamaican symbols are packaged and traded within the premises of capitalism and hence appear as commodities. These commodities—comprised of both tangible and intangible qualities—are largely sources of symbolic power. If the beholder of the original symbolic reference point loses ownership of it, the stakeholder distributing Jamaican symbolic commodities is in the position of power and can hence operate on his or her own premises. When Nike, for example, promotes a shoe with Rasta colors, it owns the judicially institutionalized brand—the Nike logo and name—and will therefore be in the more favorable position. The Jamaican symbols are thus commodified in the context of Nike—and sold within the discourse of branding—but without the judicial protection of the Rasta colors, the brand. Similarly, noted British chef Jamie Oliver stirred controversy when he sought to produce and sell a version of Jamaican cuisine he labels "jerk rice." Of course, in Jamaican cuisine jerk is only associated with and used in the cooking of meat products. In attempts to commodify Jamaican cuisine, Oliver also failed to acknowledge that the original signifier of the product is Jamaican (see McKay 2018).

The cunning nature of globalization is putting pressure on states to develop, manage, and leverage their images in ways that are conducive to capitalistic principles. The critique of the negative effects and exploitative nature of capitalism argues that the industrialized world has drained, and is still draining, the periphery and semi-periphery world of natural, economic, and human resources (Bakan 2005; Hartmann 2004; Klein 2002 and 2007; Nace 2005). In this context it is pertinent to ask if symbols are the last assets that are still possible to steal. Critics have even asserted that when the capitalistic economies are saturated, thriving off or looting less-developed nations and economies for tangible assets such as natural resources (Hyslop-Margison 2006; MacEwan 2000), they will continue to exploit the less-developed economies of intangible assets. The extension of this process is the appropriation or misappropriation of cultural and symbolic capital. The process is often cunning in nature and viewed merely as free-floating signs in a hyperreality. However, these signs are real; they have real-life references and signifiers, and such misappropriation has real-life implications.

Although intangible assets are by definition intangible, this does not mean that they cannot be depleted. An oil well can be physically drained, but the Jamaican flag will not cease to exist. However, looking at the flag and other Jamaican symbols in the discourse of commodification, to the extent that the flag is overused or misappropriated, this could drain the symbol of its strength and significance. It is a form of resource exploitation—much in the same way as Nigeria has been exploited for oil—to the disadvantage of the people, economically but also within the context of identity negotiation. It may not be feasible for Jamaica to look after its symbolic portfolio as fervently as Apple guards its logo. Yet the overuse of the Jamaican flag means that Jamaicans will to a lesser degree be able to take advantage of this resource themselves, and it may be beneficial for Jamaica to reclaim its symbolic capital and start implementing strategies to ensure a larger degree of control over its own symbolic portfolio.

Encompassed in the perspective of reclaiming ownership of symbols and their meaning lies the premise that symbolic expressions and intangible assets can be owned and also that they, in the case of Jamaica, have been misappropriated and must be reappropriated. The Jamaican cultural symbols in question will here be understood as significant entities and carriers of meaning that in the perspective of symbolic capital entail a logic in which the symbols can be owned, exchanged, bought, sold—and stolen. In addition, when it comes to the Jamaican symbolic projection, it is the people and their creative expressions that constitute the signifying base. In other words, there might be an intuitive assumption that the Jamaican people should benefit to a larger degree from such symbolic projection. If the Jamaican people did not express themselves in such an indigenous and consistently creative manner as they have, Jamaica as a sign and narrative basis would never have assumed the meaning or value it exerts today. Therefore, should not Jamaica and its people to a larger degree benefit economically and wield influence over how the Jamaican flag and other cultural symbols are appropriated and portrayed? In addition to the proprietary reasons for claiming and reclaiming ownership of Jamaica's symbols, there are also issues regarding national identity that are stake.

Cultural Symbols, National Identity, and Jamaica's Tourism Model

Jamaica has been and to some degree still is associated with certain perceptions that present the nation and its people in a particular light. Specifically, it is widely known as a land of sand, sea, and sun, as the epitome of "all right" (see Nickesia Gordon's discussion of this point in chapter 2). As such, its cultural symbols—from Bob Marley and Usain Bolt to the Rasta colors—have been used in various ways by various parties to signify these constructed sentiments. This misappropriation ultimately decontextualizes the symbols and removes them from their original significance in the Jamaican culture. Therefore, it is important to question whether the manner in which the Jamaican symbols are being sold ultimately affects the true essence of the original symbols and the identity of their originators—the Jamaican people.

Becker's (1997) perspective on labeling theory provides insight into the impact that stereotypical imageries can have on Jamaica's ability to define its own symbols and identity. Becker's labeling theory pertains to how the self-identity and behavior of an individual—or in this case a semantically constructed symbolic entity—is created and negotiated and furthermore how the image of that individual or entity is constructed and assigned by other social players in a given society. The theory focuses on the semantic tendency among social majorities to stereotype in certain ways in order to create an easily construable notion of the individual or symbolic entity. Although Becker initially used the theory to explain how marginalized groups were labeled as such and subsequently experienced difficulties in ridding themselves of the given reputation, the theory can also explain how Jamaica is stereotypically associated with certain traits (aggressive, unsafe, weed smokers, laid-back [i.e., lazy]) and is experiencing difficulties in eradicating, modifying, or inverting these persistent perceptions. In practice this would suggest that once Jamaica is labeled in a particular way and this labeling achieves acceptance as being "true," it may be hard to shift. Essentially, although Jamaica as a signifier to a large degree refers to significant but complex history and meanings, Jamaica as a sign is read in a manner that fulfills already established notions. This may explain why the stereotypical notions about life in Jamaica and about reggae, Rastafarianism, and ganja—to name a few—still persist as prominent representations.

This predicament becomes even more problematic when Jamaicans themselves feel that they have to live up to the stereotypical expectations, creating a form of self-fulfilling prophecy. According to Merton (1968), the self-fulfilling prophecy concerns a prediction that directly or indirectly causes it to be realized. This mechanism may manifest itself through a prophecy or statement—declared as true when in fact it is not—and may sufficiently influence people through covert manipulation or logical confusion so that their reactions and expectations ultimately lead to fulfillment of the false prophecy. Similarly, the contingent corruption of the Jamaican symbols—being labeled in a particular manner and the difficulties faced by Jamaicans in breaking free from these expectations—may cause Jamaicans to live up to this image to their detriment. This vicious circle continues if Jamaican authorities continue to project an idea of the nation that is confined to a position that fulfills the notion of what Jamaica is expected to be—as opposed to being given the chance to project what Jamaica itself feels is its true potential and harness the symbolic capital in a more economically beneficial manner. Such a scenario may thwart progressive cultural developments and further promote a corruption of the symbols' original meaning.

From this perspective, if there is a corruption of the symbols, they no longer represent the original signifiers, and Jamaica may be forced into a reality where it must negotiate its identity within an unrepresentative symbolic framework that is externally assigned. Jamaica's symbolism is intrinsically connected to the national culture and national identity. Hence, one may argue there is a congenial connection between Jamaica's symbolic narratives and its identity. That is, when Jamaican symbols are corrupted, this may also have disadvantageous effects on the fabric of Jamaican national identity. This predicament has forced Jamaica to negotiate its own projection of identity within the already defined and confined discourse of its labeled image and expected role—largely defined by notions of "paradise." Taking Jamaica's revolutionary heritage and its present-day (somewhat contradictory) pride into consideration, there is indeed a discrepancy between how Jamaica would like to see itself and how Jamaica may be viewed externally. Largely due to external image projection, Jamaica has been subjected to a position in which symbolic essence is extracted from the original signifier and written into presupposed paradoxical narratives of paradise, easy life, and violence.

Unfortunately, many Jamaica on the island and abroad, in ways that reflect self-fulfilling prophecy tendencies, also essentialize Jamaica and Jamaicans and contribute to the nation's limited projection of itself (see Kamille Gentles-Peart's discussion of this in chapter 3). One may then argue that the complex processes of identity negotiation has forced Jamaica to abide and comply with an externally allocated identity that is out of sync and in disharmony with its internal, organically driven forces.

Moreover, according to noted Jamaican social commentator Kadamawe K'nife, those in institutionalized positions of power have systematically neglected what Jamaicans feel is the true essence of the nation and the brand:

> The informal sector is the stone that the builder refused, which has been the head cornerstone. It is the force that has kept the economy alive and the culture alive. They have refused it and now they see that they have no other choice than to acknowledge its contribution and its potential of building Jamaica further. JAMPRO started with Brand Jamaica now, but the problem is that the people that lead that process don't believe in Jamaica—in the livity of Jamaica—in what Jamaica truly is. So most of the investment moves in a traditional way, and not necessarily to the immersion of the people. So if you look at JAMPRO and their investment portfolio they continue investing in ways that have not worked. You then look at the culture as an enterprise that comprises Brand Jamaica through music, sports, cuisine—this *is* Brand Jamaica and this is what JAMPRO has to stimulate now, and they need to understand this. (Personal interview, April 25, 2007)

In K'nife's estimation the government of Jamaica has failed to project identities that are more true to Jamaican experiences and that are essential to substantial socioeconomic betterment and progress for the nation. The government and the formal sector have for decades striven to portray Jamaica in a generic manner, as paradise—somewhat unsuccessfully—hence placing Jamaica in a precarious situation. In other words, a significant problem for Jamaica has been that the Jamaican government and the formal sector have been complicit with and have contributed to the ruling discursive perception of the nation and refused to fully acknowledge the grassroots cultural symbolic elements. For many commentators this has led to an internal conflict. Yet it may be this inverse tension—with major forces pulling in opposite directions and an inkling of a cultural inferiority complex—that creates an uncanny climate for a unified image projection. If JAMPRO is able to merge these two perspectives in a more satisfactory manner, Jamaica may to a larger degree benefit even more from Brand Jamaica initiatives, reclaim ownership of symbols and their meaning, and come to terms with its identity.

In sum, signs and their symbolic narratives assign subject position and hence allocate the framework for identity. The allocation and interpellation of identity is expedited based on the cultural narratives embedded in the signs and symbols; the symbolic projections are expressions of identity. When these symbolic expressions are misappropriated, as argued in the case of Jamaica, the sign works reciprocally back to the original referent—the Jamaican people and their notion of the nation. This not only entails a mismatch between Jamaica as a semiotic concept and the reality it is supposed to represent; the sign's acquired and redefined meaning can backfire and influence the reality created as a reflection of the semantic concept of the nation in unexpected and unintended ways. Hence, the symbolically detached yet compelling concept of Jamaica—supposedly a true reflection of Jamaica as simultaneously the embodiment of "no problem" and "sufferation"—can actually operate in a hyperrealistic dimension and change the meaning of the original signifiers. Jamaica may be forced into a subject position that is externally allocated—based on external stakeholders' notions and expectations of how Jamaica and Jamaicans are—and hence run the danger of losing touch with itself. The ultimate transcendent consequence of this may be that Jamaica loses its exclusive moral right to narrate its own discourse and thereby the exclusivity of its identity, its story, and its cultural and symbolic self-determination. It is in this politicized dimension that the need for proactive identity politics arises.

The Way Forward: IP Protection, the Jamaican Flag, and Rasta Symbolism

Jamaica's flag and colors are threatened by misappropriation, dilution, unbundling, and essentialist ideas of Jamaica as a troubled paradise. It is therefore in Jamaica's interest to proactively preserve, protect, and establish more oversight of its symbolic image. Jamaica, being in the involuntary yet advantageous position in which its flag and other symbols have assumed a self-conditioning and self-enhancing role, should now assume the affirmative narrative position so that it can reclaim its symbols and be the rightful ruler of these symbols' meanings and future embodiments. In the context of a holistic nation brand strategy, deployment of a cleverly devised IP infrastructure can constitute an important factor in ensuring success. Adequate use of IP laws gives the right to earn a return on legally protected creations—that is, logos, trademarks, brand names, slogans, designs, tangible products, and even services—and could represent a new and promising approach to the harnessing of the Jamaican symbolic economy. However, this is not easily accomplished. Proactive IP governance does not only require positive attitudes to IP but also necessitates intricate knowledge of how to best deploy adequate aspects of the IP infrastructure in beneficial ways. In order to understand Jamaica's situation with regard to IP governance, it is important to delineate several key dimensions of IP protection and the challenges of using them to protect Jamaica's cultural symbols. Carruthers and Ariovich distinguish five dimensions of (intellectual) property that, when applied to the Jamaican context, provide useful insight into the challenges facing the nation in securing IP rights for its symbols (2004, 24–31).

The first two dimensions relate to the object and subject of property. The *objects of property* describe what can be owned. This dimension has varied through cultures and times but has always had an emphasis on tangible goods. The *subject of property* speaks to who may own. While it used to be a privilege, ownership today is common. An interesting perspective here pertains to not only who has the right to own but also who should rightfully own. According to international IP jurisdiction, anyone who takes the necessary legal steps to ensure IP rights can claim ownership. This petition is covered by the Berne Convention for the Protection of Literary and Artistic Works, essentially assigning the right of the work to the creator as the work is created. It is a widely accepted principle.

In the Jamaican case, however, the application of this principle is more problematic. Jamaica's symbolic IP is of such a nature that it can hardly be labeled an invention in the technical sense. Who owns these IP rights, morally speaking? Who are the *inventors*? Much more so than the geophysical entity of the island, the Jamaican people—their creative expressions and their accomplishments—are essentially the referents that have given "Jamaica" its meaning. Hence, is it the Jamaican people who should benefit (in today's knowledge economy this IP can be transformed into meaningful revenue), or is it whoever has the ability to see the market potential of Jamaica's creative products and national symbols? In many cases it is not necessarily the inventors who are automatically entitled to the IP ownership but the stakeholders who are able to legally lay claim to it. This serves to show the potential conflict between the legal field and those basing their claims on morality—in this case the common understanding of right and wrong—which has not effectively been captured by IP legislation.

The third dimension of IP has to do with the *uses of property*. Commonly, the IP owner is awarded permission to utilize the IP freely. However, in addition to the fact that the ownership of property in question could potentially be contested, implementation of the *uses of property* dimension in the symbolic realm poses new challenges. While some uses have the ability to strengthen the symbolic value, others can be more detrimental and potentially corrupt the symbol's meaning and strength. This depends largely on the ownership of the given symbol and the interests of the owners in procuring short-term profit or long-term strengthening of the symbol.

In Jamaica's case the widespread external use of symbolic expressions has arguably strengthened the symbols and the Jamaican name, but where this use can be considered overuse, the symbols may potentially be corrupted and their significance watered down. Furthermore, intangible property, like tangible property, can be depleted, and in this respect the more this aspect of the Jamaica IP is used by external stakeholders, the less opportunities Jamaicans themselves will have to benefit from the IP.

The fourth dimension is the *enforcement of IP rights*, which focuses on the infringement of IP rights and how such infringement can be adequately tackled. The enforcement IP rights is an important aspect of a holistically grounded IP governance and should and must not be neglected. However, the installment of IP rights must come before their enforcement, and from this perspective Jamaica has a major task of first protecting its right to the IP in question.

The fifth dimension, the *transfer of property*, has an interesting manifestation and application in the Jamaican case. As discussed earlier, a major question in adequately identifying the moral and actual present-day ownership of the Jamaican symbols is: Who owns Jamaica today, and therefore who has the right to transfer its properties? If it is not the people themselves, how can the people (re)claim ownership over their own symbols and narrative?

As we can see, due to the nature of this symbol—being a flag, unlike shoe brand logos, for example—it cannot be trademarked in the judicial sense. However, this does not mean that it is legally impracticable to protect the flag. It only means that this cannot be done in the conventional manner, that is, in the same manner as other IP rights are protected.

Article 6ter and Jamaica's Symbolic Culture

One way of protecting the Jamaican uniqueness (Brand Jamaica) may be through strategically avoiding further brand proliferation, hence, ensuring that the Jamaican flag is not put on completely arbitrary products that do not convey the essence of Jamaica's spirit. This safeguarding can be accomplished by enhancing the flag's *selling power*—the symbol's uniqueness, singularity, and market appeal (Ramello 2006, 557). Boosting its selling power can best be done by vigilantly ensuring that the symbol is allowed to operate on its own premises in a symbolic sphere where it is not misappropriated or collapsed into the scope of other supernova symbols. Jamaican stakeholders and enforcing authorities must secure symbolic authority in the realms possible to regain the symbolic control that is needed for Jamaica to (re)cultivate the meanings of its signs in a manner that is conducive to manifold Jamaican identities and long-term interests.

Admittedly, a prospective challenge for Jamaica will be to develop epistemological tools to effectively appraise the potential welfare outcomes for progressive IP rights governance within the realm of narrative structures, signs, and meanings. In the absence of such a tool, Jamaica can accomplish some level of ownership of the meaning of its symbols by enacting specific international IP laws and petitions, as stipulated by the World Intellectual Property Organization (WIPO). Specifically, the Paris Convention's Article 6*ter* and geographical indications are IP governance tools that may prove to be gateways to an adequate IP protection for Jamaican symbols and culture.

The Paris Convention for the Protection of Industrial Property is widely considered as the cornerstone of the international IP system. This convention has been ratified by Jamaica, alongside 171 other nation-states. Article 6*ter* on the Protection of State Emblems, and Names, Abbreviations and Emblems of International Intergovernmental Organizations is particularly pertinent to the discussion of the protection of Jamaican symbols, especially regarding the prevalence and explicit use of the Jamaican flag for marketing purposes by both Jamaican and non-Jamaican stakeholders. Paragraph 1(*a*) states: "The countries of the Union agree to refuse or to invalidate the registration, and to prohibit by appropriate measures the use, without authorization by the competent authorities, either as trademarks or as elements of trademarks, of armorial bearings, flags, and other State emblems, of the countries of the Union, official signs and hallmarks indicating control and warranty adopted by them, and any imitation from a heraldic point of view." In other words, petitions of Article 6*ter* prohibit any nation or stakeholder from trademarking armorial bearings, national flags, and State emblems and provide guidance for the normative use of such. Although the definition of *flag* in the Paris Convention is ambiguous, pragmatic interpretation of this phrasing would imply the nation's flag as acknowledged by other nations as such. Hence, the Jamaican flag must be considered as falling under this statute.

In essence Article 6*ter* delivers a primary premise: Flags and other national symbols cannot be trademarked in the strict conventional sense, the implication being that "surrounding" IP laws—meaning IP laws that offer the best possible protection of the symbols and culture of Jamaica as well as domestic laws of a given nation—must be utilized to create appropriate protection of a similar nature. Therefore, in pursuing the obligations under the treaty, countries generally rely on national legislation that prohibits the use of such national symbols, meaning that the individual nations generally include specific local laws pertaining to the illicit or unwarranted use of national symbols. In Norway, for instance, such laws are incorporated as part of the general criminal code. This then provides a judicial framework that Jamaica may employ to achieve the IP protection and ownership. Under this treaty, in a hypothetical instance in which Jamaica experiences its IP rights being infringed, Jamaica would not be able to initiate criminal proceedings in Norway. However, Jamaica could initiate civil proceedings, pursuing a decision to prohibit such use under Norwegian jurisdiction. This essentially means that there is a judicial framework that captures these specific breaches of IP rights. This framework is intricate and requires detailed knowledge of every nation's particular laws. Therefore, legally pursuing such infringements would be a tedious and costly process to administer in every nation Jamaica deems its flag or other symbols have been misappropriated. Nevertheless, this framework can help Jamaican stakeholders to not only mobilize its symbols at market value but to leverage them on their own terms and lay some hold on their transcendental economy.

Within the Paris Convention petition it is also possible to trademark specific color combinations, such as those present in Rastafarian symbolisms—namely, the red, green, and gold of the Ethiopian flag. As relates to the Ethiopian flag itself, this obviously falls under the same legislation as the Jamaican flag and is therefore the concern of the Ethiopian authorities. When it relates to the color combination of red, gold, and green, these are fairly generic colors that are not necessarily exclusive to the Rasta movement associated with Jamaica. One could argue that these colors often operate within cultural discourses that metonymically point to a familiar Jamaican narrative. Rastafarian symbolism is one of the most recognizable symbolic manifestations of Jamaica. However, while these colors are seen in a context where the interpretation is often compellingly apparent, the colors have not been written into and signified by a specific logo or pattern. Therefore, making a claim to these colors would be difficult to fulfill according to the criteria of the Paris Convention. One way of practically approaching such a claim could be for Jamaican stakeholders to create and protect a specific Rasta logo to represent the movement.

Geographical Indications and Brand Jamaica

Another section of the Paris Convention that may be useful to Jamaica in its efforts to improve the selling power and organic meanings of its national flag and Rasta colors is the concept of "geographical indications." The main provision regarding geographical indications is the WIPO Protection of Geographical Indications Act of 2004. According to this provision, a geographical indication is

> a sign used on goods that have a specific geographical origin and possess qualities, reputation or characteristics that are essentially attributable to that place of origin. Most commonly, a geographical indication includes the name of the place of origin of the goods. Agricultural products typically have qualities that derive from their place of production and are influenced by specific local factors, such as climate and soil. Whether a sign is recognized as a geographical indication is a matter of national law. Geographical indications may be used for a wide variety of products, whether natural, agricultural or manufactured.

In other words, the concept of geographical indications leans on the same supposition as the country of origin effect. The presumption is that the link between the geographical origin of tangible or intangible goods and its quality or embodied values impacts its attractiveness and hence its market value. However, while the country of origin effect pertains to aspects concerning consumer psychology and marketing, the geographical indication deals with the judicial framework addressing a product's origin and how this relates to the marketing of that product. Notable examples of products that adhere to the logics of geographical indication are Tequila from the area surrounding the town of Tequila, Mexico; Champagne from the Champagne district in France; cigars from Cuba; maple syrup from Canada; and more peculiarly, coffee from Colombia. It is assumed that the geographical indication adds a sense of authenticity to the product, hence value. Geographic indicators can also be in effect through mechanisms of association. One example is Swiss chocolate; although Switzerland is not a cocoa-producing country, it is still considered one of the finest producers of chocolate or coffee drinks with Italian names. Italy is not a coffee-producing country, but Italians are considered coffee connoisseurs. Further examples include Danish pastry, frankfurters, and hamburgers. These three examples serve to show how geographical names often migrate into everyday language about products and to a large extent become associated with the original referent.

It is essential to highlight that geographical indications are understood by consumers to denote the origin and the quality of products. Many products characterized by their origin have acquired and embodied valuable reputations that may—if not adequately protected—be misrepresented by dishonest and/or illegitimate stakeholders. The perpetration of false geographical indications by unauthorized parties is detrimental to consumers, who are in effect misled and deceived into believing that they are buying a genuine product with specific qualities and characteristics while in fact getting an imitation. Legitimate producers are deprived of valuable business opportunities, and the established reputation of their products is cheapened and damaged by producers competing under unfair conditions.

The element of deception is central in the case of Jamaica, as widespread availability of products purporting to be Jamaican, or at least that make an unambiguous visual association with Jamaica, may give the impression that these products' association with Jamaica is officially sanctioned. The fundamental question in this respect, then, is whether any given unauthorized good produced outside Jamaica that depicts the Jamaican flag or other symbols deemed Jamaican can be considered a misappropriation—and hence an infringement—of Jamaican IP rights and therefore be the subject of litigation.

A manner in which Jamaican stakeholders can actively reposition themselves and confront this challenge is to protect products entitled to IP protection within the framework of geographical indications. In this manner Jamaican stakeholders can ensure judicial rights and reclaim market share that is capitalized on by other stakeholders. Jamaica Blue Mountain Coffee and more recently Jamaica Jerk are already protected and are thereby better able to position themselves and look after their reputations and interests as sought-after brands. Other companies such as Walkerswood, which makes traditional Jamaican foods, are not protected in this manner and could arguably benefit greatly from taking such measures to protect not only its name but also the Jamaican spirit embodied in its products. Similarly, reggae could also benefit from such protections. This music can be produced anywhere in the world. However, reggae produced in Jamaica is considered to be the genuine article and hence assumes a qualitatively higher credibility, appreciation, and significance. Same for ganja. It can be grown and produced in many countries, but Jamaica is seen to produce the "highest-grade" weed. This is because there is an intrinsic association between these specific cultural products and the nation. It is this association between cultural expressions and symbols embodying the unique, internally established flavor of Jamaica and perceived values such as vibrancy, creativity, and bold energy that ensure products associated with Jamaica experience a commercial edge. Using the framework of geographic implications can help protect Jamaican people and their products and safeguard their judicial rights and market shares.

In addition, introducing a seal of approval of tangibles and intangibles produced in Jamaica could contribute to signifying the Jamaican referent. It could be done much in the same way as the British Royal Warrant Holders Association does, whereby the BY APPOINTMENT TO HER MAJESTY THE QUEEN seal denotes exclusivity and quality, traits that are sought after by consumers. These products are deemed more attractive, essentially applying recognized market mechanisms to win against competition. This could, for example, be administered by the Bureau of Standards, which would certify that officially deemed Brand Jamaica products essentially embody the authentic flair and flavor of Jamaica. A suggestion for increasing the feasibility of this approach is—in addition to representing authenticity—to align such an endeavor with respected Jamaican designers and artists to ensure that the products not only are of better quality but also possess the creative edge with which Jamaica is already associated. The point here is that the symbols specifically associated with Jamaica could be incorporated into an overarching IP policy aimed at securing Jamaican intangible assets.

Finally, and importantly, Jamaican stakeholders may need to fully appreciate that their products embody features and characteristics that fulfill the requirements for entitlement to this IP protection. The Jamaica Intellectual Property Office works strategically in Jamaica to raise awareness of IP and how adequate IP protection can facilitate stakeholders' efforts in ensuring and promoting the economic viability of their Jamaican products. Unfortunately, the obstacle in this respect remains convincing Jamaican stakeholders that this is a profitable investment with long-term implications.

In many ways this aspect of IP touches on a fundamental assumption of our argument: Things labeled as or purporting to be Jamaican sell well, and the concept of geographical indications may well capture the mechanism of this strength. While geographical indications pertain more directly to tangible products, and hence do not necessarily encompass intangible manifestations of IP, the concept can be useful in providing an understanding of how the origin or perceived origin of an expression adds value and appeal. In this perspective one could argue that in the same way as tangible products are associated with places, so are intangible expressions, and Jamaica should be entitled to a greater share of the revenue its cultural symbols create.

In discussing the Jamaican approach to nation branding—having argued that the strong cultural and symbolic narratives bring a high level of visibility and cultural brand recognition to Jamaica—as well as providing suggestions for how Jamaica can accelerate its nation branding efforts, it is clear that Jamaica could benefit socioeconomically from a more strategic approach to nation branding. As argued consistently, one of these routes to success may be through the industrious deployment of IP governance strategies. Although there are certain shortcomings to the framework pertinent to providing legally sound protection of national IP, it is feasible to overcome these challenges so that Jamaica, through creative IP governance, can promote the socioeconomic betterment of the nation.

Furthermore, this chapter has interrogated the complex and intricate narrative mechanisms regarding the misappropriation of Jamaican cultural expressions and symbols by largely external stakeholders. This trend has notably three effects that concern Jamaica. First, the inclination for these symbolisms to be externally appropriated—first decontextualized, then recontextualized—may impact the Jamaican narrative construction and have a detrimental impact on Jamaican national identity formation. Second, given that the symbolic capital associated with Jamaica is an intangible asset that can be depleted, this external appropriation of Jamaican symbols may hinder or limit Jamaica's own ability to harness and benefit from these intangible resources. And third, the external stakeholders profit from symbolic capital that may arguably be Jamaica's prerogative to manage and distribute.

While we do not try to argue it is completely immoral of Puma, Nike, or other external stakeholders to benefit economically from their use of Jamaican symbols, it is important to critically highlight certain guidelines around this use of Jamaican symbolism: When the symbols are used, they should not be corrupted or essentialized, nor should they have negative effects on Jamaica's possibility to define itself. And Jamaica should be able to yield economic returns on its symbols and narratives that benefit the nation and its people.

Jamaican stakeholders may benefit greatly from realizing that intellectual property is a cultural and economic asset, and like other property, it can be developed, managed, and owned so that it creates an economic return. This may enable a level of competitiveness that would not be possible without higher-level strategic brand management. A more well-managed Jamaican brand may further the country's already progressive socioeconomic mode while at the same time prevent symbolic corruption and ensure that Jamaican national identity formation is organically driven by internal forces and not externally allocated. Through concerted, proactive deployment of identity politics, Jamaica can exercise its right to reappropriate its narrative and henceforth be the master of the discourse of its own narrative projection.

Final Thoughts

Hume Johnson and Kamille Gentles-Peart

There is now wide consensus that nations have become brands. Although a fairly new development, the brand of the nation (its image, identity, and reputation) has emerged in the last three decades as a vital instrument in helping nations to achieve economic advancement and sociopolitical goals. As a consequence of a fiercely competitive global marketplace, for example, all nations are forced to compete with each other for tourists, investors, aid, students, respect and attention within the international community. A powerful and positive nation brand therefore provides a massive and useful competitive advantage for countries. Indeed, national reputation is seen to be the single most valuable item of intellectual property a nation possesses; it is thus vital that developing nations such as Jamaica know how to protect, develop, and leverage this asset for sustained economic growth and international respect.

As Jamaica recognizes over fifty-five years of its independence, the nation finds itself at an interesting, critical, and historical moment with respect to its nation brand. After decades of instability and uncertainty, the Jamaican economy is showing some signs of recovery, giving Jamaicans a glimmer of hope. The nation is also in the throes of a magnificent cultural and creative renaissance. This rebirth is urging a new sense of Jamaican nationalism, which has acquired significant momentum in a country with a love for winning and success. For Simon Anholt (2006,

National Brand Index), "It is essential for countries to understand how they are seen around the world; how their achievements and failures; their assets and their liabilities; their people and their products are reflected in their brand image." Yet as Hume Johnson argues in chapter 6, Jamaica's solid cultural achievement has yet to find a real place in Jamaica's nation branding project, popularly known as "Brand Jamaica." Admittedly, over the last twenty years, much attention has been paid by Jamaican authorities to Brand Jamaica, but these efforts have been splintered and episodic at best and have focused predominantly on tourism marketing. Certainly, tourism has played a vital role in communicating attractive images of Jamaica and has helped to bolster the nation as a "destination." But as our volume has sought to illustrate, the country's branding project is problematic and demands more.

Furthermore, despite a plethora of research on Jamaica's tourism product, there has not been a scholarly interrogation of Jamaica's global image and reputation, one that examines and problematizes the practices and implications of the current overall branding project. In this regard, our volume is the first to wrestle with questions related to Jamaica's reputation, image, and brand. We ask: What are the areas of Jamaica's national identity that are foregrounded in the promotion of the nation in the global arena? Whose interests and agendas are prioritized? What are the implications for Jamaica's social, economic, and ideological well-being? The chapters presented here highlight some key areas that need to be addressed by the Jamaican authorities.

First, Jamaican authorities have largely attempted to build Brand Jamaica by relying heavily on the sentiments of foreigners and percep-tions of the elites of the nation. Their imagining of the country largely excludes the realities of ordinary (predominantly black) Jamaicans and as such has relegated their experiences and needs to the periphery of national policies. This practice marginalizes many Jamaicans, disenfran-chises them from discourses of national identity, and is deleterious to the nation's global reputation. We recommend that state leaders foster, nurture, and project images of Jamaica that is commensurate with the complexity and richness of the island. Disappointingly, destination tourism

promotion has become the most salient feature of Jamaica's nation branding project, despite the nation's multidimensional character and rich and
diverse global symbolic portfolio. Furthermore, the campaigns used to
market Jamaica to the world are replete with symbolisms and signs that
reinforce a singular idea about the nation, one that reinforces a colonial
ethos. Noted Nigerian novelist Chimamanda Adichie (2009) writes of the
danger of telling a single story about a people and a place. A single story,
she argues, "creates stereotypes. It's not that stereotypes are untrue, it's
that they are incomplete. Stereotypes make one story the only story."
She maintains that single stories not only flatten people's experiences of
that place but overlook the multiple other stories that help to form that
people and that place.

Jamaican authorities must therefore strive to establish a vision of
Jamaica that is more nuanced, multidimensional, and accurate. The national
brand should not be reduced to myths such as "authentic," "magical," or
"paradise." Instead, Jamaica should seek to promote its strong credentials
in the arts, sports, science and technology, as well as business and entrepreneurship. In short, the island and its people should be represented in
all their ethnic, cultural, territorial, economic, and political richness. In
articulating the importance of nation brand for developing countries,
Anholt (2010) asserts that most people need a sense of where they are
headed and what they are struggling for—a collective purpose, a chance
to build a new vision of a shared future—to define the country's goals
according to the values and beliefs of the population itself. Such complex
narratives of the nation have implications for national identity and cultural citizenship as well as benefits in the global economy. In other words,
for smaller countries such as Jamaica, mobilizing their identity is the
indispensable means by which to achieve growth. According to Anholt,
"Countries that aren't strong need to be interesting—they need to exercise some power of attraction, if they cannot exercise compulsion, and
the source of that attraction can only be their unique, individual identity,
their culture, their history, their land, their traditions, their genius and
their imagination" (37).

Second, we assert that Jamaican authorities must address the deficits in governance (crime, corruption, human rights abuses, poverty, and underdevelopment) in order to stave off the destabilizing impacts of these factors on its international reputation. For example, Jamaican state leaders must make greater efforts to improve education, human rights, access to justice, and unemployment. They must make more serious attempts to improve the quality of life of the Jamaican people with regard to housing, health care, and the treatment of women and children. These developments are inextricably tied to how people in the country see and talk about Jamaica and their own sense of their nation's reputation and place in the world. Most critically, the nation must undertake a program of renewal in civic values and attitudes. The socioeconomic progress and international respect Jamaica desires depends on behaviors, attitudes, and institutions that only a civil society can create (Johnson 2011). The conspicuous absence of a culture of civility, trust, and positive leadership within crucial social domains undermines Jamaica's international image and reputation.

Future Areas of Research

While our volume offers a diverse critical exploration of some of the key areas relevant to Jamaica's reputation, more work remains to be done. For example, future research may critically examine the complexities of Jamaica's sporting success (e.g., in football, track and field, cricket, and bobsled)—that is, its contribution to Jamaica's international brand image and reputation and how it can be leveraged to build a sports economy. Indeed, the ambivalent role that sports has played in promoting and resisting neocolonialism in Jamaica has yet to benefit from substantial scholarly investigation.

Additionally, the voices and lived experiences of Jamaicans themselves must find greater space in analyses of the effect of Jamaica's nation branding. Kamille Gentles-Peart begins this important work in chapter 3, but more work needs to be done to assess the psychological, social, ethnopolitical, and economic impact of the current formal branding initiatives of the Jamaican authorities on the lives of Jamaicans at home and abroad.

As Hume Johnson suggests in chapter 6, future research should also explore how Jamaica may benefit from deeper engagement in and marketing of the country's credentials in gastronomy. Although food is fundamental to Jamaica's identity and culture, no formal gastronomic industry exists there; gastronomy has been overlooked as a focus of tourism efforts, and Jamaican food and culinary traditions certainly deserve greater global recognition. Future research should consider the relationship between food and Jamaican culture, the island's culinary practices, and the extent to which food tourism can gain traction for Jamaica. In addition, we believe future research should consider Jamaica's potential to benefit from the nutraceutical products industry. With a focus on health and wellness as a future area for foreign exchange revenue for the economy, it is vital that research on these issues gets much greater attention.

Further, as we have suggested in this volume, Jamaica's pathway to future economic development will be premised in large part on the nation's innovation, creativity, and culture, that is, the creative economies of its cities and parishes. We explored what city branding might look like with a case study of Jamaica's capital city, Kingston, in chapter 6. Jamaican authorities are obliged to undertake a sustained, institutional reimagining of the country's urban spaces and centers, which ought to have as its overarching aim invigorating national pride and reforming and reviving Jamaica's international image and identity.

Finally, our investigation into Jamaica's global image and reputation exposes the consequences and limitations of the existing tourism model of marketing and promoting Jamaica ("sun, sand, and sea"). It also exposes the complexities and contradictions that constitute Brand Jamaica. This complexity demands that the concept be expanded to include not just an amalgamation of the country's cultural output but also an accounting for and understanding of the nation's image and reputation and the factors that affect them. To challenge and de-emphasize prevailing myths and stereotypes about Jamaica, future theorizing on Jamaica's nation brand needs to take account of the nation's sociopolitical realities as much as its cultural credentials and aesthetic qualities. Such an ontological and epistemological shift is essential. It is true that deeply ingrained negative stereotypes of places are difficult, sometimes nearly impossible, to change. Yet a country's reputation can be managed and changed to better represent its current reality and future aspirations.

We also posit that Jamaica develop a clear and coherent Brand Jamaica strategy defined by the proper coordination of efforts and initiatives among all sectors of the society, public and private and the citizenry as a whole, and anchored by quality governance and effective leadership. All Jamaicans have a stake in their nation's identity and should be able to communicate the same consistent, believable message about the nation, its people and cultural products, and its core values and mission. In short, effective nation branding for Jamaica cannot only focus on Jamaica's aesthetic and tourism credentials but ought to provide a way for this well-known country to showcase its fundamental qualities—the achievements of its people and its true cultural and historical identity as well as its efforts and ambitions to be a respected player in the global community.

REFERENCES

Adichie, Chimamanda N. 2009. "The Danger of a Single Story." Presentation at Ted Talks Conference. October 7.

Aguirre, Abby. 2015. "Reggae Revival: Meet the Millennial Musicians behind Jamaica's New Movement." *Vogue Magazine*, October 28. https://www .vogue.com/projects/13362670/reggae-revival-jamaica-chronixx-protoje -roots-music/.

Aïnouche, Linda. 2012. "Reggae, A Force for Dialogue." *UN Chronicle* 49, no. 3. https://unchronicle.un.org/article/reggae-force-dialogue.

Amnesty International. 2001. "JAMAICA: Killings and Violence by Police: How Many More Victims?" *Country Report: Jamaica.* April 2001. https://www .amnesty.org/download/Documents/124000/amr380072001en.pdf.

———. 2012. "Jamaica Must Tackle Shocking Wave of Police Killings." News Archives, March 8, 2012. https://www.amnesty.org/en/latest/news/2012 /03/jamaica-must-tackle-shocking-wave-police-killings/.

———. 2013. *Annual Report: State of the World's Human Rights—Jamaica.* https:// www.amnestyusa.org/reports/annual-report-jamaica-2013/.

———. 2016. *Country Report—Jamaica.* https://www.amnesty.org/en/countries /americas/jamaica/report-jamaica/.

Anholt Nation Brands Index. 2006. Special report. *Israel's International Image, Q3 2006.*

———. 2007. Special report. Q2 2007.

Anholt, Simon. 2006. "Brand Jamaica Feasibility Study." MS, February 14.

———. 2007. *Competitive Identity: The New Brand Management for Nations, Cities and Regions*. Basingstoke: Palgrave Macmillan.

———. 2010. *Places: Identity, Image and Reputation*. Basingstoke: Palgrave Macmillan.

Aronczyk, Melissa. 2013. *Branding the Nation: The Global Business of National Identity*. Oxford: Oxford University Press.

Avery, Dan. 2017. "Jamaica Insists Gay Tourists Welcome, Despite Horrific Anti-LGBT Violence." *NewNowNext*, December 7, 2017. http://www.newnownext .com/jamaica-insists-gay-tourists-welcome-despite-horrific-anti-lgbt -violence/12/2017/.

Avraham, E. 2009. "Marketing and Managing Nation Branding during Prolonged Crisis: The Case of Israel." In *Place Branding and Public Diplomacy* 5, no. 3: 202–12.

Avraham, E., and E. Ketter. 2013. "Marketing Destinations with Prolonged Negative Images: Towards a Theoretical Model." *Tourism Geographies: An International Journal of Tourism Space, Place and Environment* 15, no. 1: 145–64.

Badgett, M. V. Lee, Laura E. Durso, Angeliki Kastanis, and Christy Mallory. 2013. *The Business Impact of LGBT-Supportive Workplace Policies*. Report. Williams Institute.

Badgett, M. V. Lee, Sheila Nezhad, Kees Waaldijk, and Yana van der Meulen Rodgers. 1998. *The Relationship between LGBT Inclusion and Economic Development: An Analysis of Emerging Economies*. Report. USAID and the Williams Institute.

Bakan, Joel. 2005. *The Corporation: The Pathological Pursuit of Profit and Power*. Washington DC: Free Press.

Balliger, Robin. 2007. "The Politics of Cultural Value and the Value of Cultural Politics: International Intellectual Property Legislation in Trinidad." In *Trinidad Carnival: The Cultural Politics of a Transnational Festival*, edited by Garth L. Green and Philip W. Scher, 198–215. Bloomington: Indiana University Press.

Banerji, Aparna, Kevin Burn, and Kate Vernon. 2012. *Creating Inclusive Workplaces for LGBT Employees in India: A Resource Guide for Employers*. Report. Community Business, October 2012.

Banks, Christopher. 2001. "The Cost of Homophobia: Literature Review of the Economic Impact of Homophobia on Canada." *Gay and Lesbian Health Network*. http://www.rainbowhealth.ca/documents/english/homophobia_economic.pdf.

Barnett, Livern. 2012. "Rampaging Rapists." *Jamaica Gleaner*, March 12, 2012. http://jamaica-gleaner.com/gleaner/20120312/lead/lead1.html.

Barthes, Roland. 1972. *Mythologies*. Selected and translated by Annette Lavers. New York: NoonDay Press.

———. 1977. "Rhetoric of the Image." In *Image-Music-Text*, edited by Stephen Heath, 32–51. New York: Hill and Wang.

———. 1983a. "The Imagination of the Sign." In *A Barthes Reader*, edited by Susan Sontag, 211–17. New York: Hill and Wang.

———. 1983b. "Myth Today." In *A Barthes Reader*, edited by Susan Sontag, 93–149. New York: Hill and Wang.

Bassiouni Group. 2014. "Homophobia: The Economic Cost." Blog, November 7, 2014. http://bassiounigroup.com/homophobia-the-economic-cost/.

Baxter, Leslie. A., and Barbara M. Montgomery. 1996. *Relating: Dialogues and Dialectics*. New York: Guilford Press.

BBC. 2008. "HardTalk." Interview with Stephen Sackur. May 20, 2008. http://www.youtube.com/watch?v=YeVy5Sp6xyw.

BBCCaribbean.com. 2004. "Reggae Protesters Make Point." September 30, 2004. http://www.bbc.co.uk/caribbean/news/story/2004/09/040930_mobonight-protest.shtml.

Beauboeuf-Lafontant, Tamara. 2003. "Strong and Large Black Women: Exploring Relationships between Deviant Womanhood and Weight." *Gender and Society* 17, no. 1: 111–21.

Becker, Howard S. 1997. *Outsiders*. New ed. New York: Free Press.

Beckford, Carole. 2007. *Keeping Jamaica's Sport on Track*. Kingston: Pear Tree Press.

———. 2016. *Jamaica Is In—Sport and Tourism*. Kingston: published by the author.

Bennett, Karena. 2017. "Jamaica Ranks as Second Riskiest Country in the Caribbean to Do Business. Haiti Ranks as Riskiest in World." *Jamaica Observer*, May 12, 2017. http://www.jamaicaobserver.com/business-report/jamaica-ranks-as-second-riskiest-country-in-the-caribbean-to-do-business-8212-study-haiti-ranks-as-riskiest-in-world_98592.

Berger, Arthur A. *Media and Communication Research Methods: An Introduction to Qualitative and Qualitative Approaches*. 4th ed. Thousand Oaks CA: Sage, 2016.

Biel, A. L. 1993. "How Brand Image Drives Brand Equity." *Journal of Advertising Research* 6, RC6, RC 1.

Blackford, Richard H. 2017. "Ja's Murder Figures Tell of a State of Emergency." *Jamaica Observer*, November 6, 2017. http://www.jamaicaobserver.com/opinion/ja-8217-s-murder-figures-tell-of-a-state-of-emergency_115377?profile=1096.

Bocci, Dominic. 2014. *Quantifying the Effects of Homophobia. Advocate.com*, May 5, 2014. http://www.advocate.com/politics/2014/05/05/quantifying-effects -homophobia.

Boulding, Kenneth E. 1956. *The Image: Knowledge in Life and Society.* Ann Arbor: University of Michigan Press.

Boxill, I., E. Galbraith, R. Mitchell, and R. Russell. 2012. *National Survey of Attitudes and Perceptions of Jamaicans towards Same Sex Relationships.* Kingston: Department of Sociology, Psychology and Social Work, UWI, Mona. http:// ufdcimages.uflib.ufl.edu/AA/00/00/31/78/00001/Final_ATTITUDES _bboxhillreport.pdf.

Boyce-Davies, Carole. 2004. "Black/Female/Bodies Carnivalized." In *Black Venus 2010: They Called Her Hottentot,* edited by Deborah Willis, 186–98. Philadelphia: Temple University Press.

Boyne, Ian. 2003. "Sex, Gun and Greed: Dancehall's Threat to Society." *Jamaica Gleaner*, April 6, 2003. http://www.jamaicagleaner.com/gleaner/20030406 /focus/focus1.html.

Brown, Deon. 2015. "Gay Activists Disrupt Prime Minister's Speech at NY Diaspora Meeting." *Jamaica Gleaner*, April 6, 2015. http://old.jamaica-gleaner .com/extra/article.php?id=4147.

Brown Givens, Sonja M., and Jennifer L. Monahan. 2005. "Priming Mammies, Jezebels, and Other Controlling Images: An Examination of the Influence of Mediated Stereotypes on Perceptions of an African American Woman." *Media Psychology* 7, no. 1: 87–106.

Bryan, Chad. 2016. "Ministry Commits to Universal Access to ICT." Jamaica Information Service, November 22, 2016. http://jis.gov.jm/ministry-commits -universal-access-ict/.

Buarque, Daniel. 2015. "One Country, Two Cups—The International Image of Brazil in 1950 and 2014: A Study of the Reputation and Identity of Brazil as Projected by the International Media during the Two FIFA World Cups in the Country." *International Journal of Communication* 9:1300–1318.

Buddan, R. 2004. "Brand Jamaica: Defining Ourselves, Building a Nation." *Jamaica Gleaner*, December 5, 2004, http://jamaicagleaner.com/gleaner/20041205 /focus/focus3.html.

Carby, Hazel. 1994. "It Jus Be's Dat Way Sometime: The Sexual Politics of Women's Blues." *Advances in Discourse Processes* 30:227.

Caribbean360. 2016. "Annual Tourist Arrivals to Surpass Population Size." January 27, 2016. http://www.caribbean360.com/news/annual-tourist-arrivals -to-jamaica-surpasses-population-size.

Center for Immigration Studies. 1995. "Three Decades of Mass Immigration: The Legacy of the 1965 Immigration Act." July 9. http://cis.org/1965ImmigrationAct-MassImmigration.

Centre for Leadership and Governance. 2015. "The Economic Cost of Homophobia in Jamaica: An Exploration." University of the West Indies, Mona.

Chambers, Donna, and Bryan McIntosh. 2008. "Using Authenticity to Achieve Competitive Advantage in Medical Tourism in the English-Speaking Caribbean." *Third World Quarterly* 29, no. 5: 919–37.

Chan, Sewell. 2008. "When New York Branded Its Way Out of Crisis." *City Room* blog, *New York Times*, September 22, 2008. https://cityroom.blogs.nytimes.com/2008/09/22/when-new-york-branded-its-way-out-of-crisis/.

Chaney, Elsa. 1997. "The Context of Caribbean Migration." In *Caribbean Life in New York City: Sociocultural Dimensions*, edited by Constance Sutton and Elsa Chaney, 3–14. New York: Center for Migration Studies.

Chappell, Kate. 2018. "Kingston Says 'Get Up, Stand Up' to Win Back Tourism." *Ozy*, August 8, 2018. https://www.ozy.com/fast-forward/kingston-says-get-up-stand-up-to-win-back-tourism/88122.

Charles, Christopher. 2013. "The Anti-Informer and Anti-Snitch Discourses in Dancehall and Rap Songs." SSRN, December 26, 2013. https://papers.ssrn.com/sol3/papers.cfm?abstract_id=2372209.

Charles, Jacqueline. 2009. "Brand Jamaica: Copyrighted." *Nation Branding*, October 21, 2009. http://nation-branding.info/2009/10/21/brand-jamaica-copyrighted/.

Chevannes, Barry. *Rastafari: Roots and Ideology.* New York: Syracuse University Press.

Chow, Rey. 2013. "The Provocation of *Dim Sum*; Or, Making Diaspora Visible on Film." In *Diasporic Chineseness after the Rise of China: Communities and Cultural Production*, edited by Julia Kuehn, Kam Louie and David Pomfret, 100–110. Vancouver: University of British Columbia Press.

Clancy, Michael. 2011. "Re-presenting Ireland: Tourism, Branding and National Identity in Ireland." *Journal of International Relations and Development* 14, no. 3: 281–308.

Clarke, Colin, G. 1971. "The Development and Redevelopment of the Waterfront in Kingston, Jamaica." *Geography* 56, no. 3: 237–40.

———. 2006. *Kingston, Jamaica: Urban Development and Social Change.* Kingston: Ian Randle Publishers.

CNN. 2014. "Cities of the Future: Indian PM Pushed Plan for 100 'Smart Cities.'" July 18, 2014. http://www.cnn.com/2014/07/18/world/asia/india-modi-smart-cities/index.html.

Cobb, Russell. 2014. *The Paradox of Authenticity in a Globalized World*. New York: Palgrave Macmillan.

Collinder, Avia. 2018. "Line Already Forming for Kingston Logistics Park." *Jamaica Gleaner*, August 29, 2018. http://jamaica-gleaner.com/article/business /20180829/line-already-forming-kingston-logistics-park.

Collins, Patricia Hill. 1998. *Fighting Words: Black Women and the Search for Justice*. Minneapolis: University of Minnesota Press.

———. 2000. *Black Feminist Thought: Knowledge, Consciousness and the Politics of Empowerment*. New York: Routledge.

Comaroff, John L., and Jean Comaroff. 2009. *Ethnicity, Inc.* Chicago: University of Chicago Press.

Community Marketing and Insights (CMI). 2017. *CMI 22nd Annual LGBTQ Travel Survey Report*. https://www.communitymarketinginc.com/documents/temp /CMI_22nd-LGBT-Travel-Study-Report2017.pdf.

Conghaile, Pól Ó. 2015. "New Dublin Brand Looks beyond City Centre for 'Must-Visit' Appeal." *Independent.ie*, October 16, 2015. https://www.independent .ie/life/travel/travel-news/new-dublin-brand-looks-beyond-city-centre-for -mustvisit-appeal-34114412.html.

Cooper, Carolyn. 1995. *Noises in the Blood: Orality, Gender, and the "Vulgar" Body of Jamaican Popular Culture*. Durham NC: Duke University Press.

Cordingley, Anthony, ed. 2013. *Self-Translation: Brokering Originality in Hybrid Culture*. London: Bloomsbury Academic.

Cowell, Noel M. 2011. "Public Discourse, Popular Culture and Attitudes towards Homosexuals in Jamaica." *Social and Economic Studies* 61, no. 1 (March): 31–60.

Crenshaw, Kimberlé. 1995. "Mapping the Margins: Intersectionality, Identity Politics, and Violence against Women of Color." In *Critical Race Theory: The Key Writings That Formed the Movement*, edited by Kimberlé Crenshaw, Neil Gotanda, Gary Peller, and Kendall Thomas, 357–83. New York: New Press.

Crowder, Nicole. 2014. "Jamaican 'Rudeboy' Fashion Influences the Modern Englishman." *Washington Post*, September 17, 2014. https://www .washingtonpost.com/news/in-sight/wp/2014/09/17/jamaican-rudeboy -fashion-influences-the-modern-englishman/?noredirect=on&utm_term =.6786eb79473d.

Cutlip, Scott M., and Allen H. Center. 2009. *Effective Public Relations*. Englewood Cliffs NJ: Prentice-Hall.

Dali, Avivit A. 2014. "Depictions of Urban Landscapes in Israeli Advertisements, 1967–2008." *Israel Studies Review* 29, no. 1: 90–105.

Danquah, Meri Nana-Ama. 1998. *Willow Weep for Me: A Black Woman's Journey through Depression*. New York: One World.

Davis, Garwin. 2018. "Tourism to Benefit from Renewed Focus on Gastronomy." Jamaica Information Service. January 22, 2018. http://jis.gov.jm/tourism -benefit-renewed-focus-gastronomy/.

D'Cruz, Archie. 2016. "Does 'I Love New York' Help Create a Brand for New York City?" *Observer*, December 28, 2016. http://observer.com/2016/12/does-i -love-new-york-help-create-a-brand-for-new-york-city/.

Dennis, Denise. 2016. "Unemployment Rate Lowest in Five Years." Jamaica Information Service, November 17, 2016. http://jis.gov.jm/unemployment -rate-lowest-five-years/.

Desmond, Jane C. 1999. "Picturing Hawai'i: The 'Ideal' Native and the Origins of Tourism, 1880–1915." *Positions: East Asia Cultures Critique* 7, no. 2, 459–501.

———. 2008. "Fisherwomen Question Tourism's 'Magic.'" *National Catholic Reporter* 43, no. 42: 11.

Dicklitch-Nelson, Susan, and Chan Tov. n.d. "Only 'One Love' Allowed in Jamaica: A Longitudinal Case Study of the Repression of Sexual Minorities in Jamaica." MS, Franklin and Marshall College. ResearchGate.net.

Dinnie, Keith. 2014. *Nation Branding: Concepts, Issues, Practice*. New York: Routledge.

———. 2016. *Nation Branding: Concepts, Issues, Practice*, 2nd ed. London: Routledge.

Dodman, David. 2003. "Shooting in the City: An Autographic Exploration of the Urban Environment in Kingston, Jamaica." *Area* 35, no. 3: 293–304.

———, ed. 2004. "Feelings of Belonging? Young People's Views of Their Surroundings in Kingston." *Children's Geographies* 2, no. 2: 185–98.

Douglas, Coleen. 2018. "Cocktails with Coleen Antoinette Douglas." *Jamaica Observer*. January 14, 2018. http://m.jamaicaobserver.com/style-spotlight /cocktails-with-jan-14_122221?profile=1237.

Dreisinger, Baz. 2014. "36 Hours in Jamaica." *New York Times*, March 27, 2014. https://www.nytimes.com/2014/03/30/travel/36-hours-in-jamaica.html.

Du Bois, W. E. B. 1903. *The Souls of Black Folk: Essays and Sketches*. Cambridge MA: University Press John Wilson and Son.

Dueskar, Chandan. 2014. "The Urban Moment." *Sustainable Cities* blog. World Bank. http://blogs.worldbank.org/sustainablecities/sustainablecities/urban -moment.

Eapen, Irene. 2014. "Sports Tourism: Key Drivers of Tourism." *Voyager's World* 11, no. 11: 16–22.

Echtner, Charlotte. 2002. "The Content of Third World Tourism Marketing: A 4A Approach." *International Journal of Tourism Research* 4:413–34.

Echtner, Charlotte, and Pushkala Prasad. 2003. "The Context of Third World Marketing." *Annals of Tourism Research* 30, no. 3: 660–82.

Economist. 2012. "On Your Marks, Get Set . . . Oh." July 21, 2012. http://www.economist.com/node/21559348.

Elizur, J. 1987. *National Image.* Jerusalem: Hebrew University.

Emerson, Rana A. 2002. "'Where My Girls At?' Negotiating Black Womanhood in Music Videos." *Gender & Society* 16, no. 1: 115–35.

Fan, Ying. 2006. "Branding the Nation: What Is Being Branded?" *Journal of Vacation Marketing* 12, no. 1: 5–14.

———. 2008. "Key Perspectives in Nation Image: A Conceptual Framework for Nation Branding." Working paper, Brunel University Research Archive (BURA). https://www.researchgate.net/publication/49400582_Key_perspectives_in_nation_image_a_conceptual_framework_for_nation_branding.

Fox News. 2012. "Jamaican Lottery Scams Spread Despite Crackdown." April 17, 2012. https://www.foxnews.com/world/jamaican-lottery-scams-spread-despite-us-crackdown.

Francis, Kimone. 2019. "Jamaica Remains in Same Position on Corruption Perceptions Index." *Jamaica Observer*, January 31, 2019. http://www.jamaicaobserver.com/news/jamaica-remains-in-same-position-on-perceived-corruption-index_155917.

Franklyn, Delano. 2009. *Sprinting into History: Jamaica and the 2008 Olympic Games.* Kingston: Wilson, Franklyn, Barnes.

Gartner, William C., and Jingqing Shen. 1992. "The Impact of Tiananmen Square on China's Tourism Image." *Journal of Travel Research* 30, no. 4: 47–52.

Gaskins, Joseph, Jr. 2013. "'Buggery' and the Commonwealth Caribbean: A Comparative Examination of the Bahamas, Jamaica, and Trinidad and Tobago." In *Human Rights, Sexual Orientation and Gender Identity in the Commonwealth: Struggles for Decriminalisation and Change*, edited by Corinne Lennox and Matthew Waites, 429–54. London: School of Advanced Studies, University of London.

Gates, Theaster. 2015. "How to Revive a Neighborhood: With Imagination, Beauty and Art." Video. TED2015 Conference, Chicago. https://www.ted.com/talks/theaster_gates_how_to_revive_a_neighborhood_with_imagination_beauty_and_art.

Gentles-Peart, Kamille. 2014. "West Indian Women, Difference and Cultural Citizenship in the U.S." *Wadabagei: A Journal of the Caribbean and Its Diasporas* 15, nos. 1–2: 79–106.

Giles, Chris. 2018. "African Smart Cities: A High-Tech Solution to Over-Populated Mega-Cities." CNN. April 19, 2018. https://www.cnn.com/2017/12/12/africa/africa-new-smart-cities/index.html.

Gilpin, Jodi-Ann. 2013. "Germany, Saturn to Withdraw Flag-Burning Ad." *Jamaican Gleaner*, February 27, 2013.

Gilroy, Paul. 2005. "Could You Be Loved? Bob Marley, Anti-Politics, and Universal Sufferation." *Critical Quarterly* 47, nos. 1–2: 226–45.

Goffman, Erving. 1956. *The Presentation of Self in Everyday Life.* Edinburgh: University of Edinburgh, Social Sciences Research Centre, 1956.

Gordon, Nickesia S. 2005. "Introduction." In *Style and Meaning: Studies in Detailed Analysis of Film,* edited by John Gibbs and Douglas Pye, 1–15. Manchester: Manchester University Press.

———. 2012. "Virile Bodies, Docile Subjects: The Representation of Caribbean Masculinities in Mainstream International Media Targeting Female Tourists." In *Re-Constructing Place and Space: Media, Culture, Discourse and the Constitution of Caribbean Diasporas*, edited by Kamille A. Gentles-Peart and Maurice L. Hall. Newcastle upon Tyne: Cambridge Scholars Publishing.

Graham, Hugh. 2018. "Spiralling Murder Rate Must Be Number One Priority in 2018." *Jamaica Observer*, February 18. http://www.jamaicaobserver.com/news/spiralling-murder-rate-must-be-number-one-priority-in-2018_124980?profile=1096.

Gray, Obika. 2004. *Demeaned but Empowered: The Social Power of the Urban Poor in Jamaica.* Kingston: University of the West Indies Press.

Gray, Sherrian. 2007. "Trends in Urban Crime and Violence in Kingston, Jamaica." Case study prepared for Enhancing Urban Safety and Security. Global Report on Human Settlements. https://unhabitat.org/wp-content/uploads/2008/07/GRHS.2007.CaseStudy.Crime_.Kingston.pdf.

Gutzmore, C. 2004. "Casting the First Stone! Policing of Homo/Sexuality in Jamaican Popular Culture." *Interventions* 6, no. 1: 118–34.

Hall, Arthur. 2018. "Port Royal Redevelopment Not Abandoned—Vaz." *Jamaica Gleaner*, January 7, 2018. http://jamaica-gleaner.com/article/lead-stories/20180107/port-royal-development-not-abandoned-vaz.

Harriott, Anthony. 2000. *Police and Crime Control in Jamaica: New Challenges for Public Policy.* Kingston: University of the West Indies Press.

Harriott, Anthony A., Balford A. Lewis, and Elizabeth J. Zechmeister. 2015. *Political Culture of Democracy in Jamaica and the Americas, 2014: Democratic Governance across 10 Years of the AmericasBarometer.* USAID. Mona: Centre for Leadership and Governance, University of the West Indies.

Harrison, Sheri-Marie. 2015. "Excess in *A Brief History of Seven Killings*." *Post45*, October 24, 2015. http://post45.research.yale.edu/2015/10/excess-in-a -brief-history-of-seven-killings/.

———. 2017. "Global Sisyphus: Rereading the Jamaican 1960s through *A Brief History of Seven Killings*." *Small Axe* 21, no. 3: 85–97.

Hassan, Aisha. 2018. "Once the Music of the Marginalized, Jamaica Reggae Is Now Protected by UNESCO." *Quartzy*. November 29. https://qz.com /quartzy/1479573/unesco-protects-jamaican-reggae-malaysian-love-ballads -and-more/.

Hartmann, Thom. 2004. *Unequal Protection: The Rise of Corporate Dominance and the Theft of Human Rights*. New York: Rodale Books.

Helber, Patrick. 2015. "Between 'Murder Music' and 'Gay Propaganda': Policing Respectability in the Debate on Homophobic Dancehall." In *Reggae from Yaad: Traditional and Emerging Themes in Jamaican Popular Music*, edited by Donna P. Hope, 141–53. Kingston: Ian Randle Publishers.

Hope, Donna. P. 2006. *Inna Di Dancehall: Popular Culture and the Politics of Identity in Jamaica*. Kingston: University of the West Indies Press.

Evans, Hope. 2009. "'Gaycation' and Cruise Ship Travel." *Hospitality Jamaica* (*Gleaner* supplement), March 4, 2009, 4.

Horan, Tom. 2012. "How Jamaica Conquered the World." *Guardian*, August 4, 2012. https://www.theguardian.com/world/2012/aug/05/how-jamaica -conquered-the-world.

Human Rights Watch. 1999. "Nobody's Children: Jamaican Children in Police Detention and Government Institutions." https://www.hrw.org/reports /1999/jamaica/.

———. 2014. "Jamaica: Unchecked Homophobic Violence. Discriminatory Laws, Inadequate Police Protection." October 21. https://www.hrw.org/news/2014 /10/21/jamaica-unchecked-homophobic-violence.

Hussey-Whyte, Donna. 2011. "Doing 'Business' in New Kingston." *Sunday Observer*, August 14, 2011. http://www.jamaicaobserver.com/pfversion /Doing-business-in-New-Kingston_9445796#ixzz3npaxj5rl.

Hyslop-Margison, Emery, and Alan Seara. 2006. *Neo-Liberalism, Globalization and Human Capital Learning: Reclaiming Education for Democratic Citizenship*. Springer. International Tourism Expenditures. World Bank. http://data .worldbank.org/indicator/st.int.xpnd.

Insch, Andrea. 2011. "Branding the City as an Attractive Place to Live." In *City Branding: Theory and Cases*, edited by K. Dinnie, 8–14. Basingstoke, UK: Palgrave Macmillan.

Jackson, Angeline. 2015. "Is 'the Most Homophobic Place on Earth' Turning Around?" *Time* magazine, June 1. http://time.com/3900934/most-homophobic-place-on-earth-turning-around/.

Jamaica Forum for Lesbians, All-Sexuals and Gays (J-FLAG). 2013. Out of Many, One (Heterosexual?) People: A Symposium on LGBT Identities, Citizenship, and Activism. January 31, 2013.

Jamaica Gleaner. 2007. "2000—Bob Marley's 'Exodus' Best of the Century." July 29, 2007. http://old.jamaica-gleaner.com/gleaner/20070729/news/news6.html.

———. 2012. "Pan Chicken's Tasty Heritage." June 14, 2012. http://jamaica-gleaner.com/gleaner/20120614/cook/cook6.html.

———. 2016. "SHAME! Twenty-Four Women Killed in 2016: Former Victim of Domestic Violence Urges Women to Protect Themselves." December 18, 2016. http://jamaica-gleaner.com/article/lead-stories/20161218/shame-twenty-four-women-killed-2016-former-victim-domestic-violence.

———. 2017a. "Come Capture Kingston—Gleaner Invites Photo Enthusiasts to 24-Hour Challenge." December 13, 2017. http://jamaica-gleaner.com/article/news/20171213/come-capture-kingston-gleaner-invites-photo-enthusiasts-24-hour-challenge.

———. 2017b. "114 Murders in 20 Days—More than 1000 Jamaicans Killed since the Start of the Year." August 30, 2017. http://jamaica-gleaner.com/article/lead-stories/20170830/114-murders-20-days-more-1000-jamaicans-killed-start-year.

Jamaica Observer. 2013a. "DESPAIR—STATIN Reports Unemployment Now at 16.3%: Report Says More Women than Men Unemployed." August 16, 2013. http://www.jamaicaobserver.com/news/despair_14886016.

———. 2013b. "The Jamaican Economy and Prospects for the Future." April 19, 2013. http://www.jamaicaobserver.com/business/The-Jamaican-economy-and-prospects-for-the-future_14039624.

———. 2013c. "Justice Minister Condemns Killing of St. James Cross-Dresser." July 29, 2013. http://www.jamaicaobserver.com/news/Justice-Minister-condemns-killing-of-St-James-cross-dresser.

———. 2015. "Kingston Designated a Creative City of Music by UNESCO." December 11, 2015. http://www.jamaicaobserver.com/News/Kingston-designated-a-Creative-City-of-Music-by-UNESCO.

———. 2016. "Jamaica Homicides Jump 20 Per Cent, Highest Level in 5 Years." January 10, 2016. http://www.jamaicaobserver.com/news/Jamaica-homicides-jump-20-per-cent—highest-level-in-5-years_48331.

———. 2018a. "Dexter's Accused Denied Bail." May 9, 2018. http://www
.jamaicaobserver.com/entertainment/dexter-8217-s-accused-denied-bail
_132677.

———. 2018b. "Parliament to Extend St. James State of Emergency." January
30, 2018. http://www.jamaicaobserver.com/news/parliament-to-extend-st
-james-state-of-emergency_123927?profile=1373.

———. 2018c. "What's Going On in Barbican? Letters to the Editor." March
13, 2018. http://www.jamaicaobserver.com/editorial/what-8217-s-going
-on-in-barbican-_127678?profile=1468.

Jamaica Promotions Corporation (JAMPRO). 2014. "Trade and Investment
Jamaica: Jamaica in Numbers." http://www.jamaicatradeandinvest.org
/about-ja/jamaica-by-the-numbers.

———. 2016. *Country Brand Assessment Terms of Reference 2016*. http://www
.jamaicatradeandinvest.org/sites/default/files/tenders/ToR-%20Country
%20Branding%20Assessment.pdf.

Jamaica Tourist Board (JTB). 2015. "Annual Travel Statistics." http://www
.jtbonline.org/report-and statistics/.

———. 2016a. "Brief History." JTBonline.org. http://www.jtbonline.org/jtb/.

———. 2016b. "Tourism Development in Jamaica—A Synopsis." JTBonline.
org. http://www.jtbonline.org/tourism-in-jamaica/brief-history/.

James, Marlon. 2015. *A Brief History of Seven Killings*. London: OneWorld.

———. 2016a. *Brève histoire de sept meurtres*. Translated by Valérie Malfoy.
Paris: Albin Michel.

———. 2016b. *Breve historia de siete asesinatos*. Translated by Javier Calvo, in
collaboration with Wendy Guerra. Barcelona: Malpaso Ediciones.

JIS News. n.d. "Kingston and St. Andrew History." http://jamaica55.gov.jm
/profiles-kingston-st-andrew/kingston-st-andrew-history/.

Johnson, Hume N. 2005. "Incivility: The Politics of 'People on the Margins' in
Jamaica." *Political Studies* 53, no. 3: 579–97.

———. 2011. *Challenges to Civil Society: Popular Protest and Governance in Jamaica*.
New York: Cambria Press.

———. 2014. "JAMAICA: A Famous, Strong but Damaged Brand." In "Managing
the Reputation of Places in Crisis." Special issue, *Place Branding and Public
Diplomacy* 10, no. 3: 199–217.

Johnson, Hume, and Joseph L. Soeters. 2008. "Jamaican Dons, Italian Godfa-
thers and the Chances of a 'Reversible Destiny.'" *Political Studies* 56:166–91.

———. 2015. "See and Blind, Hear and Deaf: Informerphobia in Jamaican Garrisons." *Journal of Crime Prevention and Community Safety* 17, no. 1: 47–66.

Johnson, Lauren C. 2014. "Work at the Periphery: Issues of Tourism Sustainability in Jamaica." *Culture Unbound: Journal of Current Cultural Research* 6:949–62.

Johnston, Jake. 2013. *The Multilateral Debt Trap in Jamaica.* Issue brief. Washington DC: Centre for Economic and Policy Research.

Jørgensen, Sigrid. 2016. "Jamaica's Homophobia Forced 'Out of the Closet' by the Rainbow Flag." Council of Hemispheric Affairs. COHA.org, June 21, 2016. http://www.coha.org/jamaicas-homophobia-forced-out-of-the-closet -by-the-rainbow-flag/#_edn5.

Kaneva, Nadia. 2011. "Nation Branding: Towards an Agenda for Critical Research." *International Journal of Communication* 5:117–41.

Kaneva, Nadia, and Delia Popescu. 2011. "National Identity Lite: Nation Branding in Post-Communist Romania and Bulgaria." *International Journal of Cultural Studies* 14, no. 2: 191–207.

Kapferer, Jean-Noël. 1997. *Strategic Brand Management: Creating and Sustaining Brand Equity Long Term.* London: Kogan Page.

Kavaratzis, Michael. 2004. "From City Marketing to City Branding: Towards a Theoretical Framework for Developing City Brands." *Place Branding* 1, no. 1: 58–73.

Kerrigan, Finola, Jyotsna Shivanandan, and Anne-Marie Hede. 2012. "Nation Branding: A Critical Appraisal of Incredible India." *Journal of Macromarketing* 32, no. 3: 319–27.

Kirby, David. 1999. "Trouble in Paradise." *The Advocate: The National Gay and Lesbian Newsmagazine,* July 20, 24–33. www.advocate.com.

Klein, Naomi. 2002. *No Logo: No Space, No Choice, No Jobs.* New York: Picador.

———. 2007. *The Shock Doctrine: The Rise of Disaster Capitalism.* London: Metropolitan Books.

Kohlings, Ellen, and Pete Lilly. 2013. "From One Love to One Hate: Europe's Perception of Jamaican Homophobia Expressed in Song Lyrics." In *International Reggae: Current and Future Trends in Jamaican Popular Music,* edited by Donna P. Hope, 2–29. Kingston: Pelican Publishers.

Kotler, P., et al. 1993. *Marketing Places.* New York: Free Press.

Kotler, Philip, and David Gertner. 2002. "Country as Brand, Product and Beyond: A Place Marketing and Brand Management Perspective." *Journal of Brand Management* 9, no. 62: 249–61.

LaFont, Suzanne. 2009. "Not Quite Redemption Song: LGBT-Hate in Jamaica." In *Homophobias: Lust and Loathing across Time and Space,* edited by David A. B. Murray, 105–22. Durham NC: Duke University Press.

Lash, Scott, and Celia Lury. 2007. *The Global Culture Industry: The Mediation of Things*. Cambridge: Polity.

Latin American Public Opinion Project (LAPOP). 2010. Vanderbilt University. http://www.vanderbilt.edu/lapop/jamaica.php.

Lavers, Michael K. 2014. "Jamaica's Unique Brand of Homophobia." *Washington Blade*, May 28, 2014. http://www.washingtonblade.com/2014/05/28/jamaica -unique-brand-homophobia/#sthash.hyTigdbo.dpuf.

Lee, Sean, Ian Phau, Michael Hughes, Yu Feng Li, and Vanessa Quintal. 2015. "Heritage Tourism in Singapore Chinatown: A Perceived Value Approach to Authenticity and Satisfaction." *Journal of Travel and Tourism Marketing* 33, no. 7: 981–98.

Leed, Eric J. 1991. *The Mind of the Traveler: From Gilgamesh to Global Tourism*. New York: Basic Books.

Leonard, Mark. 1997. *Britain: Renewing Our Identity*. London: Demos Book.

Lepp, Andrew, and John Harris. 2008. "Tourism and National Identity in Uganda." *International Journal of Tourism Research* 10, no. 6: 525–36.

Lim, Margaret Ann. 2014. "A Night with Male Prostitutes. All Woman." *Daily Observer*, November 24, 2014. http://www.jamaicaobserver.com/magazines /allwoman/74207_A-night-with-male-prostitutes.

Loop Jamaica. 2018. "Kingston Creative Art Walk for Downtown Kingston on Sunday." August 18. http://www.loopjamaica.com/content/kingston -creative-artwalk-showcase-downtown-kingston-sunday.

MacCannell, Dean. 1992. *Empty Meeting Grounds: The Tourist Papers*. London: Routledge.

Maccarrone-Eaglen, Agata. 2009. "An Analysis of Culture as a Tourism Commodity." *Tourism, Culture and Communication* 9, no. 3: 151–63.

MacEwan, Arthur. 2000. *Neo-Liberalism or Democracy? Economic Strategy, Markets, and Alternatives for the 21st Century*. London: Zed Books.

Manley, Michael. 1974. *The Politics of Change: A Jamaican Testament*. Washington DC: Howard University Press.

Mann, Emily. 2016. "Story of Cities #9: Kingston, Jamaica: A City Born of Wickedness and Disaster." *Guardian*, March 24, 2016. https://www.theguardian .com/cities/2016/mar/24/story-cities-9-kingston-jamaica-richest-wickedest -city-world.

March, Elizabeth. 2007. "Shaggy: Dancehall Comes to WIPO." *WIPO [World Intellectual Property Organization] Magazine*, no. 6 (December). http://www .wipo.int/wipo_magazine/en/2007/06/article_0003.html.

Mars, Amanda. 2012. "Is the Sun Setting on Spain as a Brand." *El País*, May 13, 2012. http://elpais.com/elpais/2012/05/13/inenglish/1336914979_545825.html.

Martin, Norvan. 2013. "How Important Is Tourism to Jamaica?" *Caribbean Currents*, February 13, 2013. https://thecaribbeancurrent.com/how-important-is-tourism-to-jamaica/.

McCleod, Erin. 2014. "From Kingston's Car Parks to VH-1, Sound System Culture Puts Bass in Your Face." *Guardian*, October 2, 2014. https://www.theguardian.com/music/2014/oct/02/-sp-from-kingstons-car-parks-to-vh-1-soundsystem-culture-puts-bass-in-your-face.

McElroy, Steven. 2014. "Finding Comfort and Safety as a Gay Traveler." *New York Times*, May 30, 2014. https://www.nytimes.com/2014/06/01/travel/finding-comfort-and-safety-as-a-gay-traveler.html.

McFee, Rochelle, and Elroy Galbraith. 2016. "The Developmental Cost of Homophobia: The Case of Jamaica." *Washingtonblade.com*, January 2016. http://www.washingtonblade.com/content/files/2016/01/The-Developmental-Cost-of-Homophobia-The-Case-of-Jamaica_2016-1.pdf.

McKay, Jessica. 2018. "Jamie Oliver Jerk Dish a Mistake, Says Jamaican-born Chef Levi Roots." *Guardian*, August 20, 2018. https://www.theguardian.com/uk-news/2018/aug/20/jamie-olivers-jerk-rice-dish-a-mistake-says-jamaica-born-chef?cmp=share_btn_link.

McKenzie, Clyde. 2010. "Dancehall's Decline." *Jamaica Observer*, April 4, 2010. http://www.jamaicaobserver.com/entertainment/dancehall-s-decline.

Mead, Nick, and Jo Blason. 2014. "The 10 World Cities with the Highest Murder Rates—in Pictures." *Guardian*, June 24, 2014. https://www.theguardian.com/cities/gallery/2014/jun/24/10-world-cities-highest-murder-rates-homicides-in-pictures.

Merton, Robert K. 1968. *Social Theory and Social Structure*. Enlarged ed. New York: Free Press.

Middleton, Alan. C. 2011. "City Branding and Inward Investment." In *City Branding: Theory and Cases*, edited by Keith Dinnie, 15–25. Houndmills, UK: Palgrave Macmillan.

Ministry of Tourism [Jamaica]. 2002. "The Tourism Master Plan for Sustainable Growth: JAMAICA." http://www.mot.gov.jm/page/tourism-master-plan.

Miller, Kei. 1992. *Communication Theories: Perspectives, Processes and Contexts*. New York: McGraw-Hill Higher Education.

———. 2014. "*A Brief History of Seven Killings* by Marlon James review—bloody conflicts in 70s Jamaica." *Guardian*, December 10, 2014. https://

www.theguardian.com/books/2014/dec/10/brief-history-of-seven-killings
-marlon-james-review.

Moghaddam, Mohammad, et al. 2013. "Examining the City Brand Theory and Presenting Some Solutions for Implementing It in Iran." *Civil Engineering and Architecture* 1, no. 4: 120–24.

Moramollu, Gülrah. 2016. "Ideology and Literature." *Humanities and Social Science Review* 6, no. 1: 455–60. https://www.academia.edu/30731580/IDEOLOGY _AND_LITERATURE?auto=download.

Morgan, Michael, and James Shanahan. 2010. "The State of Cultivation." *Journal of Broadcasting and Electronic Media* 54, no. 2: 337–55.

Morgan, Nigel, and Annette Pritchard. 1998. *Tourism Promotion and Power: Creating Images, Creating Identities.* Chichester: Wiley.

Mose Brown, Tamara. 2011. *Raising Brooklyn: Nannies, Childcare and Caribbeans Creating Community.* New York: New York University Press.

Mostashari, Ali, Friedrich Arnold, Mo Mansouri, and Mathias Finger. 2011. "Cognitive Cities and Intelligent Urban Governance." *Network Industries Quarterly* 13, no. 3: 4–7.

Munroe, Trevor. 1999. *Renewing Democracy into the Millennium: The Jamaican Experience in Perspective.* Kingston: University of the West Indies Press.

Mussche, Steffen Patrick. 2008. "Wi Likkle but wi tallawah: Narratives of Nation Branding: Intellectual Property Governance and Identity Politics in Jamaica." Master's thesis, Department of Sociology and Human Geography, Faculty of Social Sciences, University of Oslo.

Myers, John. 2014. "Brand Jamaica Worth $Billions." *Jamaica Gleaner* online. November 24, 2014. http://jamaica-gleaner.com/gleaner/20141124/lead /lead5.html.

National Geographic. 2011. "Top Ten National Dishes." September 13, 2011. https:// www.nationalgeographic.com/travel/top-10/national-food-dishes/.

Nelson, Jaevion. 2014. "Zero Tolerance for Homophobic Bullying." *Jamaica Gleaner,* April 2, 2014. http://jamaica-gleaner.com/article/commentary /20150402/zero-tolerance-homophobic-bullying.

Nelson, Leah. 2010. "Jamaica's Anti-Gay 'Murder Music' Carries Violent Message." *Intelligence Report,* no. 140. Southern Poverty Law Center.

Nettleford, Rex. *Caribbean Cultural Identity: The Case of Jamaica.* Los Angeles: UCLA Latin American Centre Publications, 1979.

Nixon, Angelique. 2015. *Resisting Paradise: Tourism, Diaspora, and Sexuality in Caribbean Culture.* Jackson: University Press of Mississippi.

North, Samantha. 2015. "The Cultural Capital of the Caribbean: How Kingston, Jamaica, Went from Murder Capital to Creative Capital." *City Metric.* August 11. https://www.citymetric.com/politics/cultural-capital-caribbean-how -kingston-jamaica-went-murder-capital-creative-capital-1308.

Nworah, Uche. 2008. *Rebranding Nigeria Critical Perspectives on the Heart of Africa Image Project.* http://www.brandchannel.com/images/papers/40_rebranding nigeria-critical perspectives.pdf.

Nye, Joseph, S. 2004. *Soft Power: The Means to Success in World Politics.* New York: Public Affairs.

Okwodu, Janelle. 2015. "Meet the Man behind Jamaica's Model Wave." *Vogue,* October 28, 2015. https://www.vogue.com/article/saint-international -interview-jamaica-model-wave.

Olins, Wally. 2000. *Trading Identities: Why Countries and Companies Are Taking on Each Other's Roles.* London: Foreign Policy Centre.

Oliver, Rochelle. 2017. "The Jamaican Beef Patty Extends Its Reach." *New York Times,* May 23, 2017. https://www.nytimes.com/2017/05/23/dining/jamaican -beef-patties.html.

Olympic.org. 2014. "The Jamaican Bobsleigh Team Is 'The Hottest Thing on Ice.'" *IOC News,* February 3, 2014. http://www.olympic.org/news/the-jamaican -bobsleigh-team-is-the-hottest-thing-on-ice/2 22740.

O'Shaughnessy, John, and Nicholas J. O'Shaughnessy. 2000. "Treating the Nation as a Brand: Some Neglected Issues." *Journal of Macromarketing* 20, no. 1: 56–64.

Overseas Security Advisory Council (OSAC). 2016. *Jamaica 2016 Crime and Safety Report. United States Department of State.* https://www.osac.gov/pages /ContentReportDetails.aspx?cid=19562.

Padgett, Tim. 2006. "The Most Homophobic Place on Earth?" *Time,* April 12, 2006. http://content.time.com/time/world/article/0,8599,1182991,00.html.

Panzaru, Olga. 2012. "Semiotic Interdependence between Text and Visual Image." *Lucrari Stiintifice* 55, no. 2: 409–12.

Patterson, Chris. 2017. "Redevelopment of Downtown Kingston on Stream." Jamaica Information Service, April 17, 2017. http://jis.gov.jm/redevelopment -downtown-kingston-stream/.

Patterson, Percival James "P.J." 1993. "Budget Presentation." In *The Challenges of Change: PJ Patterson Budget Presentations, 1992–2002,* edited by D. Franklyn. Kingston: Ian Randle.

————. 2014. "Caribbean Creativity the Way Forward." *Jamaica Observer*, November 10, 2014. http://www.jamaicaobserver.com/news/Caribbean-creativity-the-way-forward--p-j-Patterson_17908968.

Pattullo, Polly. 2005. *Last Resorts: The Cost of Tourism in the Caribbean*. New York: Monthly Review Press.

Pelan, Rebecca. 2012. "Brand Ireland or Ireland Branded: Versions of Irish Identity." *ANQ: A Quarterly Journal of Short Articles, Notes and Reviews* 25, no. 1: 3–9.

Perkins, Anna Kasafi. 2012. "Throwing Words across the Fence: Church and Dancehall in National Development." Paper presented at Jamaica 50-50 Conference, Sir Arthur Lewis Institute of Social and Economic Studies, Kingston, August 20–25.

————. 2016. "More than Words: Evangelicals, the Rhetoric of Battle and the Fight over Gay Rights in the Caribbean." *Journal of Eastern Caribbean Studies* 41, no. 1: 13–46.

Pertierra, Ana Cristina, and Heather Horst. 2009. "Introduction: Thinking about Caribbean Media Worlds." *International Journal of Cultural Studies* 12, no. 2: 99–111.

Petridis, Alexis. 2004. "Pride and Prejudice." *Guardian*, December 10, 2004. http://www.theguardian.com/music/2004/dec/10/gayrights.popandrock.

Pew Research Center. 2013. *The Global Divide on Homosexuality: Greater Acceptance in More Secular and Affluent Countries*. Report. PewGlobal.org, June 4, 2013. http://www.pewglobal.org/2013/06/04/the-global-divide-on-homosexuality/.

Pfefferkorn-Winfield, Julia. 2005. "The Branding of Cities: Exploring City Branding and the Importance of Brand Image." Master's thesis, Syracuse University. http://www.culturaldiplomacy.org/academy/pdf/research/books/nation_branding/The_Branding_Of_Cities_-_Julia_Winfield-Pfefferkorn.pdf.

Piccard, David. 2011. *Tourism, Magic and Modernity: Cultivating the Human Garden*. New York: Berghahn Press.

Pillai, Manusha. 2017. "Cities as Building Blocks of the Nation Brand." *Branding News*, July 27, 2017. https://www.bizcommunity.com/Article/196/82/165294.html.

Place Brand Observer. 2017. "Interview with Diane Edwards on Brand Jamaica, Country Branding and Investment Attraction Strategies." *PlaceBrandObserver.com*, November 9, 2017. https://placebrandobserver.com/interview-diane-edwards/.

———. 2018. "New York City: Performance, Brand Image and Reputation." *PlaceBrandObserver.com*, March 21, 2018. https://placebrandobserver.com/new-york-city-performance-brand-image-reputation/.

Planning Institute of Jamaica (PIOJ). 2012. *Economic and Social Survey of Jamaica.* http://www.pioj.gov.jm/Home/tabid/37/Default.aspx.

———. 2013. *Vision 2030 Jamaica.* National Development Plan. http://www.vision2030.gov.jm/.

Portes, A., and R. Grosfoguel. 1994. "Caribbean Diasporas: Migration and the Emergence of Ethnic Communities in the U.S. Mainland." *Annals of the American Academy of Political and Social Sciences* 533 (May): 8–69.

Portes, Alejandro, Carlos Dore-Carbral, and Patricia Landolt. 1997. *The Urban Caribbean: Transition to the New Global Economy.* Baltimore: Johns Hopkins University Press.

Poushter, Jacob. 2016. "Favorable Views of the UN Prevail in Europe, Asia and U.S." *Pew Research Center: Global Attitude and Trends.* http://www.pewresearch.org/fact-tank/2016/09/20/favorable-views-of-the-un-prevail-in-europe-asia-and-u-s/.

Pratt, Mary Louise. 2008. *Imperial Eyes: Travel Writing and Transculturation.* 2nd ed. New York: Routledge.

Ramello, Giovanni B. 2006. "What's in a Sign? Trademark Law and Economic Theory." *Journal of Economic Surveys* 20, no. 4: 547–56.

Ramkissoon, Haywantee. 2015. "Authenticity, Satisfaction, and Place Attachment: A Conceptual Framework for Cultural Tourism in African Island Economies." *Development Southern Africa* 32, no. 3: 292–302.

Rawlins, William. K. 2008. *Friendship Matters: Communication, Dialectics and the Life Course.* New Brunswick NJ: Transaction Publishers.

Reed, Tim V. n.d. "Textual Analysis." https://public.wsu.edu/~amerstu/471/471syl.html.

Regan, Michael P. 2019. "Welcome to Jamaica, Home of the World's Best-Performing Stock Market." *Bloomberg Businessweek*, January 18, 2019. https://www.bloomberg.com/news/features/2019-01-18/the-jamaican-stock-exchange-is-the-world-s-best-performing-market.

Ries, Al, and Laura Ries. 2002. *The 22 Immutable Laws of Branding.* New York: HarperCollins.

Roberts, Dorothy. 1995. "Punishing Drug Addicts Who Have Babies: Women of Color, Equality, and the Right of Privacy." In *Critical Race Theory: The Key Writings That Formed the Movement*, edited by Kimberlé Crenshaw, Neil T. Gotanda, Gary Peller, and Kendall Thomas, 357–83. New York: New Press.

Rose, Tricia. 1994. *Black Noise: Rap Music and Black Culture in Contemporary America*. Hanover NH: Wesleyan University Press, University Press of New England.

Rouse, Margaret. 2018. "Smart City." WhatIs.com, TechTarget, IoT Agenda. https://internetofthingsagenda.techtarget.com/definition/smart-city.

Roy, Abhik. 1998. "Images of Domesticity and Motherhood in Indian Television Commercials: A Critical Study." *Journal of Popular Culture* 32, no. 3: 117–34.

Roy, Ishita Sinha. 2007. "Worlds Apart: Nation Branding on the National Geographic Channel." *Media, Culture and Society* 29, no. 4: 569–92.

Salman, Saba. 2008. "Future of Cities: Brand of Gold." *Guardian*, September 30, 2008. https://www.theguardian.com/society/2008/oct/01/city.urban.branding.

Sanger, David. 2017. "In a Week, Trump Reshapes Decades of Perceptions about America." *New York Times*, January 29, 2017. https://www.nytimes.com/2017/01/29/us/donald-trump-perception-foreign-policy.html?_r=0.

Scott, Noel, Ann Suwaree Ashton, Peiyi Ding, and Honggang Xu. 2011. "Tourism Branding and Nation Building in China." *International Journal of Culture, Tourism and Hospitality Research* 5, no. 3: 227–34.

Selby, Keith, and Ron Cowdery. 1995. *How to Study Television*. London: Palgrave.

Seligson, Mitchell, and Amy Smith. 2010. *The Political Culture of Democracy: Democratic Consolidation in the Americas in Hard Times*. Kingston: Centre for Leadership and Governance, University of the West Indies, and Vanderbilt University.

Sevin, Efe, and Emma Bjorner. 2015 "A New China: Media Portrayal of Chinese Mega-Cities." *Journal of Place Branding and Public Diplomacy* 11, no. 4: 309–23.

Sharpley, Richard. 1994. *Tourism, Tourists and Society*. London: Elm Publication.

Sheller, Mimi. 2003. *Consuming the Caribbean: From Arawaks to Zombies*. London: Routledge.

Sherlock, Phillip, and Hazel Bennett. 1998. *The Story of the Jamaican People*. Kingston: Ian Randle Publishers.

Silvera, Janet. 2014. "LGBT Tourism Makes Regional Splash." *Hospitality Jamaica. Jamaica Gleaner*, November 19, 2014.

Sims, Glenda. 2004. "Schools Are Not Zones of Tolerance." *Sunday Gleaner*, March 7, 2004. http://old.jamaica-gleaner.com/gleaner/20040307/focus/focus3.html.

Small, Kimberley. 2018. "Kingston Creative Determined to Elucidate the City as an Art District." *Jamaica Gleaner*. July 12, 2018. http://jamaica-gleaner.com/article/entertainment/20180712/kingston-creative-determined-elucidate-city-art-district.

Smith, Charlene L., and Ryan Kosobucki. 2011. "Homophobia in the Caribbean: Jamaica." *Journal of Law and Social Deviance* 1:1–55. http://www.lsd-journal .net/archives/Volume1/Homophobia%20in%20the%20Caribbean.pdf.

SoulRebels.org. n.d. "Sizzla Is Not Respecting His Signature of the Reggae Compassionate Act." https://www.soulrebels.org/dancehall/w_compassionate _012.htm.

Spartacus International Gay Guide. 2017. "Gay Travel Index." February 28. https:// spartacus.gayguide.travel/blog/gay-travel-index-2019/.

Star Newspaper. 2015. "New Regulations Coming for Taxis." December 10, 2015. http://www3.jamaica-star.com/article/news/20151210/new-regulations -coming-taxis.

———. 2018. "I Love MoBay Campaign Kicks Off Tomorrow." February 16, 2018. http://jamaica-star.com/article/news/20180216/i-love-mobay-campaign -kicks-tomorrow.

Statistical Institute of Jamaica (STATIN). 2016. "Employment and Earning Tables." http://statinja.gov.jm/LabourForce/Newemploymentstats.aspx.

Stephenson, Marcus, and Howard Hughes. 2005. "Racialised Boundaries in Tourism and Travel: A Case Study of the UK Black Caribbean Community." *Leisure Studies* 24, no. 2: 137–60.

Stone, Carl. 1992. *Values, Norms and Personality Development in Jamaica.* Kingston: University of the West Indies.

Stothard, Michael. 2017. "Barcelona Brand Suffers after Independence Turmoil." *Financial Times*, November 30, 2017. https://www.ft.com/content/dd1436ac -d5c6-11e7-a303-9060cb1e5f44.

Strachan, Ian Gregory. 2002. *Paradise and Plantation: Tourism and Culture in the Anglophone Caribbean.* Charlottesville: University of Virginia Press.

Strasser, Max. 2014. "Top Twelve Most Homophobic Nations." *Newsweek*, February 27, 2014. http://www.newsweek.com/top-twelve-most-homophobic -nations-230348.

Sullivan, Jacob, and Michael Hegenauer. 2017. "LGBTQ Travel Index: Which Countries Are the Most Gay Friendly?" *Kayak*, "Travel Hacks." April 4, 2017. https://www.kayak.co.uk/magazine/gay-travel-index-2017/.

Swann, W. B. 1987. "Identity Negotiation: Where Two Roads Meet." *Journal of Personality and Social Psychology* 53:1038–51.

Swash, Rosie. 2007. "Beenie Man, Sizzla and Capleton Renounce Homophobia." *Guardian*, June 14, 2007. http://www.theguardian.com/music/2007/jun /14/news.rosieswash.

Tatchell, Peter. 2004. "The Queer Killing Fields of Jamaica." *PeterTatchell.net* (blog), October 4, 2004. http://www.petertatchell.net/international/jamaica /jamaica/.

———. 2009. "Jamaica: A Grim Place to Be Gay." *Gays without Borders.* https:// gayswithoutborders.wordpress.com/category/boycott-jamaica/.

Taylor, Frank Fonda. 1993. *To Hell with Paradise: A History of the Jamaican Tourism Industry.* Pittsburgh: University of Pittsburgh Press.

Taylor, Orville. 2012. "Fish, Foul Swimmer and Scammers." *Sunday Gleaner*, July 15, 2012. http://jamaica-gleaner.com/gleaner/20120715/focus/focus4.htm.

Telegraph (UK). 2014. "Jamaican Swimmer Alia Atkinson Becomes First Black Woman to Win World Title." December 6, 2014. https://www.telegraph.co.uk /sport/olympics/swimming/11277795/Jamaican-swimmer-Alia-Atkinson -becomes-first-black-woman-to-win-world-title.html.

Thomas, Christopher. 2012. "Bebe Granted Bail." *Gleaner*, July 9, 2012. http:// jamaica-gleaner.com/power/38445.

Tingling, Marlon. 2016. "Over \$2 Billion in Tourism Earnings to Date." Jamaica Information Service, December 16, 2016. http://jis.gov.jm/2-billion-tourism -earnings-date/.

Tomei, Renato. 2016. "Language Redemption: Bob Marley in Translation." In *Descriptions, Translations and the Caribbean: From Fruits to Rastafarian*, edited by Rosanna Masiola and Renato Tomei, 99–134. Basingstoke, UK: Palgrave Macmillan.

Tomlinson, Maurice. 2013. "Not Cashing In on Gay Tourist Dollar." *Gleaner*, September 30. http://jamaica-gleaner.com/gleaner/20130930/cleisure /cleisure3.html.

Townsend Gilkes, Cheryl. 2000. *If It Wasn't for the Women . . . : Black Women's Experience and Womanist Culture in Church and Community.* Maryknoll NY: Orbis.

Transparency International. 2013. "Country Reports—Jamaica." Transparency International Corruption Perceptions Index. https://www.transparency .org/country/JAM.

Trujillo, Jesus, and Joseph Parilla. 2016. *Redefining Global Cities: The Seven Types of Global Metro Economies.* Brookings Institution: Global Cities Initiative.

Tymoczko, Maria, ed. 2010. *Translation, Resistance, Activism: Essays on the Role of Translators as Agents of Change.* Amherst: University of Massachusetts Press.

United Nations Office of Drugs and Crime (UNODC). 2013. *Global Study on Homicides: Trends, Contexts, Data.* https://www.unodc.org/documents/gsh /pdfs/2014_global_homicide_book_web.pdf.

UNESCO. 2017. "Kingston: Creative Cities Network." https://en.unesco.org/creative-cities/kingston.

Valaskivi, Katja. 2016. *Cool Nations: Media and the Social Imaginary of the Branded Country*. Abingdon, UK: Routledge.

Van Ham, Peter. 2001. "The Rise of the Brand State: The Postmodern Politics of Image and Reputation." *Foreign Affairs* 80, no. 5: 2–6.

Venuti, Lawrence. 1995. *The Translator's Invisibility*. New York: Routledge.

———. 1998. *The Scandals of Translation: Towards an Ethics of Difference*. New York: Routledge.

Viosca, Charles, Blaise Bergiel, and Phillip Balsmeier. 2005. "Country Equity: South Africa, a Case in Point." *Journal of Promotion Management* 12, no. 1: 85–95.

VisitJamaica.com. n.d. http://www.visitjamaica.com/downtown-kingston-heritage-walking-tour.

Walker, Karyl. 2014. "Gun-Toting Gays Drive Fear in Citizens of Garrison Communities." *Jamaica Observer*, June 8, 2014. http://www.jamaicaobserver.com/news/Gun-toting-gays-drive-fear-in-citizens-of-garrison-communities_16826316.

Wang, Yifei, Songshan Huang, and Aise Kyoung Kim. 2015. "Toward a Framework Integrating Authenticity and Integrity in Heritage Tourism." *Journal of Sustainable Tourism* 23, no. 10: 1468–81.

Watkins-Owens, Irma. 2001. "Early Twentieth-Century Caribbean Women: Migration and Social Networks in New York City." In *Island in the City: West Indian Migration to New York*, edited by Nancy Foner, 25–51. Los Angeles: University of California Press.

Weiss, Robert. 1994. *Learning from Strangers*. New York: Free Press.

West, Keon, and Kate Houlden. 2016. "The Marlon James Conundrum." Small Group Project. *Independent Social Research Foundation*. http://www.isrf.org/about/fellows-and-projects/fg2-10/.

White, Patrick. 2014. "Get Off Anti-Gay Bandwagon." *Sunday Gleaner*, November 9, 2014.

Wike, Richard, Jacob Poushter, and Hani Zainulbhai. 2016. "As Obama Years Draw to Close, President and U.S. Seen Favorably in Europe and Asia." Pew Research Center. Report, June 27, 2016. http://www.pewglobal.org/2016/06/29/as-obama-years-draw-to-close-president-and-u-s-seen-favorably-in-europe-and-asia/pew-research-center-balance-of-power-report-final-june-29-2016/.

Wilkes, Karen. 2016. *Whiteness, Weddings, and Tourism in the Caribbean: Paradise for Sale*. New York: Nature America.

Wilets, James D. 2011. "From Divergence to Convergence? A Comparative and International Law Analysis of LGBTI Rights in the Context of Race and Post-Colonialism." *Duke Journal of Comparative & International Law* 21, no. 3: 631–86. https://scholarship.law.duke.edu/djcil/vol21/iss3/5.

Williams, Densil. 2013. "Beyond the Grave: Is Manley's Economic Philosophy Relevant to the Advancement of Contemporary Jamaica?" In *PNP: People's National Party at 75: The Party of the People*, edited by Delano Franklyn. Kingston: Wilson Franklyn Barnes Publishers.

Williams, Lawson. 2000. "Homophobia and Gay Rights Activism in Jamaica." *Small Axe: A Caribbean Journal of Criticism* 4, no. 1: 106–11.

World Bank. 2009. *World Development Report: Reshaping Economic Geography*. Washington DC: World Bank. http://documents.worldbank.org/curated/en/730971468139804495/pdf/437380revised01blic1097808213760720.pdf.

———. 2018. *Doing Business 2019: Training for Reform—Jamaica*. http://documents.worldbank.org/curated/en/394171541138539718/Doing-Business-2019-Training-for-Reform-Jamaica.

World Bank Group. 2017a. *Doing Business Report: Equal Opportunity for All*. http://www.doingbusiness.org/data/exploreeconomies/jamaica.

———. 2017b. "The World Bank in Jamaica—Jamaica Overview." April 11, 2017. http://www.worldbank.org/en/country/jamaica/overview.

World Economic Forum. 2015. "What Is Creativity Worth to the World Economy?" https://www.weforum.org/agenda/2015/12/creative-industries-worth-world-economy/.

Zabus, Chantal. 1991. *The African Palimpsest: Indigenization of Language in the West African Europhone Novel*. Amsterdam: Rodopi.

CONTRIBUTORS

Kamille Gentles-Peart (PhD, University of Michigan, 2007) is a critical cultural studies scholar and Associate Professor of Communication and Media Studies at Roger Williams University, Rhode Island. Her research explores the intersections of race, gender and body politics in the lives of Caribbean black women, with specific focus on how power regimes are mobilized through the body and how black Caribbean women make meaning and life in the context of race and gender hegemonies. She is the author of *Romance with Voluptuousness: Caribbean Women and Thick Bodies in the United States* (2016) as well as the coeditor of the award-winning anthology *Re-Constructing Place and Space: Media, Culture, Discourse and the Constitution of Caribbean Diasporas* (2012). Dr. Gentles-Peart is also cofounder of the Collaborative for the Research on Black Women and Girls.

Nickesia S. Gordon (PhD, Howard University, 2007) is Associate Professor of Communication at Rochester Institute of Technology, Rochester NY. Her research focuses on globalization, media and culture, communication for social change, as well as mass media and popular culture. She also has an active research agenda in critical cultural studies as it relates to gender, race, and nationality. She is coeditor of *Reflections on Gender from a Communication Point-of-View* (Peace Studies: Edges and Innovations Series, 2017) and *Still Searching for Our Mothers' Gardens: Experiences of New, Tenure Track Women of Color at "Majority" Institutions* (2012). She is also author of *Media and the Politics of Culture: The Case of Television Privatization and Media Globalization in Jamaica, 1990–2007* (2008).

Hume N. Johnson (PhD, University of Waikato, New Zealand, 2007) is a branding and communications strategy consultant and Associate Professor of Public Relations at Roger Williams University, Rhode Island. A political scholar and former broadcast journalist, she is the author of *Challenges to Civil Society: Popular Protest and Governance in Jamaica* (2011), as well as two books on personal branding. Her scholarship explores various aspects of governance; political participation and civil society in developing countries; the intersections between politics and the media; and the public relations of nation-states. Dr. Johnson is also founder of The Re:Imagine Jamaica Project and a noted speaker on Brand Jamaica.

Steffen Mussche-Johansen (MSc, University of Oslo, Norway, 2008) is a Norwegian Irish sociologist and entrepreneur. His research interests include country branding and intellectual property, with specific application to Jamaica. Mussche-Johansen is an emerging player in product branding, having started the rapidly growing Oslo Brewing Company and male grooming brand Bad Norwegian. Based in Oslo, he likes to spend as much time as possible in his adopted second home, Jamaica. If it's on a beach in Portland, in buzzing Kingston, or in tranquil Irish Town in the cool Blue Mountains, there's no place he feels more alive than in Jamaica.

Anna Kasafi Perkins (PhD, Boston College, 2004) holds degrees from St. Michael's Theological College / University of the West Indies, Mona Campus, Jamaica; Cambridge University; and Boston College. Her research interests include sex and sexuality, religion and popular culture (especially dancehall), gender and justice. She is the author of *Justice as Equality: Michael Manley's Caribbean Vision of Justice* (2010) and coeditor of *Justice and Peace in a Renewed Caribbean: Contemporary Catholic Reflections and Quality in Higher Education in the Caribbean* (2012, 2016). Her current book project is tentatively entitled "Throwing Words: Christianity, Ethics, and Popular Culture in Jamaica." She is currently the Senior Programme Officer, Quality Assurance Unit, University of the West Indies, Mona Campus.

Laëtitia Saint-Loubert (PhD, University of Warwick, England, 2018) is a literary translator and researcher in Caribbean and Translation Studies. She completed a doctorate in Caribbean studies and is currently working at the University of Reunion Island (E.A. [Équipe d'Acceuil] DIRE). Her research investigates Caribbean literatures in translation and addresses, more specifically, issues related to transversal, non-vertical modes of circulation for Caribbean literatures and languages inside and outside the region as well as trans-pelagically.

Collins, Patricia Hill, 52, 53, 54
colonialism, xxi, xxii, 33, 40, 41, 42, 56,
    69, 169; tourism and, 49
colonization, 9, 40, 56; anthropology
    of, 38; branding and, 41
colors: combinations, 160; Ethiopian,
    148–49; Rasta, 146, 150, 152, 161
Colthirst, Miz, 105
Comaroff, Jean, xxviii, xxix
Comaroff, John L., xxviii, xxix
"come and feel all right," 17
"Come Back to Jamaica," 37, 38
"Come to Jamaica," 37, 40, 46
"Come to Jamaica and feel all right," 43
Commission of Enquiry, 18
Commonwealth Games (1966), 29n1
communication, xiii, 124; brand,
    120; dialectics and, 7; networks,
    123; nonverbal, 37; secondary,
    120; tertiary, 120; word-of-
    mouth, 120
community, xxv, 59, 143; culture and,
    135; diasporic, 68; domestic, 94; gay,
    xxxi, 20, 21, 30n5, 78, 80, 83, 86, 87,
    88–89, 90; international, 167
Community Marketing and Insights, 87
competition, xiii, xvi–xx, 2, 11, 117, 130,
    165
consciousness: collective, 57; double,
    54, 62–68, 71
Constant Spring, 140
consumption, xxiv, 93; cultural, 99, 112;
    external, 48–49
Cool Britannia campaign, xvii
Cool Runnings (film), 6, 30n3
Copenhagen City, 95, 99
Coronation Market, 137, 141
corruption, xix, xxii, xxvii, xxx, 1, 2, 8,
    9, 11, 22, 23, 28, 29, 68, 127, 153, 170;

perceptions of, 16–17; reputation
    for, 52; symbolic, 165
Corruption Perceptions Index (CPI), 1
Country Report—Jamaica (Amnesty
    International), 79
Cowen, Brian, xviii
creative arts, 24–26
Creative City of Music, 115, 129–31,
    131–33, 143
creative industries, xxxi, 94, 130
"Creative Kingston," 139
creative moments, xxxii, 116, 131,
    133–35, 136–38
credentials: cultural, 3, 116, 131, 171;
    Jamaican, 24–26
Crenshaw, Kimberlé, 53
crime, xxiii, xxviii, 1, 2, 6, 9, 22, 28, 29,
    126, 140, 170; aesthetics and, 139;
    hate, 18, 76–77; ignoring, 16; impact
    of, 12–13, 128; narrative of, 129;
    nonviolent, 14; upsurge in, 12, 24;
    violent, xxx, 8, 13–14, 15, 116, 146
C Sharp, 132
cultural assets, 34, 165
cultural expression, xxxii, 4, 163, 165
cultural markers, 64, 112
cultural products, 29, 42, 146, 163
cultural references, 98, 103, 104, 149
culture, xvi, xxv, 9, 15, 56, 58, 62, 63,
    103, 112, 116, 122, 123, 124, 142, 146,
    154, 159, 171, 172; commodification
    of, xxxiii; community and, 135;
    complex, xi; construction of, 68;
    cosmopolitan, 138; creativity and,
    135; dancehall, 5, 82, 89; diasporic,
    63; diverse, 25; dynamics of, 32; edu-
    cation and, 64; food, 136–37, 138,
    171; homophobia and, 20; identity
    and, 147, 169, 172; language and, 4,

governance, xxvi, xxxi, 119, 124; bad, 22, 25, 52; challenges of, 29; deficits in, 169–70; good, xxii, 116; improving, 23; IP, 145, 146, 148, 156, 158, 159, 164; quality, 17, 139–44; urban, 120

La guagua aérea (Sánchez), 114n10

Guerra, Javier, 92

Guerra, Wendy, 92, 104, 107

Guldner, 84

Gutzmore, C., 82

Half Way Tree, 141

Halfway Tree Road, 110, 111

Hall, Stuart, 66

The Harder They Come (film), 127

HardTalk (BBC), 20

Harris, E. Nigel, 128

Harrison, Sheri-Marie, 97, 114n11

Hart-Celler Immigration Bill, 73n1

Hawthorne, Lowell, 137

Headley, George, 29n1

health care, 10, 60, 66, 71, 123, 140, 141, 144, 170

Hegenauer, Michael, 88

Helber, Patrick, 75

heritage, xvi, xvii, xxv, xxviii, 56, 63, 66, 129; attractions, xiv; cultural, 61, 115, 137; food, 138

High School Boys and Girls Athletic Championships, 136

history, 24–26, 119, 124, 125–27, 138; adoption/decontextualization of, 132; sports, 136

"Home of All Right," 37, 46

homophobia, xxii, xxvii, xxviii, 1, 2, 68, 75, 76, 79, 146; Brand Jamaica and, 89, 90; culture and, 20; emerging, 88; extreme, 77, 78; impact of, 21–22; perceptions of, 8, 77; rampant, 82–83; reputation of, 52; tourism and, 86, 87–89

homosexuality, 65; attitudes toward, 21, 79; outlawing, 20, 80, 81; plantation societies and, 82; religious conservatives and, 87

homosexuals: human rights of, 86, 88; threats against, 21; treatment of, 82, 83

Hope, Donna, 5

Hope Botanical Gardens, 133, 141

Hospitality Jamaica (Gleaner Company), 89

human rights, xxiii, 4, 8, 28, 77, 79, 170; brand and, 18–22; declining, xxx, 2; homophobia and, 20; homosexuals and, 86, 88; improving, 23; violations of, 18

Human Rights Watch, 19, 128

I and I, 101, 102

IBM, trademark for, 147

identity, xi, xx, xxvi, xxvii, xxix, xxx, xxxii, 42, 48, 52, 57, 62, 63, 65, 78, 96, 116, 119, 122, 143; allocation of, 154; articulation of, 24–25; black, 4, 130; brand, xii, 92–93, 121; cultural, 32, 135, 147, 169, 172; diasporic, 58, 68, 73n2; distinctive, 124, 135; expression of, 25, 155; formation, xvii–xviii, 165; international, 27, 171; Jamaican, xxi, xxiv, 22, 24, 25, 28, 39, 62, 66, 91–92, 158; markers, 107; national, xvi, 31, 32, 42, 49, 78, 95, 97, 151–55, 165, 168, 169;

sociopolitical realities, 4, 167, 171

Somerset House, 132

"Sound System," 130

space: colonial, 41; economic, 142; modern, 67; place and, 31, 39

Spanish Court, 142

Spanish Town, 124, 125

Spartacus International Gay Guide, 88

speech: black, 106; depoliticized, 47; transplanting, 101

sports, xiv, xxii, 2, 3, 24–26, 28, 29, 79, 117, 129, 136, 143, 169; economic growth and, 26; tourism, 7

stakeholders, xiii, 119, 138, 143, 149, 155, 161, 164; external, xxiv, 157, 165; IP ownership and, 157; Jamaican, 121, 146, 158, 159, 160, 162–63

St. Andrew, 15, 125–26, 139

Starsky and Hutch (television show), 108

stereotypes, xxvii, xxviii, xxix, xxx, 23, 35, 37, 49, 52, 57, 65, 75, 100, 118, 129, 146, 152; black female, 53; creation of, 169; gendered, 56; internalization of, 67–68; negative, 3, 171

Stone, Carl, 127

Stonewall Inn, 83

"Stop Murder Music" campaign, 84–85, 85 (table), 86

Strachan, Dean, 76

Strasser, Max, 81

strategy, xvii, 96–100, 141, 146; brand, xvi, xix, xx, 121, 122, 138, 156; business, 38; communication, xiv, 120; national, xviii; promotional, xxvii; urban, 117

Strictly the Best (album), 84

St. Williams Grant Park, 134

Sullivan, Jacob, 88

Supreme Court, 17, 134

symbols, 1, 4, 57, 130, 164; corruption of, 153; cultural, xxix, 19, 151–55, 156; Jamaican, 146, 147, 148, 149–50, 151, 152, 153, 158, 159, 160, 162, 165; meaning of, 157; misappropriation of, 152, 165; narrative and, 146; national, xxxii, 160; ownership of, 151, 155; Rastafarian, 155–58, 160; supernova, 158

Tatchell, Peter, 79, 84

technology, xxvii, 2, 132, 169; information/communication, 124; telecom, 123

texts, 34; mass media, 34–35; verbal, 34; visual, 36–37

Third World, 4, 62, 64, 66; marketing of, 54–55

Third World (Marley), 4

Thompson, Elaine, 5

Time, 1–2, 4

Ting, 6

Tivoli Gardens, 15, 99

Tomlinson, Maurice, 89

tourism, xiii, xiv, xxiii, xxxi, xxxiii, 9, 16, 24, 27, 29, 46, 75, 92, 129, 135, 137; attracting, 124, 141; authenticity of, 38; campaigns, 54, 72; Caribbean, 31, 33; colonialism and, 49; conceptualization of, 43; controlling images and, 52–57; dancehall music and, 83; destination, xi, xii, xxv, xxix, xxx, 2, 3, 6, 28, 48, 55, 60, 118, 124, 142, 168–69; dynamics of, 32; economy and, xxxi, 44–45, 51; environmental burdens of, 45; focus

violence (*cont.*)

cycle of, 13; decoupling, 99; filmic, 127; history of, 9; homophobic, 20, 76, 128; increase in, 12; narrative of, 129; political, xvii–xviii; presentation of, 99; reputation for, 52; sexual, 19; structural, 81; upsurge in, 24

Viosca, Charles, xix

Vision 2030 plan, 142

Vogue, 132

Volkswagen, Super Bowl advertising for, 6, 24, 148

Vybz Kartel, 84, 131

Wales, Josey, 99, 109

Walkerswood, 163

"War" (Marley), 4

Ward Theatre, 134

Wary and Nephew Jamaica Rum, 26

Washington Post, 132

welfare, 53, 149, 158–59

West Kingston Business Park, 141

white supremacists, xix, 54, 56

Wike, Richard, xix

Wilets, James D., 82

Wilkes, Karen, 41, 48

Williams, Delroy, 139

Wint, Arthur, 5, 29n1, 136

WIPO. *See* World Intellectual Property Organization (WIPO)

Women's Football World Cup, 26

World Bank, xxiv, 11–12, 128, 129

World Economic Forum, 129–30

World Games, 136

World Intellectual Property Organization (WIPO), 159; Protection of Geographical Indications Act (2004), 161

World Tourism Organization, 23

Zainulbhai, Hani, xix

Zabus, Chantal, 114n7

www.ingramcontent.com/pod-product-compliance
Lightning Source LLC
Chambersburg PA
CBHW030024300326
R18045400001B/R180454PG41914CBX00004B/3/J